★ ★ ★

"Guaranteed to spark interest in any military reader, it serves as a beguiling introduction to the more detailed critical analysis of military history absolutely essential 'to anyone,' as Clausewitz put it, 'who wants to learn about war from books' "

—Harry G. Summers Jr.,
author of *On Strategy*

"*Leaders and Battles* is an easy reading experience. . . . This work clearly has the potential for use as a leadership study guide. It can stimulate many hours of thoughtful group discussion. At the very least, it will also serve as an introduction to the practical value of studying military history. . . . Although Marines have never lacked in military spirit, this book will serve to enhance and invigorate."

—*Marine Corps Gazette*

"Wood shows that battles have been won by the minds of skilled leaders, that the attributes of leadership are found in the individual himself and that these statements have been true throughout the history of warfare."

—*Military Review*

"Fascinating and easy reading without losing the main lessons the author wishes to bring out. One feels that Napoleon would have approved this approach despite the relatively humble ranks of most of those commanders examined. 'Read and meditate upon the wars of the greatest captains,' the 'Corsican Ogre' once enthused. 'This is the only means of rightly learning the science of war—and we might add, the 'art' as well."

—David Chandler

Daniel Morgan, portrait by Charles Willson Peale

LEADERS
AND
BATTLES
The Art of
Military Leadership

W. J. WOOD

PRESIDIO

For Barbara

Published by Presidio Press
505 B San Marin Dr., Suite 300
Novato, CA 94945-1340

Printing History
First published in cloth by Presidio Press in 1984
Fitrst paperbound edition published in 1995

Library of Congress Cataloging in Publication Data

Wood, W. J. (William J.), 1917–
   Leaders and battles.

   Bibliography: p.324
   Includes index.
   ISBN: 0-89141-185-2 (cloth)
   ISBN: 0-89141-560-2 (paper)
   1. Leadership—Addresses, essays, lectures. 2. Military history—Adresses, essays, lectures. I. Title.
U210.W66   1984   355.3'3041   84-6905

Printed in the United States of America

Contents

Permissions for use of illustrations and quoted material in LEADERS AND BAT-TLES by William Wood

Quote from "The New Army with New Punch" by Robert S. Dudney reprinted with permission from *U.S. News and World Report, Inc.* September 20, 1982. Copyright 1982.

Quotation from "John Brown's Body" by Stephen Vincent Benet is from *Selected Works of Stephen Vincent Benet.* Holt, Rinehart & Winston, Inc. Copyright renewed 1955, 1956 by Rosemary Carr Benet. Reprinted by permission of Brandt & Brandt Literary Agents.

"The Taking of Lungtungpen" section reprinted from *Soldiers Three and Military Tales, Part II* by Rudyard Kipling. New York: Charles Scriber's Sons, 1899.

Illustrations.

Reproduction of the painting of Daniel Morgan by Charles Willson Peale is from Don Higginbotham's *Daniel Morgan: Revolutionary Rifleman.* University of North Carolina Press, 1961.

Maps of "Battle of Cowpens" and "Stony Point" reprinted with permission from the Boatner *Encyclopedia of the American Revolution,* copyright David McKay, 1976.

Reproduction of "Le Bataille d'Auerstadt" (1806) by Gobaut with permission from Roger Viollet, Paris.

"Zulus rallying to renew an attack" is taken from *A History of Warfare* by Field Marshal Montgomery. New York: World Publishing Company, 1968; reprinted from Louis Creswicke's *South Africa and the Transvaal War, 1900–02.*

Portrait of Henry Bouquet is from *The Battle of Bushy Run* by Niles Anderson. Pennsylvania Historical & Museum Commission, 1975.

Reproduction of "Black Watch at Bushy Run" by C. W. Jeffries courtesy of Public Archives, Canada.

Portraits of Custer, Reno and Benteen courtesy of Custer Battlefield Historical and Museum Association.

Drawing by John W. Thomason, Jr. of Marshal Lannes is reprinted from *The Adventures of General Marbot* with the permission of Charles Scribner's Sons. Copyright renewed 1963 by Leda B. Thomason.

Photo of General von Lettow-Vorbeck and photo of "Natives' Hives to Attract Wild Bees at Tonga" from *Duel for Kilimanjaro* by Leonard Mosley. Weidenfeld & Nicolson, 1963.

Drawing of Marshal Lannes on page 256 is by John W. Thomason, Jr. reprinted from *The Adventures of General Marbot* with the permission of Charles Scribner's Sons. Copyright 1935 Charles Scribner's Sons; copyright renewed 1963, Leda B. Thomason.

Maps by Martin Wilkerson (except for Cowpens and Stony Point).

Jacket painting by Robert Wilson, copyright Hubert Hendricks, Spartanburg, SC.

Introduction

HAVE YOU EVER read an account of a battle and wondered why the author seemed so incisive and the leaders so bumbling? I have, many times, and have found that it doesn't require military genius to find the answer. It takes simply an awareness that the indoor sport of Monday-morning quarterbacking can be played outdoors to allow the author to occupy what could be called an omniscient observation post. From his cozy O.P. the writer is able to see all and know all. Then, you may ask, what about the leaders who are under scrutiny? In fairness, they could not have seen everything, let alone have known everything, so why did they act as they did?

There are no pat answers to the question. Yet the reader is entitled to a clear answer, and that is why this book was written. The idea of a book which would show the general reader that leadership in battle is a practical art had been gnawing at my mind for years. Only recently has the idea been propelled into action by two persuasive prime movers. The first stimulus was James Fallows' illuminating book, *National Defense*,[1] particularly the passages pointing out the Army's growing need for team leaders of men who live, train, and fight as combat units. There is neither need nor space here to go into the details of requirements that Fallows treats so lucidly. It is sufficient to note that Fallows concludes his insights by suggesting "in broad terms, the efforts that should be made to impose more constructive patterns on national

1

defense." The recommendation that heads his list of proposed efforts: "To restore the military spirit."[2]

The second prime mover, a close ally of the first, was the growing awareness that a new Army is beginning to emerge from the troubles that plagued it during the 1970's, such as too many school dropouts, too few re-enlistments, the departure of officers and non-commissioned officers with essential skills, and rapidly deteriorating weapons and equipment. The new Army's emergence—really a rebirth—has been described in an article by Robert Dudney:

> The old battlefield doctrine of depending on massive firepower alone to crush foes is being scrapped in favor of a blend of maneuver, deception, and speed. The goal: Disorient an enemy that may be larger and more heavily armed. Known as "AirLand Battle", the concept emphasizes small, stripped-down units that can move swiftly. Battlefield commanders will have a rare degree of freedom to exploit enemy weaknesses, and their troops will be trained to fight for long periods without rest [and the Army Chief of Staff adds] . . . It's an awful lot for any organization to digest. It's going to take some of the greatest leadership we've ever had to get through this period.[3]

The aim of this book is to aid in restoring the military spirit by setting itself three goals. The first is to show Americans that battles can be won by the minds of leaders, those who are skilled in the art of leadership. The second is to demonstrate that the art of leadership is embodied in the man, not in some set of abstractions. The third is to establish that the art must be based on certain attributes which are found in leaders who have proved themselves in battle. When this book has attained those goals it can provide something else of value: It should point the way toward correcting the neglect of military history by showing how to sort out and use *real lessons* from the past.

Since this book is intended for the general reader, it should demonstrate that recognition of the art of leadership in battle represents a quantum stride toward appreciating the contribution that this art can make to the military spirit and hence to the national defense.

What then is meant by an *art* of leadership? Certainly the leader in combat is not exercising a set of aesthetic principles. Clearly his art is a practical one, a means of applying ideas that govern his craft. We are, therefore, concerned here with *an exceptional skill in conducting a human activity*.[4] Accordingly, my sights are set on examining the personal attributes of leaders whose thoughts and actions during critical battles can be deduced from the record.

When one's attention is fixed on such an examination, it is readily apparent that to include a discussion of war as a human institution would be irrelevant. Entanglement in an issue of morality would serve no purpose here and can be avoided by keeping a realistic eye on the book's aim. I have sought to do that by acknowledging the conclusions of two authorities whose backgrounds are as different as their views on the history of war are in agreement. The first, Gen. J. F. C. Fuller, the foremost twentieth century writer on the history and conduct of warfare, wrote: "Whether war is a necessary factor in the evolution of mankind may be disputed, but a fact which cannot be questioned is that, from the earliest records of man to the present age, war has been his dominant preoccupation. There has never been a period in human history altogether free from war, and seldom one or more of a generation which has not witnessed a major conflict: great wars flow and ebb almost as regularly as the tides."[5] The other source, Will and Ariel Durant, two humanists reviewing the lessons of history in the epilogue of their life work, *The Story of Civilization* (1968), wrote: "War is one of the constants of history, and has not diminished with civilization or democracy. In the last 3,421 years of recorded history only 268 have seen no war."[6]

When one descends from the mountain top view of war—from the omniscient observation post—one may scramble down the slopes toward the sound of battle, but not into battle—not yet. First, one should fix a perspective, and that means gaining the ability to look into the minds and natures of men who have led in battle. For we are going to see battle through *their* eyes and thoughts, to see how they think, act or react—without depending on hackneyed narratives or analyses.

Before we look into those minds and hearts we must recognize the forces that oppose and test the best qualities of the leader. These forces must be understood in order to appreciate their terrifying potential. I call them the Dynamics of Battle. After scanning more than 1,500 battles, from the earliest times (Megiddo, 1469 B.C.) to the present (don't we always have one going on somewhere "at present"?), I have observed six dynamics appearing with regularity and consistency.

The first—*danger*—should emerge as a surprise to no one.

It is scarcely necessary to tell anyone that the battlefield is a dangerous place. But in the context of the art of leadership, I do not refer to the personal, physical dangers that threaten the soldier, nor do I have in mind the dangers to a leader's person. What is under consideration throughout the battle scenes is a danger to the leader's command or a major part of it. As an example take the threat of encirclement, or an unexpected attack against a flank or the rear, or units taken by surprise and in danger of being overrun.

Chance, the second dynamic, is one that can upset the best-planned operation or present a leader with an unanticipated opportunity to strike his enemy a decisive blow. Clausewitz, the soldier-scholar-philosopher, tells us that "War is the province of chance . . . it increases the uncertainty of every circumstance, and deranges the course of events."[7] Chance should not be confused with luck in this context, for that will be considered later.

Exertion is the third force operating against the plans of the commander. It may affect the troops and the leader himself. It may run a gamut from the simple stress of climbing a hill under fire to the limits of human suffering such as the combined horrors of extreme thirst and Saracen arrow barrages at night which were suffered by the Crusaders at Hattin at the end of the Second Crusade.

Uncertainty may be defined as a lack of knowledge essential to the accomplishment of a mission. It can be a dearth of combat intelligence regarding a leader's units or those of his enemy. Uncertainty seems to infiltrate even operations that have been going according to plan. This demon is always lurking just behind the commander's shoulder, but is never visible when he looks around.

I have called the fifth dynamic *apprehension*, and find a dictionary definition fitting: "anticipation of adversity, dread or fear of coming evil."[8] A leader can himself feel apprehensive, but he must always be on guard against apprehension among his troops. It may further be regarded as the child of uncertainty and the father of fear; left to grow unchecked it may even become the grandsire of panic.

I have left the sixth dynamic, *frustration*, for last, because it is the hardest to portray to minds that have never experienced war. It was Clausewitz who first defined it and his definition remains the classic reference. He labelled it "friction", but I have elected to call it *frustration* because that term seems to mean more to the American reader. Terminology aside, here is the gist of what Clausewitz said in *On War*: "Everything is very simple in War, but the simplest thing is difficult. These difficulties accumulate and produce a friction which no man can imagine exactly who has not seen war. . . . This is one of the great chasms which separate conception from execution."[9]

Clausewitz goes on to use an analogy from civil life which concerns a traveler who, at the end of a trying day, finds his travel plans falling apart, with coach horses missing, and finally ending up at miserable accommodations. Clausewitz's parallel is apt enough in its nineteenth century manner, but too mild I think to show its meaning to modern readers. I prefer the story told by a friend in the good old days when automobiles were first coming out with automatic transmissions. He couldn't get his car started on a frosty winter morning until a neighbor pulled her car alongside his and asked if she could help. Delighted at the prospect of getting a push he was quick to accept the offer, then remembered to caution her that his Cadillac had an automatic transmission. He made it quite clear (in his version of the event) that the cars would have to reach a speed of thirty-five miles per hour before he could get his engine running. She nodded her understanding and proceeded to back up—almost the length of the block, as he recalled. After checking to see that his transmission lever was in the proper position, he looked in his rear-view mirror to see if the lady was bringing her car up to the rear of his. She was. To his horror he saw her bearing down on his rear—at thirty-five miles per hour!

That is frustration. It comes as close to its battlefield definition as I can imagine. In a broader sense frustration is the vast difference between plans and their execution, between expectation and reality. Oddly enough, the accumulation of difficulties mentioned in Clausewitz has been described graphically by a man who never saw a battle. Stephen Vincent Benét sketches such things lucidly as he recounts the opening of the Battle of Bull Run in *John Brown's Body*:

> If you take a flat map
> And move wooden blocks upon it strategically,*
> The thing looks well, the blocks behave as they should.
> The science* of war is moving live men like blocks,
> And getting the blocks into place at a fixed moment.

*Benét's terms, not mine. I would have used "tactically" instead of strategically and "art" instead of science, but then I am *un pauvre soldat* who has never been issued a poetic license. For a discussion of strategy and tactics see Appendix A.

But it takes time to mold your men into blocks
And flat maps turn into country where creeks and gullies
Hamper your wooden squares. They stick in the brush,
They are tired and rest, they straggle after ripe blackberries,
And you cannot lift them up in your hand and move them . . .
It is all so clear in the maps, so clear in the mind,
But the orders are slow, the men in the blocks are slow
To move, when they start they take too long on the way—
The general loses his stars and the block men die . . .
Because still used to being men, not block parts. . . ."[10]

I could never put it as engagingly as Benét, so simply bear in mind: Frustration=difference between plans and reality.

Fortunately for commanders in the past all six dynamics have rarely appeared in a *concerted combination* in a single battle. When such a rarity has occurred (like the notorious case of the collapse of the French Army at Waterloo) a leader has gone down, and one recalls the mournful truism that for every battle won, someone had to lose it.

In fact, when such a disastrous combination has arisen, it usually has been the fault of the leader who has allowed the dynamics to accumulate against him. Avoiding that accumulation is an essential element of the art of leadership. Avoidance, however, is only the secondary or negative theme of this writing. The main theme is positive in its nature, for its purpose is to bring out the *attributes of the leader*. These are the personal qualities without which there can be no base on which to build an art of leadership. These are the counterforces that have enabled the successful leader to overcome the dynamics of battle that oppose and threaten to destroy him. I call the personal counterforces *attributes*, not only because the word is more fitting than "characteristics," but also because the whole art of leadership can be attributed to them.

How to present attributes to the reader became the cause of more mental travail and just plain sweat than I have ever endured in a single project. To toss some kind of list in front of my reader would be an unthinkable affront, and a detailed discussion of abstract qualities at this point could result in something equally tedious. Yet negative aspects can sometimes provoke the mind into positive thought; that is what happened in my case. The positive side forced me to recall my promise to come up with answers by looking at leaders in action; not by probing into abstractions, but by looking at success in battle through the minds and eyes of leaders. This put me back on track, pointed toward realistic goals.

Along that track I came to think of the leader as a quarterback (certainly not the Monday morning type), as a *tactical leader on the field*. I was not concerned with leadership at the higher levels, since that should be left to the coaches and their staffs who represent the strategists. I soon found that the character of the quarterback/leader could be seen in a less complex and more understandable way by thinking of his attributes as the underpinning, the basis of his art. The whole of his art could then be seen as the sum of its parts. The idea of the whole being the sum of its parts is anything but new; however, what *is* new is that attributes can be brought to life when shown as parts of the art which have assured a leader of victory in battle.

Yet attributes cannot be displayed on isolated slides to be viewed under the microscope of the mind. They must be seen in the heat of action where they are forced to confront the dynamics of battle. In the Prologue that follows we will see a multi-faceted show of dynamic forces massing to overpower a leader.

Prologue: The Dynamics of Battle

Dan Morgan at the Battle of Cowpens, 1781

DAN MORGAN DISMOUNTED, swinging his six-foot frame from the saddle as lightly as he could without showing signs of the rheumatic twinges shooting down his legs. He managed it in the graceful motion that had always marked his movements, but now he had to act it out consciously to hide his pain from the others. Bad enough their commander having this cursed affliction in his first independent command without him having to put up with side glances and helpful gestures. He'd have none of that.

He snatched the map his aide-de-camp was handing to him, and glared down at it for the fifth time that afternoon. Kosciuszko, General Greene's engineer, had done a good job of charting rivers and creeks, but here, west of the Catawba River, he had barely sketched in the main roads. And it was no main road that Morgan's column was stumbling along now as it filed past him. In fact, calling it a road would be doing it proud—as they put it in the Carolinas—since it was no more than a cattle trail, scarcely visible through the bare branches of winter underbrush.

As the branches of laurel and dead briars were whipped back and forth by the passing infantrymen, Morgan looked up long enough to recognize the dark blue regimental coats with red facings as the uniform of a company of Howard's Maryland Continentals. They marched in open column keeping to their files as well as they could on the rough trail. Yet who could care about drill ground formations here in this wilderness? They looked fit enough, though fatigue was showing in the faces of men who had been on forced march for over ten hours—and with half their breakfast rations left behind on the cooking fires. That was how quickly he had hurried them off on this march from Burr's Mill, after getting the reports that Tarleton was close on his trail.

His keen glance took in the column as far as the woods would allow. The Continentals showed all the marks of veteran infantry, from the muskets slung butt-up with their locks wrapped against the winter damp, to the way knapsacks were carried high behind the shoulders. Even the files were silent, with none of the jabbering that went on with a column of militia. The only sounds here were the clink of a bayonet scabbard or the rattle of twigs against a musket stock. He could almost hear their breathing, though that may have been an illusion caused by the sight of their wisps of breath on the wintry air.

His glance swung around, first toward Major Giles, then to portly Col. William Washington. He caught himself in time to stifle the grin that almost creased his rough face when he looked at Washington. *My God*, he thought, *how can the man be such a rare cavalry commander and stay so damned fat?* His mind turned back to business.

"Well, Colonel, how far are we from the Broad if we keep heading in this direction?" Morgan asked.

"We're on the watershed about midway between Thicketty Creek on our left and Gilkey Creek on our right. That'll put us about ten miles from the river, right about there," Washington jabbed a thick forefinger at the map.

"Any other word about the river?" Morgan asked.

"Same scouts' reports—she's still up to her banks and flowing fast."

"Can we still make it across the ford?"

"Yes, but we'll need plenty of time to rig the lines and get things set for the infantry and then the wagons."

"How much time is plenty?"

"Sir, we'll need at least two hours, and you know we can't do it at night," Washington said.

Morgan looked back at the map, and spoke half-aloud, so low that Washington and Giles had to strain to follow his words.

"Only four hours of daylight left. It'll take all of that just to reach the river, with no time left to cross. Then too, if Tarleton marches at night like he often does, tomorrow morning he'd be on us when we'd be trying to make it across. And can't you just see what Tarleton's dragoons could do to our militia—caught milling around with their asses to the river? Hell, those that didn't disappear in the swamps would be slaughtered like hogs at a county butcherin'."

He raised his voice, looking back at Washington. "Just two more questions, Colonel. Since we can't make a proper crossing today, what about that place you mentioned—the ground where the farmers let their cattle range?"

"That would be Hannah's Cowpens; open grazing land with a lot of trees. It would be about five miles from here, near the upper end of Thicketty Creek. But I must warn you, General, that whole area is cavalry country. Exactly the kind of ground Tarleton would love to have for maneuvering his dragoons," Washington said.

"I realize that. Now, how far do you reckon we're ahead of Bloody Benny?" Morgan asked.

"A half-hour ago my scouts spotted his van about four hours behind our rearguard, and that won't have changed much. But one more thing, Sir. Pickens' messenger has been waiting while I sent for Major McDowell." Washington pointed toward the two mountain men making their way through the underbrush.

"Why McDowell? What does he have to do with Pickens who isn't even here?"

"It's McDowell himself that's important right now. He and some of his North Carolinians were through this way three months ago on their way to whip Ferguson at Kings Mountain. The overmountain men used the Cowpens for an assembly area before heading east for Kings Mountain," Washington explained.

Morgan motioned a silent order to the two men in worn hunting shirts for them to stay in the saddle. Pickens' man made his report: his commander was on his way with 150 men to join General Morgan. Join him where? Colonel Pickens hadn't said, the messenger guessed he'd just catch up with the General.

Morgan shook his head, half in disgust, half in secret amusement. "The Old Wagoner," with five years of war behind him, knew so well what this mountaineer would never have considered—that one "where" unanswered could cost a commander a campaign. He turned to Major McDowell, a stocky Scotch-Irish frontiersman whose blue eyes met Morgan's without wavering.

"You know why you're here," Morgan said, "tell us about it."

McDowell described the Cowpens. The area consisted mostly of rolling or flat ground with scattered stands of hickory, pines, or red oaks. There was no underbrush, and the long grass made fine pasturing for the cattle that the Carolina farmers marked and turned loose to forage through the open forest. The center of the area, marked by the Green River Road, was about five miles from the Broad River and the same distance from Morgan's present location. At the mention of forage Morgan's eyes had lit up.

"By God, Washington, you know how bad we're needing that for the horses! Now, hold on just a minute, gentlemen. I won't keep you waiting long," Morgan said.

His head was bent over the map for silent seconds. Then, as he looked up, orders followed decision as one footstep follows another.

"We'll go to the Cowpens. You"—he looked at Pickens' messenger—"get back to Colonel Pickens and tell him to meet me at the Cowpens, as fast as he can make it.

"Colonel Washington, go ahead and scout out the area. I'll meet you there with my commanders. We'll ride on ahead of the column. When you pass the advance guard, have it bear left around the head of Thicketty Creek, toward the Cowpens.

"Major Giles, ride back down the column and round up the commanders, then rejoin me at the Cowpens.

"Come on, Major McDowell, let's get going."

Morgan and Washington met on the Green River Road in the fading light of the January day. The senior commanders, with the exception of Pickens who would not arrive until after nightfall, rode behind their general—Lieutenant Colonel Howard, commanding the Continentals, followed by the militia commanders. Morgan left them to wait and look over the near terrain while he and Washington reconnoitered the larger expanse of the area.

Looking to the northwest Morgan saw before him a wide and deep stretch of grassland studded with the trees McDowell had described. The ground in front of him sloped gently upward until it was topped by a low crest about four hundred yards away. Beyond that he could see a higher ridge, really two hills, and farther a glimpse of a low swale, and beyond, the highest hill of the area. It was all rolling terrain with gentle slopes, none of the high spots exceeding twenty-five yards above Morgan's position.

Washington guided him back and forth across the tract. As they rode Washington pointed out the key terrain features. Morgan listened and observed, yet his thoughts were racing throughout the conversation.

This will have to be it, he thought, *the ground I'll fight on . . . time is running out, Tarleton will be only four hours away . . . and what if he rolls his men out in the dark as he usually does? That means I've got to be ready to take on his advance guard at first light . . . Washington's reports are always reliable and they tell me that Bloody Ben has over a thousand men. I may have near that tonight if all my militia show up . . . But, my God, what a difference! His veteran regulars outnumber mine three to one, and except for Triplett's two-hundred Virginians my militia are an untrained, scraggly lot, as liable to disappear as to fight, though there are good riflemen among them . . . Tarleton's got three-hundred cavalrymen to Washington's eighty . . . and then there's this ground (will it be my last battlefield?) that I'll have to deploy on . . . the militia will know that the river is behind them, I'll see to that, and it will spark their "fighting spirit" because there'll be no swamps to disappear into . . . but that means that I'll have nothing to protect my flanks against Benny's dragoons; they'll be wide open . . . that's a chance I'll have to take, but it can be weighed against two things—Benny always comes up fast and hits as hard as he can straight on. He will only maneuver later if he's forced to. I'll keep Washington's cavalry as my fast-moving reserve to counterattack the flank or rear of any maneuvering force of Tarleton's . . . all of which means that I've got to deploy my force in depth. Well, the ground lends itself to that, so that's the way I'll fight . . . yet if I'm planning to fight a pitched battle, how will that fit into the meaning of my mission as I got it from Nathanael Greene?* "This force—and such others as may join you—you will employ against the enemy on the west side of the Catawba River, either offensively or defensively, as your prudence and discretion may direct, acting with caution and avoiding surprises by every possible precaution . . . The object . . . is to give protection to that part of the country and spirit up the people, to annoy the enemy in that quarter."[1]

Well, at this point how can I "spirit up the people" if I don't get Bloody Benny off their backs—and mine? So now my "prudence and discretion" are telling me to stop running and fight—either offensively or defensively—and I'll have to do that in reverse order, first on the defense then over to the offense. Damned if this isn't like an old, rheumatic hound being brought to bay by a feisty three-year-old, with all his sharp young teeth snappin' at the old one's arse.

His mind made up, he and Washington rode back to the others. He was no longer a cornered hound dog, but Brig.-Gen. Daniel Morgan, commanding the Southern Department's Army in the West. He waved his commanders to close in around him, keeping them on horseback as he spoke.

"I'm giving you the guts of my plan now while there's still light enough to see it on the ground. We'll talk over the details tonight, so now I'll take only questions about what I'm pointing out here.

"We'll post the infantry in three lines. The road we're standing on will mark the center of our deployment. All indications are that Tarleton will come at us from the east on this road, just as you came up it a while ago.

"The first line will be made up of picked riflemen. They will be the first to bring Benny's cavalry under fire when they advance to scout us out. Majors McDowell and Cunningham will each command half of this line, and it will be spread out along the lower slope—right across here.

"The second line will be a hundred and fifty yards farther back, midway up the slope—back there. It will contain the rest of the Carolina and Georgia militia. Colonel Pickens will be in overall command of the second line.

"The third line will consist of the Continentals as well as the Virginia militia and Beaty's South Carolinians, and it will be commanded by Lieutenant Colonel Howard. The line will be formed along the main crest and just down the slope with its center astride this road.

"Colonel Washington's cavalry will be in reserve, posted out of sight behind the second hill—back there. The whole idea is to lead Benny into a trap, so we can blast his cavalry and infantry as they come up these slopes. When they've been cut down to size by our fire, we'll attack *them*. All right, any questions?"

He looked around a ring of faces registering a gamut of reactions ranging from disbelief to delight. Major Triplett of Virginia spoke first.

"Sir, those militia out in front will run, sure as we're

standing here. They'll never face the bayonets of Tarleton's regulars."

"Don't you think I know that, Major? Hell, we're going to tell them to run—after they've gotten off at least two shots. Then the first line riflemen can run back and fall in with the second line's militia. On Pickens' command that whole bunch will get off at least two shots. Then Pickens' line will file off to the left and take position on the left of Howard's line. Remember this—if they're running on orders they won't panic. And we'll give 'em a little extra courage by reminding 'em the Broad River is still back there, five miles behind us, and if they run again they'll never get across it before Tarleton's dragoons catch up with 'em."[2]

That brought a laugh that ran around the circle of officers. They knew down-to-earth logic when they heard it, especially when it came from a man with Morgan's reputation as a fighter. As the laughter died Colonel Brannon of South Carolina spoke.

"We're with you, General, but what about our flanks?"

"We can bank on everyone's experience with Tarleton. When his dragoons find our position he'll go for us hell for leather, straight ahead, sure's you're born. He'll think he's got us far surpassed because he has some of the finest troops in the British Army, so it will never occur to him that he's taking a risk. I've thought this out, Colonel, and that's why Washington's cavalry will be hidden there in reserve. Then too, if Pickens and his officers can rally and reform the militia we'll be able to bring fire to bear on the flanks of Benny's formations at a time when they will be least expecting it."

As Morgan looked around for the final time he thought, *they may be tired, but they're spoiling for a fight—now that they know what to do and believe they can do it.*

"Very well then," Morgan's voice rose in its wagoner's bawl, "tonight as the men bed down, we'll get them educated too, so there'll be no confusion when they're posted in the morning."

Morgan was making his rounds an hour before first light, his rheumatism reminding him that it was very much with him. He kept his silence—trying though it was—until all was going as it should. He observed that the men were fed, the campfires stamped out, and the baggage loaded on the wagons. The militia companies were falling in, with all the jostle and noise that always marked their assembling. Howard's

Maryland and Delaware Continentals had already marched off silently to their positions on the rise. They were used to forming up and marching in the dark.

Morgan had kept silent for too long. He bellowed at the wagonmasters, his voice hoarse from the night's exertions, until the trains began to move out of sight through the trees, barely visible in the graying dawn.

After the last militia company had trudged away Morgan followed it as far as the Green River Road where he turned off to find his first line. Major McDowell's North Carolinians and Major Cunningham's Georgians had just finished filing off into their skirmishers' positions. Morgan joked with them as he rode past them, but there was deadly meaning in his "Aim for the epaulet men. Kill them first. Kill them and you've done a day's work.

"Remember to run straight back. Pickens' men will be leaving spaces for you in their line."

He rode back to the second line and met Pickens for a review of his Carolina and Georgia militia. Together they rode the full three hundred yards of the line, Pickens keeping his customary silence, Morgan joking and exhorting—

"Sit down, men. Ease your joints. No need to stand now, just keep in your places.

"You there, Georgia boy, no need to look so glum! We're going to have plenty of amusement mighty shortly.

"Remember, you owe me at least two fires, and when you take off, be sure it's to the left flank."

He left the taciturn Pickens at the end of his line and rode around the north side of the hill, far enough to see the long white coats of Washington's cavalrymen, standing alongside their horses in orderly lines in the swale behind the hill. He turned his horse and rode up the rear slope of the rise where Howard had taken post behind his four hundred Continentals and veteran militia. As he rode he could tell himself: *The men have been rested and fed well. They've been posted quietly, with no confusion. Now I can only hope that Tarleton's men will have been turned out hours ago, to march in the cold darkness across creeks, ravines, and rough trails, always stumbling over unknown terrain, watched all the time by my scouts. That ought to take the fighting edge off King George's mighty regulars. But if I don't get blessed by Tarleton's misfortune, I do have three blessings for sure in having Washington, Howard, and Pickens as senior commanders. I don't take kindly to Pickens when he's being preacher-like, but his militia will fight for him. Washington, in spite of being tubby, is the*

*finest cavalry commander I could have found; he's all over the place
and always in control. And John Howard, sitting his horse like a
statue up there. He's maybe seventeen years younger than me, but
just as cool in a fight, with five years of war and a half-dozen big
battles behind him. He's a quiet man, never showing off his fine education, but he's mean as a cornered bear in battle. Yes, I'm lucky,
though I'll need a lot of luck this morning.*

Morgan and Howard stood side by side on the crest of
the hill. Behind them their horses were tethered amid a cluster of staff officers. Fifty yards below them on the forward
slope the double-ranked line of Continentals had hunkered
down on the hillside.

Another two hundred yards down the hill the line of
Pickens' militia was harder to see; their brown hunting shirts
and homespun had blended into the winter grass. The men
had "eased their joints", lying or sitting half-hidden on the
dun hillside.

Even Morgan's keen eye could not make out the skirmish
line of McDowell's and Cunningham's riflemen, three-hundred
and fifty yards away. The sharpshooters had taken cover be-

Continentals await the British attack at Cowpens
(a Bicentennial reenactment)

hind trees and in the long grass in their natural fashion, so it was not remarkable that their line remained out of sight.

A settled silence hung over the nine hundred men like their ghosts of breath in the frosty air of the rising dawn. Even Morgan had fallen silent, musing in the strange way that comes to men before battle.

Just as well, he thought, *that I can't see that line of skirmishers. If I can't, knowing where they are, then it's sure the British can't. What could be better? Well, it could be better, back there in Frederick County where I thought I'd gone into an earned retirement. Especially after that damned Congress had seen fit to pass over COLONEL Morgan. That is, until they had second thoughts about needing an old war horse, and pulling him out of his pasture. And thinking of pastures, I surely hope that Abigail isn't having trouble with those cattle getting loose again. That's no fit task for a woman, having to manage that farm by herself. Seems strange it could be Wednesday morning too, back there in Virginia, with everything quiet and—*

He was jarred back to reality by Howard's sudden movement. The infantry commander had brushed against Morgan's arm when he had raised his hands to frame his eyes.

"It's them all right, General, see them?" Howard was pointing toward the distant black treeline beyond the American skirmish line.

Morgan, staring, could see the tiny figures of mounted men in Lincoln-green jackets moving out of the woods. A thin scattered line emerged into the open and halted at the foot of the long slope. Their brass dragoon helmets began to reflect the growing light.

"Tarleton had come with the sun."[3]

As Morgan and Howard watched, scarlet jacketed cavalrymen appeared at the edge of the woods, followed by a green-jacketed officer. The little figure rode forward, its black helmet plume waving in the wind. It gestured to its front and the line of dragoons spurred forward. They must have seen several of the riflemen, for they broke from a walk into a trot. Morgan fancied he could hear the drumming of the hooves on the hard ground, but he knew that must be his imagination. It was not his imagination when he saw little puff balls of smoke blossom among the trees where the riflemen were lying. The rattle of rifle fire came on the clear air. Morgan saw saddles emptied as other horses were pulled up short when their riders wheeled them about and galloped for the rear.

"Now that's shooting!" Morgan boomed, exulting, "I count a dozen down. Right, Howard?"

"At least, Sir, maybe a half dozen more," Howard replied.

They saw the dragoon officer waving his saber in a futile effort to rally the fleeing cavalrymen, but they swept past him and disappeared into the woods.

"Well, by God, Benny should know for certain we're here now. What'll be the next act in his program?" Morgan said.

As if in reply, the panoply of Tarleton's army began to unfold from the forest, columns marching off to wheel into line where the Green River Road entered the Cowpens. A company of British dragoons led off to the British right, followed by the scarlet coats and white breeches of infantry companies wheeling into line with drill ground precision. A small blue-coated section followed the infantry, then there was a second column of infantry in green jackets. Behind it another scarlet and white column debouched from the forest and came up into precise line to the left of the green jackets. Another dark blue section moved up alongside the scarlet infantry, and finally another company of green dragoons took post on the British left flank. Sergeants dressed the ranks into rigid lines that became a brilliant array of scarlet, green, blue, and white. The colorful line was topped with a glittering line of bayonets as the British infantry shouldered arms, and the long line came marching forward, drums rolling and regimental colors rippling in the wind.

"Now you see Tarleton's order of battle," Morgan said. "He has posted British Legion dragoons on each flank. Then, going from his right to his left, there are companies of British infantry, then a grasshopper* where those blue coats are, then Legion infantry in the green jackets, another grasshopper, then more British infantry. And now I see his Highlanders, look at the kilts, moving into reserve behind his left flank, and it looks like at least two more companies of Legion dragoons going into reserve there with the Highlanders."

The British drums began to beat the long roll, and the line came on, battalions aligning on the colors. There were more puffs of smoke among the trees that sheltered the riflemen. Then they were jumping to their feet and running

---

*Soldier slang for a 3-pounder artillery piece carried on horseback for transport. It got its name from its recoil, which made it appear to jump when fired. The two guns at Cowpens were making a colorful history: captured from the British at Saratoga (October 1777), recaptured by the British at Camden (August 1780), taken back by Morgan's men at Cowpens, only to be lost to the British again at Guilford Courthouse two months later.[4]

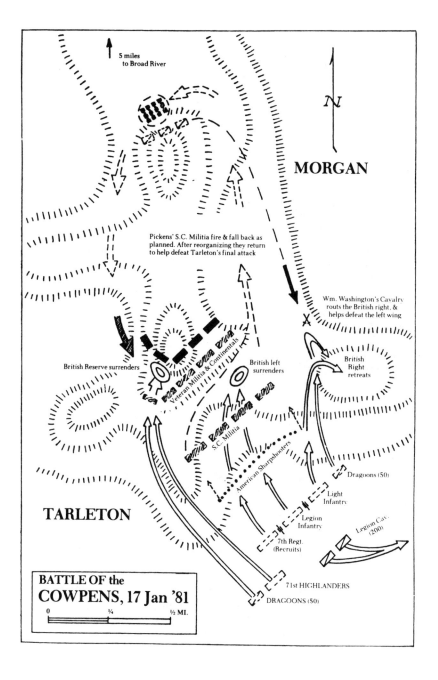

5 miles
to Broad River

N

MORGAN

Pickens' S.C. Militia fire & fall back as
planned. After reorganizing they return
to help defeat Tarleton's final attack

Wm. Washington's Cavalry
routs the British right, &
helps defeat the left wing

British
Right
retreats

British Reserve surrenders

British left
surrenders

Veteran Militia & Continentals

S.C. Militia

American Sharpshooters

Dragoons (50)

Light
Infantry

TARLETON

Legion
Infantry

Legion Cav.
(200)

7th Regt.
(Recruits)

71st HIGHLANDERS

DRAGOONS (50)

BATTLE OF the
COWPENS, 17 Jan '81

0   ¼   ½ MI.

back toward Pickens' line. Some were reloading and firing as they ran, a feat that always amused Morgan because it never failed to confound the British who were trained to load and fire only at a halt. Morgan looked at his watch and snapped its cover shut.

"I've got five minutes after seven," he said to Howard. "I'm going down to look again at Pickens' line."

He walked his horse through company intervals in the line of Continentals, then trotted forward to join Pickens. They watched the militia officers walking up and down behind the line, cautioning the men to hold their fire.

"Good, good," Morgan muttered to Pickens, "let 'em get within fifty paces before our first volley."

The British line swung up the slope, deadly in its grim beauty, muskets leveled at Charge Bayonet. Morgan saw the Carolina company officers glancing back over their shoulders at Pickens who was holding his right arm stiffly upright. Pickens dropped his arm, and the officers shouted "Fire!" The volley crashed into the British. The scarlet and green line could be seen reeling through the smoke, but it recovered, closing its ranks as it halted. British Army discipline ruled over shock, and a return volley was thrown at the Americans, though most of its effect ripped into the sod in front of Pickens' men.

There was a fatal pause as the British reloaded. This was the golden moment Pickens had been waiting for: catching the enemy standing stock still, within easy rifle range where even the muskets of his militia farmers could reap their toll of British casualties. Pickens' officers were shouting "Fire!" again, and another volley tore into the enemy ranks. Redcoats were going down, among them the lion's share of the "epaulet men" that Tarleton would lose that morning.

Incredibly the British were reforming, and their thinned but realigned line came on with leveled bayonets. This was the critical time that Morgan had dreaded. If Pickens' militia broke and ran, panicking, straight back toward Howard's Continentals, there would be chaos. Morgan peered through the drifting powder smoke, and almost cried out in relief. Yes, the militiamen were running, like the devil himself was on their heels, but the rush of men poured like a swift current off to the left flank, heading to pass around the slope where Howard's men stood like a dam before a flood.

Yet as Morgan stood in his stirrups, straining to see beyond the smoke, the next of his fears was materializing to his left front. He could see well enough now to make out Tarleton's right flank dragoons trotting off to their right oblique to pass around the British infantry, obviously maneuvering into position to launch a charge against the running American militia. Morgan's mind was racing, trying to put himself in Tarleton's thoughts. How would he be assessing the situation? Then he had to calculate how he should deal with Tarleton's cavalry:

Yes, Tarleton must have jumped to the conclusion that the running Americans were a horde of fugitives fleeing in panic as militia always had before a British bayonet assault. And so, Bloody Ben would be committing this cavalry to saber down the "routed" militia. He would try and use those dragoons to turn the rout into a flood that would pour over the Continentals' line, raising havoc to allow the British infantry to overwhelm Howard's men in the confusion. Well. The Old Wagoner was not going to let that happen. He must get word to Washington in time to have him smash Tarleton's dragoons on their right flank.

He bawled for Major Giles, unaware that his aide was at his left elbow, "Get back to Colonel Washington as fast as that nag will carry you. Tell him to attack around this hill and charge those dragoons on their flank, I want 'em wiped out or swept off this field."

Giles spurred his horse up the hill, his dark blue cloak

Colonel Washington's troopers (a Bicentennial reenactment)

streaming out behind him. Morgan rode up the hill at a walk. Aides could fly to the rear at a gallop, but the troops should not see their general move with anything but dignity, especially when he had turned his back to the enemy. Pickens rode beside him as they passed through an interval in Howard's line. When they had cleared the rear rank Morgan put his horse to a trot, and moved toward the left end of the line. They halted on the crest of the slope. Below them the Continentals and the veteran militia were standing at the ready. Farther down the slope Pickens' men were now a strung-out river flowing around the bottom of the east slope of the hill where Morgan stood. But they had not halted as he had directed! Instead they were heading toward the rearmost knoll that hid Washington's cavalry. Morgan sensed at once what had caused this failure to follow his orders.

I should have known, he thought, *that most of those militia have their horses picketed in the trees in rear of Washington's assembly area. And, by God, they're heading for those horses. Pickens and I will have to stop them and get them reformed. But right this minute my place is here, until I can make sure that Washington is coming up to counterattack. Damn, what a sorry plight I've gotten myself into . . . .*

He looked along Pickens pointing arm to see the white coats of Washington's dragoons coming over the rearward hill. The cavalry swept down across the swale, bearing left to avoid Pickens' men. In seconds that seemed hours to Morgan, stout Colonel Washington was drawing saber and shouting commands to his leading company. The company wheeled into line followed by another forming a second rank. Looking back to his left Morgan saw Tarleton's leading dragoons break formation to ride down the last of Pickens' militia.

It's going to be mighty rough on some of those men who'll feel those British sabers. But there's going to be reward in this, for Washington will be charging into a disorganized enemy and into their flank to boot.

He and Pickens watched long enough to see Washington's cavalry smash into Tarleton's horsemen. The British rear dissolved under the impact to become a flurry of fugitives fleeing to escape the American sabers. There was no time to stay and watch Washington's pursuit. Morgan and Pickens galloped back across the swale, all dignity forgotten, in their rush to get to the mass of fleeing militia.

Morgan would never forget the transformation of Pickens from a reticent iceberg of a man to a whirling dervish on horseback. The man was everywhere at once, shouting at one knot of men, grabbing at others to halt them and bring them to their senses. Between them, Pickens and Morgan got hold of officers, got the streaming flood halted and turned into a mass of milling men who at last could be rallied and formed back into companies and battalions.

There was no time for Morgan to remain here, either, to await an outcome. He paused long enough to hear a renewed rattle of musketry that was increasing to a rolling roar. He knew what was happening, the British infantry and the American third line had clashed and the intensity of the firing told Morgan they were slugging it out.

He left Pickens to reorganize his command, after directing him to send mounted messengers when his troops were ready to move out. He was off again at a gallop to rejoin Howard and resume command. When he reached the crest of the hill the battle was unfolding below him. The roar of the volleying had fallen away to scattered firing, and Morgan saw that the British line, center and wings together, had withdrawn halfway down the hill to reform a new line. The reason for their reorganizing was all too evident. The scarlet coats and green jackets of dead or wounded British littered the slope between the two forces. Morgan looked down to his right front and saw Howard trotting off toward his right flank, and in a flash he saw the cause of Howard's concern. Far beyond the right of Howard's line he could see Tarleton's battalion of Highlanders, the famed 71st or Fraser's Highlanders, marching in column and swinging wide to clear the British left flank. Tarleton was committing his only infantry reserve to envelope Howard's line and roll it up.

Well, no need for me to go rushing down there. Howard is one of the finest infantrymen I've ever known. He'll handle things, probably refuse that right flank* by pulling back a company or two. But God in heaven! What is he doing? What are they all doing?

To Morgan's horror Howard's right flank company, Wallace's Virginians, had faced about and was marching to the rear, backs to the enemy! And to make it more mystifying they appeared to be marching in perfect order. All down Howard's line other commanders, apparently believing that

---

*Refusing a flank means changing the front of a flank unit to face it toward the enemy threat thus protecting the force's flank.

a general withdrawal had been ordered, were facing their units about and marching them rearward, aligning on the Virginians. Morgan could see Howard riding back and forth in front of his marching line. He was giving orders as he rode, but he was too far away for Morgan to hear the commands.

He could certainly not afford to stay out of this. Such an appalling change coming at the critical moment in his battle could cost him the whole affair in minutes. He rode like the wind until he could rein up alongside Howard.

"What is this retreat?" Morgan demanded.

"I am trying to save my right flank. I had intended to wheel Wallace's company in order to refuse the flank, but there's been a misunderstanding, so I'm taking up a new position," Howard's words came rapidly but his voice was steady.

"Are you beaten?" Morgan asked.

"Do men who march like that look as though they were beaten?" Howard said, as coolly as if on parade. Morgan stifled a gasp of relief that might have been heard for yards.

"Right!" he said, "I'll choose you a second position. When you reach it, face about and fire."

He was off again down the reverse slope of Howard's hill and up the forward slope of the hill that had screened Washington's cavalry. As he mounted the slope two buckskin-clad horsemen rode over the hill to meet him. They were Pickens' messengers, the first to speak saying that Colonel Pickens wanted to know on what point to direct his march. Morgan pointed back toward Pickens' rallying ground, then swept his arm in a great arc that encompassed the American rear and Howard's right flank, and ended by pointing at the distant Highlanders.

"Tell Colonel Pickens that he has already gone halfway around the battle. I want him to complete the circuit by moving with all the speed he can muster and hit those Highlanders and any other British he comes across in their rear. Got it? Get going!"

He scanned the hillside for a suitable halting place for Howard. It appeared that any point midway up the hill would provide good ground. He looked back to see Howard's marching line coming toward him with the same steadiness that had marked it from the beginning. He turned his horse to go down the slope when Pickens' other man called out to him: "Another messenger comin', General."

It was one of Washington's officers on a black stallion whose sides were streaming with sweat.

"Sir, Colonel Washington sends his respects and—"

"Get on with it," Morgan snapped.

"He says to tell you those British infantry are coming on like a mob. Give them one fire and I'll charge them." The young lieutenant panted out the message, his eyes shining in his excitement.

"Tell Colonel Washington that is exactly what I want him to do. Tell him to move out around the hill so he can launch his attack when he sees Colonel Howard's men open fire."

The lieutenant was gone as quickly as he had come, and Morgan looked again at Howard's approaching line, then beyond it at the slope of the other hill. It was covered with scarlet coats of charging British infantry like masses of red leaves swirling over a brown field. Yes, Washington had called the shot. The enemy was coming on like a mob, no longer in ordered ranks, but like a shouting rabble, bayonets bobbing up and down in any direction.

"Like a damned dismounted foxhunt," snorted Morgan, "and this is one they'll never come back from."

He rode toward Howard, raising his right arm in the signal to halt. Howard waved his sword in acknowledgement, and gave his commands. His timing was perfect. The double ranks of Continentals and militia came to a parade-ground halt, faced about, and sent their volley crashing into the enemy. It was done so quickly that the Americans had fired from the hip, at a range of thirty yards, into the packed mass of howling British infantry. The shock that followed was a boxer's knockout blow. The enemy who were still standing reeled back in stunned confusion, and Howard, no longer the calm statue or the leader on parade, was shouting: "Give them the bayonet!"

The pent rage of men who had been retreating against their will needed no command to release it. They charged into the staggering redcoats, thrusting and slashing until those who could not escape were bellowing for quarter, some kneeling, others throwing themselves full length on the ground.

Morgan rode back far enough to survey the whole field, in time to watch Washington's dragoons in a thundering charge that swept around the hill to smash into Tarleton's right flank. The British Legion dragoons did not wheel to face the American charge, instead they scattered and fled. The American horsemen, unopposed now, rode down the British infantry, sabers rising and falling, until the light infantry and fusiliers broke and ran. Lieutenant Colonel McCall of Washington's command pursued the mass of fugitives (Morgan estimated it to number two hundred men), surrounded it, and made prisoners of them all.

The British center and right were collapsing before Morgan's eyes. Legion infantry and the 7th Fusiliers were dropping their muskets and throwing their crossbelts and side arms on the ground. But all was not over yet. Triplett's Virginians and South Carolinians, the right flank men who had fought like Continentals that day, were still engaged in a hot fight with the Highlanders. That battalion of Scots under their fighting commander, Major McArthur, was the only infantry unit of Tarleton's army that had not become casualties or prisoners. Yet their gallant fight was to prove hopeless. Pickens' men, reformed into their units, fell into firing line on the Highlanders' left rear. A rallied company of Tarleton's Legion cavalry rode toward the beleagured Scots in an attempt to prevent their encirclement, but they met a blast of fire from Pickens' riflemen. They broke and fled for the last time. In a matter of minutes the Highlanders were surrounded on three sides by Howard's and Pickens' men, and were being slaughtered under a hail of rifle and musket bullets. Pickens called on their commander to surrender, and Major McArthur had to tender his sword to Pickens to save his battalion from certain annihilation.

Now the only British soldiers left fighting were the Royal Artillery gun crews with the two grasshoppers. The blue-coated gunners continued to "serve their pieces" in the finest artillery tradition, but the full fury of Howard's nearest infantry was turned upon them. Howard ordered the guns taken. They were, as the gunners were cut down to a man.

Lieutenant Colonel McCall rode up to Morgan to make his report on the fate of Tarleton's cavalry. Evidently Tarleton had tried to lead his reserve of 250 Legion dragoons in a desperate attack to free the Highlanders and save the gunners. It was a final and futile gesture, for "the dragoons forsook their leader and rode off, bearing down any officer who opposed their flight."[5] And Washington himself had gone in pursuit of Tarleton, though there was yet no report of the outcome.

Morgan was for once speechless. He could not believe the extent of his victory. It is said that he was so exuberant that he picked up a nine-year-old drummer boy and kissed him on both cheeks. He had planned to lead Tarleton into a "fire trap" that would administer a stinging repulse to Tarleton's attack, severe enough to make him lick his wounds while Morgan got his army across the Broad. Instead he had wiped out Tarleton's army in a double envelopment that would sparkle as a tactical gem in anyone's military history. With his thousand men he had crushed Tarleton's army whose losses totaled 110 killed, 830 prisoners (including 200 wounded), 2 regimental colors, 2 artillery pieces, 800 muskets, 35 baggage wagons, 60 Negro slaves, 100 cavalry horses, large stores of ammunition, and all of the British "field musick." Morgan's losses were 12 killed and 61 wounded. The comparative losses in combat power: Tarleton's over 85 percent; Morgan's .7 percent. In another meaningful sense, Tarleton had lost 25 percent of Cornwallis' invasion army in one hour.

Before this prologue I said that we would see in this battle a show of the dynamics of battle massing to overpower a leader. Let us take a retrospective look at Cowpens in search of those dynamics.

Danger. There was danger aplenty. Morgan's little army had no logistical base and was all on its own with only the supplies it could carry. It was too far from any friendly force for even a prayer of support. Greene's other "half" of his army was 120 miles away, a week's march in those days, and Cornwallis' main army was between him and Morgan. Add to these dangers Tarleton's mobile task force, a more powerful force than Morgan's in terms of regular infantry and cavalry, capable of pursuing Morgan anywhere he could go and destroying him if he were trapped. And Morgan was, in a way, trapped between Tarleton and the Broad River.

Chance. Morgan had to take the calculated risk that Tarleton would attack with his usual impetuosity, straight ahead at whatever was in his way. Risk? Yes, because Tarleton would have the time and favorable terrain to feel out Morgan's flanks, then maneuver to strike a vulnerable area. But Morgan knew all about Tarleton's character and took the chance, just as Lee and Jackson would, eighty years later, against Union commanders whose characters they knew well.

Exertion. Morgan demanded the most of his men and

himself, though it is certain that no one was pushed to the verge of suffering. On the other hand, we have seen Morgan showing a strength of will just to keep on going with the physical exertion required of him. This was significant in his case because of his being plagued with the constant pain of rheumatism or sciatica (since there were no medical records we cannot know which an accurate diagnosis would have shown). In fact, he soon became so disabled by his ailment that he was unable to mount a horse, and less than three weeks after Cowpens he had to go into permanent retirement.

Uncertainty. There was uncertainty throughout and before the battle. How far was Tarleton behind Morgan at any time? Where or how fast could Tarleton move to corner or attack him? How could he cross the Broad and still hold on to his militia, with Tarleton poised to spring on him while he was in the act? Where was Pickens, and when and where would he join Morgan? Would the militia in the first and second battle lines heed his orders and move out as directed after firing two shots? Was Washington's cavalry, even with its augmentation of McCall's men, strong enough to accomplish the mission of counterattacking British threats to the flanks? Could Pickens' militia be rallied and recommitted to action in time to play a decisive role in the battle?

Apprehension. This dynamic Morgan had to deal with in handling militia. He knew their capabilities and limitations, and the major limitation was their fear of the measured advance of British infantry behind its hedge of leveled bayonets, if for no other reason than that the militia had neither bayonets nor training to counter the threat. Morgan counted on that fear to "inspire" the men after they had given him "his two fires." But that fear was on the verge of becoming panic until Morgan and Pickens had halted and rallied the fleeing militia.

Frustration. Robert Burns, certainly never a soldier, has put it neatly nevertheless: "The best laid schemes o' mice an' men/Gang aft agley," and Morgan's fortune with his "schemes" at Cowpens was neither better nor worse than any other successful commander's. This can be recognized in two events. The first occurred when Morgan discovered that Pickens' men—running after firing their two rounds—were not going into the designated "rallying ground," but, instead, heading for their horses picketed behind Washington's reserve area. If the flight had been allowed to continue, in all probability the militia would have mounted up and been long gone when Morgan needed them most. The second occasion, equally serious in its potential for disaster, was the sudden and unexpected withdrawal of Howard's line which could have been catastrophic. Howard, it will be remembered, had decided to refuse his right flank in order to cope with an impending envelopment by the Highlanders. Accordingly he gave orders that his right flank company, Wallace's Virginians, change its front ninety degrees. To execute Howard's order the company should have been given the command to face about, followed by the command to wheel to the left and halt. In actuality, the company faced about, but instead of wheeling to the left, marched straight ahead, i.e., to the rear. The error could easily have been corrected, but before that could have happened the error was compounded by other commanders in Howard's line who thought that Wallace was obeying an order for a general withdrawal. They proceeded to follow suit. But Howard, understanding what had happened, handled the situation with the coolness we have seen.

So much for the dynamics of battle; they have shown the dark side of Cowpens. What did Dan Morgan bring to the bright side?

First of all, *courage,* the indispensable attribute. He consistently showed physical courage at the most critical and dangerous turns in the battle. Equally evident was his moral courage, that other quality required to take the risks involved in making a bold plan and sticking to it to see it executed to the finish.

When one considers Morgan's *intellect* there is little doubt that he exhibited those qualities that go to make up that attribute: imagination, flexibility of mind, and sound judgment. He was able to seize the opportunity to innovate because of his knowledge of human nature in general and the frailties of militia in particular. This was demonstrated when he told Pickens' men to run, because he knew they would, in any event, once confronted with British bayonets. It was his way of controlling the uncontrollable, allowing the militia to run away and fight another day which, in effect, they did.

Flexibility of mind also contributed to the attribute of *intellect,* shown in the case of Howard's "retreat." "This was the climax of the battle and the crucial decision. If Morgan had panicked or not gone along quickly with Howard, the Cowpens would have had a different ending. As it was, the misunderstood order called for a lightning-like decision, an almost intuitive reaction. Daniel Morgan met the crisis superbly."[6] In taking the action he did at this critical turn of events he further showed his good judgment.

Then there are Morgan's qualities which add up to the attribute of *will*. It would be difficult indeed to find a finer example of a leader coping with that most unpredictable dynamic, frustration. Morgan was exposed to it time and again; the most critical events have been covered in the analysis of the dynamics of battle. The other contributing qualities of boldness and staunchness which were also the manifestation of Morgan's will can be seen in his reactions to situations wherein his best-laid plans could have blown up in his face. He had to have known that such frustrations can occur—and usually do.

Finally, the sum of Morgan's attributes shown at Cowpens—*courage, intellect,* and *will*—were welded together into a tactical art. The combination enabled him to achieve that most sought-after effect in battle, surprise.

Tarleton reacted exactly as Morgan calculated he would by attacking frontally without reconaissance or maneuver. Furthermore, Tarleton was taken in by the flight of Pickens' line which he thought was acting like militia always had when on the wrong end of British bayonets. This led him to continue his frontal attack, and let it get out of hand when the false sense of exhilaration spread through his infantry, causing it to rush forward in a disordered mass. No one could have been more astounded than Tarleton when he saw this miniature Cannae happening to *him*! In his own words, he and his men were the victims of ". . . some unforeseen event, which may throw terror into the most disciplined soldiers, or counteract the best-concerted designs."[7] Some of us who were not there might call it surprise.

The summing up of this inside look at Cowpens might be compared to an arrow of Robin Hood's in the contest at Nottingham. If the shaft were straight and the aim true, he had a bullseye. Our shaft has been Dan Morgan's character, and the aim to show that a leader's attributes are the substance of his art. In Cowpens we have watched three such attributes come to life. As I have recognized five in all, the following chapters will be devoted to the examination of a leader's attributes in the light of the contribution of each to the art of leadership.

Part One

COURAGE

Anthony Wayne at
Stony Point, 1779

Louis Nicolas Davout
at **Auerstadt,** 1806

COURAGE

"This marshal [referring to Davout after his victory at Auerstädt] displayed distinguished bravery and firmness of character, the first qualities of the warrior."
—Napoleon in a bulletin to the *Grande Armée*

"We know from experience that the valor of the troops consists solely in the valor of the officers—a brave colonel, a brave battalion."
—Frederick the Great, *Die Werke Friedrichs des Grossen*

"I have formed a picture of a general which is not chimerical. . . . The first of all qualities is courage."
—Marshal de Saxe, *Reveries on the Art of War*

"War is the province of danger, and therefore courage above all things is the first quality of a warrior."
—Clausewitz, *On War*

Is an array of four epigraphs necessary to demonstrate the importance of courage? In this case, yes, for the intent has not been to overwhelm the reader with quotations, instead to suggest that something more than coincidence has caused three great commanders and a renowned theorist to agree that courage is the first attribute of the leader.

When one examines the histories of successful commanders, one soon finds that each invariably manifested not just simple bravery but two kinds of courage—the physical and the moral. And when one looks deeper he will realize that the dichotomy is not a historical nicety; there are indeed wide differences between the two.

Physical courage in battle, as the adjective indicates, involves the exposure of the body to the threat of wounds or death. Moral courage belongs to the domain of the mind. Yet, as we shall see, the two are often employed together and in combination with other attributes. For our purposes, however, I will first consider each separately with a view toward bringing them into balance at the chapter's end.

Physical Courage

FACING UP TO FEAR, to danger, is the focus of our interest as we consider men and their fears in battle. At the outset let us dispose of an encumbrance, the "fearless man." We have all heard of such men or have seen them in the movies, but fortunately they are about as scarce as politicians on the battlefield. I say "fortunately" because I have known (and known of) such men, and I wouldn't want them around in combat, much less leading men whose lives were my responsibility.

Let us see how one great mind has dealt with the idea of courage as opposed to fearlessness. Plato in the *Laches* has Nicias present his view of the issue: "I do not call animals . . . which have no fear of dangers, because they are ignorant of them, courageous, but only fearless or senseless . . . There is a difference, to my way of thinking, between fearlessness and courage. I am of the opinion that thoughtful courage is a quality possessed by very few, but that rashness, and boldness, and fearlessness, which has no forethought, are very common qualities possessed by many men, many women, many children, many animals . . . my courageous actions are wise actions."[1]

Plato is seconded by Aristotle when he observes that "drunken men often behave fearlessly and we do not praise them for their courage." In the light of such observations it is apparent that defining courage in the leader must embrace

33

the concept of "thoughtful courage," the ability to distinguish between the danger itself, and the necessity to get the job done in spite of it. For the leader to make decisions in battle he should be expected to act or react with thoughtful courage while being guided by his professional values.

Consequently we can disregard the "fearless man" and concentrate on the great majority of men, men who acknowledge fear while realizing they must act positively in spite of it. This lies at the core of the enigma that confronts the soldier in battle. Unfortunately he has neither the time nor the environment to study his problems and arrive at reasonable solutions, as we can do so calmly in these pages.

It is the soldier and his fears that demand attention before we can refocus on his leaders. My own experience tells me that it would take a lifetime of research to do justice to the combat soldier's travail. We are in luck, however, in being able to rely on the findings of two men who have delved deeply into the subject and whose writings are universally respected.

The first, Col. Ardant du Picq, was mortally wounded by a German artillery shell while leading his regiment into its baptism by fire at Longville-les-Metz in the Franco-Prussian War. A professional infantry officer in the French Army and a veteran of three campaigns, du Picq was the first nineteenth-century writer to investigate the behavior of men in battle. His early researches made him an unpopular fellow with his brother officers, for his original approach was based on a questionnaire which he circulated among them. According to John Keegan in *The Face of Battle:* "The questionnaire was not a success, most who received it finding its tone impertinent or its completion tedious. But his questions were intelligent and original and, when applied by du Picq (whose rebuff by his brother officers had not extinguished his curiosity) to documentary material, elicited fascinating answers."[2]

I can sympathize with du Picq, having made a similar attempt at the Army Command and General College a century later. My responses from some three hundred combat officers may have been more numerous than those received by du Picq but scarcely more rewarding. Therein lies a trace of irony: The veteran officer seems to be as cautious in expressing his opinions about men in battle as he is bold at leading them in combat. So cautious, in fact, as to supply inadequate answers on this less tangible aspect of behavior. In his small book, *Battle Studies,* du Picq found answers by recognizing clearly the nature of fear in battle and its effects on combat units. He came to two major conclusions, and one is still applicable to ground combat in our times. His first finding was that, in ancient times, organized masses of men approached each other with the apparent intention of coming into violent collision. The collision never really occurred except in a front rank. One side would hesitate, slow down, even halt on some occasions, then break and turn away. The first and foremost in flight were those soldiers in the rear who had not yet come face to face with the enemy. Then the forward ranks gave way and joined in the flight. After that came the wholesale slaughter of the defeated, so common in ancient warfare, because the fleeing men had exposed their backs to the enemy.

Du Picq's second conclusion—of far greater interest to modern readers—was that modern soldiers from civilized nations can be made to realize through reasoned discipline and realistic training, that the greater danger lies in flight, for safety, in some measure, can be found in maintaining the integrity of the soldier's unit. In this light several of du Picq's contributory findings are interesting:

> How many men before a lion, have the courage to look him in the face, to think of and put into practice measures of self-defense? In war when terror has seized you, as experience has shown it often does, you are as before a lion . . .

> Four brave men who do not know each other will not dare to attack a lion. Four less brave, but knowing each other well, sure of their reliability and consequently of mutual aid, will attack resolutely. There is the science of the organization of armies in a nutshell . . .

> To fight from a distance is distinctive in man. From the first day he has worked to this end, and he continues to do so. It was thought that with long range weapons close combat might return. On the contrary troops keep further off before its effects . . .

> The theory of strong battalions is a shameful theory. It does not reckon on courage but on the amount of human flesh. It is a reflection on the soul. Great and small orators, all of whom speak of military matters today, talk only of masses. War is waged by enormous masses, etc. In the masses, man as an individual

disappears, the number only is seen. *Quality is forgotten, and yet today as always, quality alone produces real effect**. . . .[3]

The other writer whose work is authoritative was the late Brig.-Gen. S. L. A. Marshall, who has deservedly been called the successor of du Picq. Slam Marshall (Samuel Lyman Atwood Marshall) succeeded where du Picq did not, for he lived to see his conclusions and chief recommendations bear fruit. He was able, in Keegan's words, "to persuade the American army that it was fighting its wars the wrong way."[4]

It became relatively easy for Marshall to draw the conclusions he did because his innovative methods produced the bases for the widely acclaimed campaign histories of the American army in World War II. Probably of greater importance was the quality and quantity of data about men in battle which now provides invaluable aid to historians and other analysts. It was Marshall who sold the high command in the European Theater his idea of debriefing, i.e., historical teams holding mass interviews with combat infantrymen *on the spot just as their companies came out of combat.* He developed techniques for getting the men talking—to an extent that unabashed and unembarrassed soldiers were sounding off freely—so that one man's recollections were reinforced and often amended by those of his comrades. In fact the stories, from memories fresh and uncluttered by subsequent events, poured out so freely and fast that the skills of the historical teams were often strained in trying to get down all the interrelated accounts. Yet they succeeded in an amazing tour de force.

Marshall's most disturbing discovery, at least to army officers and military analysts, was that

> a commander of infantry will be well advised to believe that when he engages the enemy not more than one quarter of his men will ever strike a real blow unless they are compelled by almost overpowering circumstance or unless all junior leaders constantly 'ride herd' on troops with the specific mission of increasing their fire. The 25 percent estimate stands even for well-trained and well-seasoned troops. I mean that 75 percent will not fire or will not persist in firing against the enemy and his works. They may face the danger, but they will not fight.[5]

In searching for a way out of this dilemma, Marshall had

---

*Italics added

found a key clue when he said: "Men who have been in battle know from first hand experience that when the chips are down, a man fights to help the man next to him, just as a company fights to keep pace with its flanks."[6]

Another contributor who helped find a key to controlling fear and behavior was none other than Charles Darwin. In his study of the development of intellectual and moral faculties in prehistoric man, he wrote:

> We may therefore conclude that primeval man, at a very remote period, was influenced by the praise and blame of his fellows. It is obvious, that the members of the same tribe would approve of conduct which appeared to them to be for the general good, and would reprobate that which appeared evil. To do good unto others—to do unto others as ye would that they should do unto you—is the foundation stone of morality. It is, therefore, hardly possible to exaggerate the importance during rude times of the love of praise and the dread of blame. A man who was not impelled by any deep, instinctive feeling, to sacrifice his life for the good of others, yet was aroused to such actions by a sense of glory, would by his example excite the same wish for glory in other men, and would strengthen by exercise the noble feeling of admiration.[7]

I believe that Marshall would have read this assertion of Darwin's with satisfaction, and I believe that he would agree with me when I sum up the gist of the solution in two key words—honor and companionship. These words are not meant to be used as guides in a crusade which would ennoble soldiers to a point where every company would contain a hundred Damons and an equal number of Pythiases. But Du Picq and Marshall have shown us the way. Marshall lived to see a major recommendation adopted by the Army dealing with the reorganization of fighting units at the lowest level, the infantry squad. This resulted in restructuring squads into small groups called fire teams. Marshall's concept included centering the fire teams on "natural fighters." Such a fighter might be exemplified by Stephen Crane's Henry Fleming in *The Red Badge of Courage*. Henry was the boy who ran from his first fire fight, then returned to become a man by leading a charge of his company and capturing the enemy's regimental color. This part of Marshall's proposal is difficult to implement in peacetime training, for it has only been in battle's natural process of selection that such fighters emerge.

Thus far we have focused on the problems of aiding the soldier to overcome "freezing" in combat. What about the leader? He cannot look to companionship for help in overcoming his fears. In fact the very nature of command makes the lot of the commander one of the loneliest conditions known to man. Since he cannot look outside for help he must look into himself for moral sustenance. That alone should remind us that du Picq was right when he spoke of quality as the only producer of "real effect." For nothing can exceed in importance the selection of officers and non-commissioned officers for positions of leadership. That selection should take heed of what William James termed the "heroic mind": "When a dreadful object is presented, or when life as a whole turns up its dark abysses to our view, then the worthless ones among us lose their hold on the situation altogether . . . But the heroic mind does differently . . . It can face them if necessary, without . . . losing its hold upon the rest of life. The world thus finds in the heroic man its worthy match and mate . . . [for] he can *stand* this universe."[8]

When one reflects on James's heroic mind would it not— once presented with a "dreadful object" or looking into one of "life's dark abysses"—resort to the kind of thoughtful courage propounded by Plato's Nicias? It would seem that any other kind of courage—such as so-called fearlessness— would not be consistent with such a mind.

If this is so, should we expect all our leaders to possess heroic minds? Not necessarily. I believe James's use of such a grand adjective as heroic was only a way of dramatizing what we commonly call a person with a "strong mind." For example, I would feel uneasy, if not downright embarrassed, telling someone that I thought that Harry Truman had a heroic mind. Strong, yes indeed; heroic, no.

In the event of a full scale mobilization we will not be afforded the luxury of a discriminating search for leaders with truly heroic minds. If we can find enough strong-minded men for leaders, experience has shown that courage can be expected to accompany their other qualities.

Honor should be considered concomitant with courage. It is the very heartbeat of the leader's role, for if his actions are not exemplary, what is he doing in that position? If he is doing his job, his presence among his men (where he belongs if he is really leading and not just operating some electronic device in a command post) places him under constant scrutiny. And the nature of that scrutiny rules out any kind of phoniness, for soldiers soon develop an uncanny sense for separating the counterfeit from the genuine. Any officer who has led in battle will tell you that such awareness is one of the first things acquired if one expects to succeed as a leader. It is a fact that has been around as long as warfare, and that is a long, long time.

Now it is time to show leaders in action, to observe battle through their eyes and minds. We have already witnessed one such action. This time the accent is on what Napoleon called "two o'clock in the morning courage," as we see Anthony Wayne and his light infantry leaders prepare for:

The Storming of Stony Point

The July night was still warm long after midnight. Its quiet had been unbroken until the baying of the running hound had brought the patrol to a halt. The four infantrymen sank down in their tracks and waited silently for their sergeant to come back down the trail. In seconds his broad bulk loomed alongside the first man in the file. The sergeant reached out in the darkness and tapped the two nearest men on the shoulder.

The two rose without a sound and disappeared, Indian-like, into the treeline that separated the trail from the clearing. The sergeant squatted beside the other two men, and all three listened intently. There was a low whistle and the sound of the dog lunging into the brush. The barking broke out again, this time rising in the ringing bay of the hound charging the intruder. The baying rose, then ended abruptly in a sharp yelping that broke off as quickly as it had begun.

The sergeant led the patrol forward on the trail to join the two men he had sent out. They fell in at the end of the file, the last man pausing long enough to wipe his bayonet on a handful of pine needles from the forest floor.

Washington rested his field glass on Anthony Wayne's right shoulder and turned his attention again to the abatis* encircling the outermost fieldworks of Stony Point. He shifted the focus of his glass slowly until he had taken in the lower artillery batteries, then repeated his surveillance of the inner

---

*Abatis—an obstacle formed by felling large trees so that the ends of their branches are pointing at possible enemy avenues of approach.

ring of abatis. Satisfied, he took another look at the British frigate anchored in the middle of the Hudson a mile and a half away. The reflection of the afternoon sun on the sparkling surface of the river was almost blinding, so much so that the commander-in-chief was quick to lower his glass.

"That's the *Vulture,* is it not?" Washington asked.

"You're correct, Sir. The British have kept her moored there ever since they took Stony Point on the first of June," Wayne replied.

"And so they have done all this fortifying in just five weeks. Busy work, and fast, for British soldiers," Washington said.

"But not too fast for our plans. You'll remember that part of Captain McClane's report about the incompleted wall on the west side of the citadel, a gap wide enough to march a platoon through in line abreast."

"That report is one of the chief reasons I'm on this reconnaissance with you. I believe that Major Lee* got McClane into the fort under a flag of truce where he made the observations in his report."

"Right again, Sir. McClane told me that the British commandant, Lieutenant Colonel Johnson, was so confident of the strength of Stony Point's fortifications that he did not have McClane blindfolded," Wayne said.

"McClane was in the fort just two days ago, and you made your own reconnaissance two days before that, on July 2. But before we say more about the fort, what is your latest estimate of the garrison's strength?" Washington asked.

"Hardly an estimate any longer, Sir, just cold fact. We've not only been watching the British with Lee's Legion, but we have all kinds of reports from civilians and the like. What the garrison amounts to is Colonel Johnson's 17th Regiment plus the grenadier company of the 71st Highlanders, a detachment of the Loyal Americans, and fifteen guns manned by Royal Artillery crews. In all, the total comes to a little over six hundred men."

Washington nodded his understanding as he seated himself on a boulder, motioning Wayne to do the same. The two generals had spent the past hour oblivious to everything except their observations and exchanges. Now the commander-in-chief relaxed, looking down the pine-clad slopes of the

---

*Light Horse Harry Lee, famed cavalryman and father of Robert E. Lee. Lee's Legion, made up of cavalry and infantry companies, was under Washington, with Lee reporting to Wayne.

View of Stony Point today

mountain toward distant Stony Point. The two were shielded from the warm July sun by the pines of the Buckberg and the rock outcropping they had used for cover. A hundred yards below them, just visible through the pines, they could see Light-Horse Harry Lee and Alexander Hamilton, Washington's senior aide, pacing impatiently back and forth as they waited for the generals to break off their reconnaissance and rejoin them. Wayne paid them no heed as he leaned forward to hand Washington the sketch that had been drafted by Colonel Putnam and added to by Wayne himself.

"I'm ready to talk about the details of my mission, if you are, Sir," Wayne said.

Washington took the sketch, pretending to examine it while his mind's eye was studying the man who had handed it to him.

I must have no doubts now, he thought, *that I've chosen the right man for this operation, for it seems all risk and with nothing but damaged reputations, even ruined careers, if it fails. I can't afford failure. I can't afford any more Long Islands or Germantowns, though we've come a long way in those three years since Long Island.*

*Wayne has shown all the dash and daring needed for this work;
now I need to know that he can plan it well, and carry out that plan.
I must know that he will calculate as would I. Yet he must have the
freedom of action he needs, for how else am I ever going to get generals fit for independent command, generals I can trust?*

Washington looked up from the sketch that had been im-
printed on his memory hours before this reconnaissance. His
steady gaze fixed on Wayne's hazel eyes as he spoke.

"There are no more details to discuss here. I expect you
to furnish enough of those in your finished plan to assure
my approval. In the meantime I will confirm my ideas in writing, to reach you in at least four days, say by July 10. Now,
since we're agreed on a general plan, let me summarize it.
To begin, it must be a night attack, planned with the utmost
secrecy, and made known only to senior officers who must
be trusted with it. We are agreed, too, that the British outworks and the citadel itself must be taken by surprise. Yes, it
must be stormed—"

An animated Wayne was on his feet, his hazel eyes lit
with such excitement that he forgot he was interrupting his
chief.

"General, if you give me permission, I'll storm Hell itself
for you," Wayne said.

The briefest gleam flickered in Washington's eye.

"Perhaps you had better try Stony Point first," he said.

Wayne flushed as he became aware of his breach of military courtesy. He started to stammer an apology, but Washington's quiet smile and outstretched hand restrained him.
The two wasted no time on formalities as they went back over
Washington's guidelines to his chosen commander of the newly-
formed Light Infantry Corps. Washington recounted each
main point pausing only to answer Wayne's questions. The
assault would be made by Wayne's light infantry alone. The
thirteen-mile approach march, starting from Wayne's camp
at Sandy Beach, must end under cover of darkness, observing
the strictest security measures. Sole reliance must be placed
on the bayonet, all muskets unloaded. When he got to that
point Washington eyed Wayne, wondering if they both were
thinking of the disastrous rout of Wayne's division by a British surprise attack at night, back in September of '77.

I know he still smarts at the memory of it, Washington thought.
*Although he was fully acquitted by the court-martial he had de-
manded, Wayne will never get over it—nor should he. Surprised in*

the dead of night by the British general whose deed won him the title of "no-flint" Grey, Wayne's fifteen hundred men were overrun at Paoli where he lost a good tenth of his command in casualties and prisoners. It was a British victory won by careful planning, surprise, and reliance on the bayonet. I can see by his face he needs no more reminders: his appetite for revenge alone will assure that he has learned his lesson, one that he can turn to good account against the enemy at Stony Point.

Washington went on to recall their agreement on the composition and direction of the main attack. The approach should be toward the south side of the peninsula that formed the base of Stony Point, across a sunken sandbar where the marsh surrounding the landward side of Stony Point ended. Wayne had already pointed out two critical factors that made the approach over the sandbar an invaluable aid to a *coup de main*. First, the British were unaware of the existence of the sandbar, for they had not set a night picket to cover that avenue of approach. Second, since the Hudson in the area was actually an estuary rather than a river, the marsh and the sandbar were flooded at high tide, but the bar could be crossed by wading at low tide.

Washington added that it was common practice for night attacks to be made a little before first light. Since the garrison should be well aware of that, however, and would keep a more vigilant watch at that time, it would be better to launch the assault near midnight on a moonless night. He went on to cover what he considered adequate forces for the main and secondary attacks: assault columns preceded by "forlorn hopes"* whose carefully selected leaders would make sure that paths would be cleared through the abatis while driving in the British outposts; advance parties to follow through the obstacles, composed of one to two hundred men; and, finally, the main bodies of the selected regiments which would assure enough weight of support to accomplish the mission.

Washington concluded by repeating his concern for the secrecy and security so essential to a successful surprise, even if it meant securing civilians who might observe the approach of Wayne's force. When Washington stood to indicate that the conference was at an end Wayne was on his feet with a final assurance.

"My plans already include such measures, for the farm-

---

*In today's journalese, suicide squads.

ers and their families, but I'm also going to be sure that not even a dog's barking will give away our approach march."

The fine July weather continued to grace the Hudson Highlands, and now on Thursday morning of the fifteenth Wayne's Light Infantry Corps stood in ranks for inspection in the sun beating down on the Sandy Beach camp. The four regiments were aligned, each in a two-battalion front, under Baron von Steuben's approving eye. Anthony Wayne's eye was not so approving. "Dandy"[9] Wayne winced inwardly as he looked down the ranks of the smartly-turned-out battalions. He knew he would never be happy with his corps on parade as long as the men had to wear the uniforms of the various regiments from which they had been drawn. To his mind, with its love of orderly display, these splendid men had been done an injustice in not being issued one distinctive uniform. The discordant array jarred his military sensibility. Here they were, handpicked men from six states, each still in the uniform of his own line. The overall cut of the uniforms was similar, but the color of the facings clashed, and there were the brown coats (obtained the previous year from France) worn by Continentals from Virginia, Pennsylvania, and Massachusetts alongside the blue of the North Carolina, Connecticut, and Maryland Line. Washington had given Wayne first priority on arms and equipment but he had flatly refused Wayne's request for a single uniform for the elite corps. Although the non-uniformity would continue to irk their commander the men in the ranks never gave it a passing thought. (One wonders: if the Light Infantry had contained a counterpart of an earlier Bill Mauldin in its eighteenth-century ranks, would he not at times have seen Dandy Wayne as the same pain-in-the-ass as the World War II G.I. cartoonist saw pistol-packing General Patton? Both generals loved color and dash, while sharing the same regard for discipline symbolized by a correctly turned-out uniform.)

Nevertheless, Wayne comforted himself as he gazed down the ruler-straight ranks, *I've still got the finest men in Washington's army, all 1,350 picked from the forty-six infantry battalions of the Continental Line. And the commander-in-chief had personally passed on every officer from ensign to colonel before he chose me for commander of the corps. What an irony lies behind that selection! It has been said that the choice was narrowed down to Dan Morgan and myself. Then, once Washington's decision had been made, I came*

*out of three months retirement, and Dan Morgan retired in disgust
to his farm in Virginia. So here I am only eighteen days in command
of the finest body of men in America—oh, the gleam in von Steuben's
eye when he watched the precision of their drill a half-hour ago—
and yet not a man jack aware that he is about to march off to take
part in the most dangerous operation ever attempted in this army.
Yes, only a little over twelve hours from now how many of those fine
men standing there will be blasted to earth by a British bullet or
grapeshot? Only the mighty Jehovah can answer that. Now here comes
my aide, Henry Archer, and I know he is going to tell me that the
Baron has declared the inspection complete and Brigade Major
McCormick can order the battalions to pass in review.*

As Wayne rode his horse at a walk to take post behind
the Brigade Major the commands began to ring out as he
approached the front of Colonel Febiger's 1st Regiment.

"Battalion! Present—Arms!"

The drums on the right wing began beating the salute
as Wayne returned the salutes of the officers. The drums on
the left of the regiment took up the roll as the commands
came from the battalion he had just passed.

"Shoulder—Firelocks!

"Rear rank! Close to the front—March!

"Rest!"

At the last command young Lt. George Knox in the 1st
Battalion, 1st Regiment relaxed and shifted his weight to the
espontoon* held upright in his right hand. The seven-foot
shaft of the pike was still awkward to his hand; the officers
had been issued the weapon only three days before and the
only practice in their handling had been the bayonet-like drill
which was clearly intended as combat training. Knox, formerly of the 9th Regiment of the Pennsylvania Line, was well
aware of Dandy Wayne's reputation for show, but the issue
of officers' espontoons and the practice that followed was
puzzling. If the weapons had been meant for show—as they
seemed to be in this parade—then why the battle drill?

If any officer, Knox thought, *can figure out Dandy Wayne's
plans he deserves to be a general himself. We've been marched and
drilled and inspected until the men are getting restless. We know by
now that we're bound for some special mission some day and that
we're as sharply-trained as men can get. Yet I hope the men don't go*

---

*Espontoon (or spontoon)—a pike with a wooden shaft from six to eight feet long. Wayne got
them for all his officers through a letter to Washington, and the weapons were issued to the
Light Infantry officers by July 12.

over that fine edge. This inspection was the strictest yet, by far. I've seen that every man in my platoon was "fresh shaved and well powdered" by brigade order, and I've checked every item of uniform from neck stocks to gaiters a dozen times per man. I've counted musket flints and inspected cartridge boxes, by brigade order, until I've been blue in the face. For what? Another march through the Highlands?

Knox's thoughts were cut short by a volley of commands from his battalion commander, Lieutenant Colonel Fleury.

"Battalion—Attention!

"Shoulder firelocks—

"Battalion—

"By platoons to the left—Wheel! March!"

All right then, fine. The men stepped out smartly in time with the marching beat of the drums. This was what they had been waiting for: the march past their general that would end this tedious day of inspection and parade. Soon they could fall out and relax in the shade of their tents, stretching out on the grass while the camp kettles were heated up for the noon meal.

Knox marched alongside his platoon with the swinging stride of the Light Infantry, which had already become accustomed to parading to the quick step. He cut his eyes to the right to locate the camp "street" where his battalion would be dismissed in front of its row of tents.

But what was happening? He could see the head of the battalion passing the end of their street. Fleury was not the kind of commander to allow a mistake like that, yet he could see Fleury's ramrod-straight back still aligned firmly to the front. Knox was marching at attention and could not turn his head, but he was sure they had passed their street. And in minutes they had left the camp behind. What was happening? The question was in every man's mind, and confusion was compounded by Fleury's next commands.

"Take care to break off by sections of four!

"Sections of four! Break off!"

The sections of the platoons were obliquing inward to form the column of fours required for a road march. Then the battalion *was* off on a march, this time headed south along the Hudson on the road to Fort Montgomery.

It had been straight-up noon when the whole of the Light Infantry—four regiments strong and all in one column for the first time—had left the camp at Sandy Beach. They had route-marched past the ruins of Fort Montgomery, turning

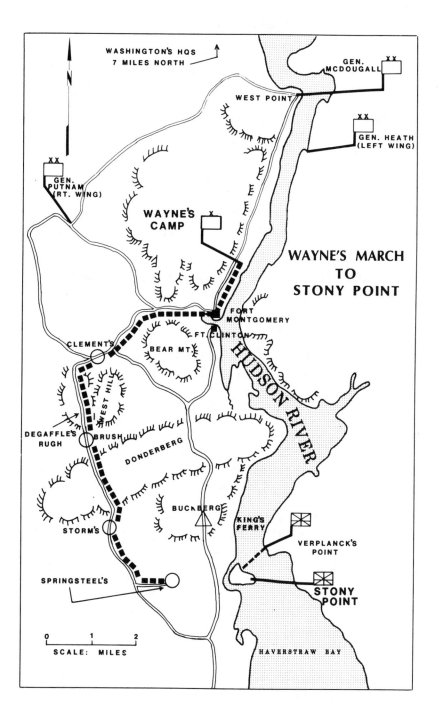

westward to pass between Torn Mountain and the mass of rugged Bear Mountain. They had forked left to the south-west and at two o'clock Wayne had ordered the first halt near the solitary house of a farmer named Clement.

While the corps fell out to rest along the roadside, the Brigade Major gave the assembled regimental and battalion commanders the orders for the rest of the march. Major McCormick finished by saying that the commander had directed that no soldier would leave the ranks, for any reason, except at a scheduled halt, and then only under the eyes of an officer. "Yes," the major said in reply to a query, "if it means a lieutenant has to take his platoon en masse off the road for a quick piss, that is exactly what he'll have to do."

The first half of the next leg proved to be the roughest part of the march. The rutted dirt road dwindled into a narrow, bouldered path as it crossed Degaffle's Rugh, until the column had to ascend and descend the tortuous way in single file; nothing new to these veterans, most of whom had seen years of war. The men sweated under their full field equipment, up and down steep ravines in the July heat, but none was allowed to slow the march, nor did any soldier want to. They picked their way through the pines down the Rugh, and then had to ascend painfully the steep slopes of the Donderberg.

By 6:00 P.M. the column was approaching Storm's farmhouse, and not a man had been lost to straggling. Wayne found Light Horse Harry Lee awaiting him, and the two went into the house for a final exchange of information.

The march continued through late afternoon into the July evening until, with dusk closing around them, the corps closed into its assembly area around David Springsteel's farm, a mile and a half directly west of Stony Point. Wayne had already dispatched Col. Richard Butler (commanding the 2nd Regiment), along with Maj. Tom Posey and Maj. Harry Lee, to a covered post where they could observe Stony Point and its garrison. Wayne left Springsteel's after he had issued his orders for the organization for combat, and went directly to join Butler. He took with him Col. "Old Denmark" Febiger* of the 1st Regiment, Col. Return Meigs of the 3rd, Maj. William Hull commanding the 4th, and their battalion commanders.

---

*So called because he had emigrated from Denmark to Virginia in 1774. He joined the colonists the following year, and in the army had proved himself a leader at Bunker Hill and Quebec.

In the failing light Wayne was still able to point out critical terrain features: the details of the fort's defenses, avenues
of approach for the assault columns, and the objectives for
each column. An elated Anthony Wayne then led the command group back to Springsteel's over the approach route
the corps would take before it would split into two assault
columns. Wayne had reason to be elated. He had closed his
command in its assembly area with not a man lost, and more
important, every security measure had been carried out so
that he was able to say he had observed to the letter Washington's warning: "Knowledge of your intention ten minutes
previously obtained can blast all your hopes."

When the command group had reassembled in the
Springsteel house, Major McCormick spread out the enlarged
sketch of Wayne's battle plan on David Springsteel's dining
table and weighted its corners with candle holders. Before he
spoke Wayne looked across the candlelight at the circle of
faces above the battle plan. *This is the moment they've been waiting for,* he thought, *and with the exception of four of them, this
will be their first exposure to my plan.*

"I'll be brief," he said, "and cover only the main points.
Then Major McCormick will go over the written order in detail.* Later, you can give it to the troops. But first, a question—have the white patches for the hats been issued?"

"Every man has been given a square of white paper and
the NCO's are making sure that each man fastens it to the
front of his hat," Major McCormick said.

"Very well, here is the plan. As you see, there are two
attacks—two assault columns—which will penetrate the British defenses and seize their joint objective, the citadel of the
fort—here."

Wayne's forefinger rested on the highest, innermost point
in the fort. His hazel eyes shone and his handsome, bold-
nosed face showed its high color in the candles' glow as he
continued.

"The main attack is on the right and I will lead it myself.
It will come from the south following Route Number 1, crossing the marsh and the submerged sandbar which we should
be wading over near midnight. This column will be preceded
by a twenty-man forlorn hope under a selected officer, followed by the advance party led by Lieutenant Colonel Fleury—

*Appendix contains Wayne's order in full.

all from Colonel Febiger's regiment. The main body, following close on Colonel Fleury's 150 men, will consist of Colonel Meigs' 3rd Regiment which will be followed by Major Hull with the 1st Battalion of the 4th Regiment."

Wayne's finger traced the movements across the plan, pointing to each unit as he referred to it.

"Colonel Butler will command the secondary attack on the left, on the north over Route Number 2, and that attack will be made in a similar fashion, that is, led by a forlorn hope, followed by Major Stewart with 150 men of the 2nd Battalion of Colonel Butler's regiment, that makes up the advance party. It will be followed by the remainder of Colonel Butler's regiment.

"You can see the routes for the two attacks, but there is a third element which has a mission just as important as the two attacks. That is the diversionary force made up of Major Murfree's North Carolinians. He will lead his two companies, and his orders direct him to follow the rear of Colonel Butler's column until all are across the causeway over the marsh—here. At that time Major Murfree will break off with his men and advance toward the British center, prepared to conduct a diversion, commencing to fire as soon as the British pickets open fire on any element of our corps.

"Now note this, gentlemen. Major Murfree's command is the only one authorized to fire during the operation. All others will move to the assault with unloaded, shouldered muskets, so that their sole weapon will be the bayonet—and the officers' espontoons. Note also that I have included in my written order that any soldier who attempts to fire, unless so ordered by an officer, will be put to death by the nearest officer.[10] Finally, the matter of the watchword, 'The fort is ours', which will be shouted only when our men have broken into the inner walls of the fort. All clear then?"

Wayne answered the few questions from the group, then turned to his other aide, Major Fishbourne, who put the shaft of an espontoon into his general's outstretched hand.

"In case you are wondering, gentlemen, I'm not carrying this just to show it off to the troops. I trust you have the same intent in mind with your own. Our conference is dismissed. We will move out at 11:30, that gives you ample time to make your preparations," Wayne concluded.

Lt. Col. François Louis Teissedre de Fleury (plain Fleury to the Americans), scion of a French noble family of Provençal, commanding the 1st Battalion of the 1st Regiment, was a logical choice to lead the advance party of the main attack. Logical because of his outstanding record and reputation for gallantry, made as a volunteer in the American service in which he had enlisted three years before. In less than one year, starting in May of 1777, he had distinguished himself in a siege, a raid, and two major battles—Brandywine and Germantown. He had earned the thanks of Congress and the official gift of a horse for the first, then had the horse killed under him in the second, where he also took a wound in the leg. These actions and others had him promoted, in rapid succession, from captain to major to lieutenant colonel, all in the same year.[11]

Now that quick French mind was bent to the tasks of organizing his battalion for that most dreaded of operations, a night attack. To Fleury's mind the first task was ensuring that the officer who led the forlorn hope was thoroughly grounded in his mission and all that it entailed. He took Lieutenant Knox to one side while the advance party was being formed up.

"You are aware that you have been assigned the most rewarding duty in all the corps," Fleury said, his face only inches away from Knox's in the close darkness.

"Responsible, Sir—but rewarding?" Knox's voice carried the surprise that Fleury was not able to see in his face.

"Ah yes, the glory. What else? What greater opportunity will any lieutenant ever have? But you are ready, yes?"

"Well, if you mean me myself, I suppose so, Sir."

"Of course I mean you. You will have plenty of time to inspect your men, their equipment, all that. But are you prepared in your mind—so you see each thing that must be done?" Fleury asked, his tone almost fatherly in spite of his realization that, at the age of thirty, he could hardly have fathered a lieutenant.

"I have much concern about my route. I've not had the chance to see it but once in daylight, and since I will be in the lead—"

Fleury's sudden interruption was eased by his reassuring hand laid on Knox's shoulder.

"Two reasons for not worrying. I will be beside you even though my post might be thought to be at your rear. Also we will have as a guide one of Major Lee's best scouts, a sergeant who has been reconnoitering the fort and its approaches for a week, night and day. But now, do you have the plan of the fort fixed in your head?" Fleury asked.

In his mind's eye Knox saw again the rocky promontory rising 150 feet above the river and the marsh, a natural fortress now studded with outworks and gun emplacements and guarded by a double ring of abatis, each extending all the way around the rocky peninsula, the whole surmounted by the citadel with its stone bastions. To Knox's young mind, it was truly the Gibraltar of the West as the British had proclaimed it.

"Yes," Knox said, "I've had my turn at looking at the map and the order, but I am concerned now about the approach to the first British picket."

"First you must remember that Stony Point is really an island because of the salt marsh all around the landward side.

We will approach, first across the marsh, then over the sandbar which should be covered by only inches of water at midnight. The first picket will be to your left flank as we come out of the water on the beach of the Point—which we will follow for fifty paces to make sure that we have gotten around the south or water end of the first row of abatis. Then if the picket fires at us we will keep on going because he will draw the fire of Murfree's men, and that will keep the British occupied."

"And then?"

"And then comes the vital part of your mission, your double task."

"Double task? I don't follow you."

"Double because two things must be done at once if the whole attack is to succeed. Some of your men must take care of the nearest outpost while others, with axes and billhooks, must clear enough of the abatis to make a path for my advance party. Do you see?"

"I do now, Sir. Is that all?"

"Surely it is enough, is it not? Is it that I have found a fire-eater in this lieutenant? Yes, fire-eater, one final thing. You must not let the tales of this 'little Gibraltar' cause fear in you. It is far from being impregnable, and you must trust me when I say that surprise overcomes all. Now, back to your men. By this time they will have been issued their tools, and you must organize them for their work." The white outline of Fleury's face faded away in the dark.

At five minutes before midnight Knox and his men had forded the marsh, wading through marsh grass and ankle-deep saltwater. He halted, waiting for his men to close up, and tried to peer through the blackness. It seemed to Knox that the night had become a black curtain dropped across a darkened stage. The night sounds were reassuring though, the crickets and frogs making a background chorus over the subdued sloshing of the wading men. It was eerie here amid the clinging stink of the marsh air and all too quiet with hundreds of men yet to follow in their wake. *Yes, all going too well. Here they were stepping out to wade the sandbar only a few yards to their front, and still no sound from the British outposts.*

Knox felt the chill of the tidewater rising to his knees as he pressed forward, and then, incredibly, to his thighs and over his waist. Fleury too had felt the chilling surprise—"*Mon dieu,*" he muttered as he struggled forward. *My God, yes,* thought Knox, *if this is the ankle-deep sandbar, what in hell next?*

What-in-hell-next happened all too soon. The men behind Knox had slung their muskets in order to free their hands for carrying their axes. When the cold water became waist deep the soldiers started to unsling their muskets and hold them overhead with their axes. A swinging musket struck against the bayonet of the next infantryman with the unmistakable clang of steel against steel, and off to the left came the British picket's challenge—"Who goes there?"

Knox and his file leaders pushed on in silence, breasting the tide, their feet on the sand bottom giving them the foothold they needed. All of the forlorn hope was still in waist-deep water when the first British sentry fired. The flash and bang of the shot triggered off a ragged volley from other pickets, the bullets ricocheting off the water or whistling overhead. In seconds Murfree's companies opened up with a roar, and the night to the left and front of Knox's men was aflame with the answering fire of British muskets. Knox felt the water receding as he made his way onto the beach and felt his boots dig into dry sand. He heard the shouted commands of British sergeants as reinforcements charged down from the citadel and artillery gun crews ran to man their guns.

Knox and Fleury, side by side, were running along the beach, the forlorn hope on their heels when the first British cannon shot crashed out from the emplacement a hundred yards above them. The artillerymen had fired high and the whirring of the grapeshot ripped through the air overhead. Luckily for Knox, he was running with the point of his espontoon thrust forward when the blade glanced off a leveled tree branch. He was in the edge of the second row of abatis. He thrust the blade of his weapon into the ground and yelled his file leaders into their task of chopping and pulling aside the interlaced branches of the obstacle. No need for keeping silent now, the night had exploded into a red roar, with British muskets and artillery firing with such intensity that the slope in front of the Americans was lit by the discharges. No time for anything now but clawing and tearing at the abatis until bloodied hands were doing better work than axes. But British artillery had gotten the range and the rounds of grapeshot were rattling off the tree limbs and into the forlorn hope. Sergeant Baker, to Knox's left, took wounds in arm and leg but kept tearing his way forward.

We've got to get through here now, by God, Knox thought, trying to see an end to the tangle of branches, *or we will die here. I've got to get them forward, it's the only way they'll survive.*

He snatched up his espontoon and used its upper half like a club to batter his way through. He heard Fleury getting men to open another path. They were in the clear now, and the first files of Fleury's advance party were widening the gaps made by Knox's men. Fleury and Knox were running up the slope between the British gun emplacements.

Anthony Wayne and Old Denmark entered a gap in the abatis at the head of the main body, Wayne's once-fine uniform coat a mass of dripping mud—like those of his men— from the chest down. He grounded his espontoon and tried to shout above the crash of musketry to direct Major Posey and his men toward the gap.

"Over this way! Incline the column to the right—" Wayne's commands stopped short. He felt a searing stab on his forehead. There was a whirling rush of stabbing stars across his eyes. The ground rushed up at him, and he was down among the logs of the abatis.

Ben Fishbourne and Henry Archer, Wayne's aides, were on either side of their general and felt rather than saw him fall. Archer was the first to realize that Wayne had a head wound, and was probing in his commander's bloody hair when he regained consciousness. Wayne winced at feeling Archer's fingers touch the wound.

"Help me up to the fort. I must get to the head of the column." Wayne had gotten back his command voice.

"Let me get my handkerchief around your head and we'll get you moving," Fishbourne's tone was as firm as Wayne's.

The aides found that their general had taken a scalp wound, a bullet crease above the forehead, and in seconds had his head bandaged, and had him standing between them.

"All right, let's get moving," Wayne ordered, and the three moved alongside Febiger's column until they found an interval between companies. In minutes Wayne was back in command, directing elements of the main body forward and up to the citadel at the summit.

Fleury, outdistancing Knox by only yards, was the first to charge through the sallyport on the citadel's south side. He was followed by Knox, then Sergeant Baker of Virginia (now four times wounded), Sergeant Spencer of Virginia, and Sergeant Donlop of Pennsylvania, both twice wounded.[12] Fleury rushed to the flagstaff, shouting "the fort is ours!" He freed the halyards and hauled down the British flag. His men, pouring through the sallyport, took up the cry, but the watchword in itself could not assure that British resistance was finished.

For a quarter of an hour the inner walls and the works around it were bloody confusion as knots of British fought back with bayonets and swords. But it was soon evident the British cause was doomed. The head of Butler's column, led by Major Stewart, charged over the north side of the citadel where they were greeted by Maj. Tom Posey. While the mopping-up had gotten under way Fleury, Stewart, and Posey held a hurried conference, and they soon realized how the overall action had gone.

"Murfree's demonstration had achieved its purpose, and Colonel Johnson charged down the hill with half his garrison—six companies of the 17th—to meet what he thought was the main threat. He was cut off and captured by Febiger's Regiment when he tried to regain the fort. The others tried to hold out but were isolated into little packets where they vainly tried to resist the bayonets, swords, and spontoons— for about fifteen minutes the hilltop was the scene of a mad turmoil, and the British then began to throw down their arms and cry quarter. It is a further tribute to Wayne's discipline that Stony Point did not join the list of Revolutionary War 'massacres'."[13]

In less than an hour and a half after leaving Springsteel's farm the Light Infantry Corps had accomplished its mission. Anthony Wayne, wearing that archetype of heroic emblems, the bloody bandage around the head, sat down in the British colonel's quarters to pen his *veni, vidi, vici* to his Commander-in-Chief:

> Stony Point, 16th July, 1779
> 2 A.M.

> Dear Gen'l,—The fort & garrison with Col. Johnson are ours.
> Our officers and men behaved like men who are
> determined to be free.
> Yours most sincerely,
> Anth'y Wayne

He handed the dispatch to the waiting Major Fishbourne who took off in a hell-for-leather gallop for Washington's headquarters at New Windsor. Outside the commandant's quarters the American artillery detachment under Captains Pendleton and Barr was busily turning the British cannon to bear on the *Vulture* in mid-river as well as the enemy fortifications across the Hudson at Verplanck's Point. It was all over but the shouting.

In 1779 Stony Point was something to shout about. Anthony Wayne and the Light Infantry had delivered a stroke that fired the imagination and admiration of the Patriots. He and his men had done the impossible—taken the impregnable—and in the doing had given the Colonists' cause a badly needed "shot in the arm" while having the opposite effect on the British. From a historical perspective two factors should be recognized. The first and less significant factor was that Stony Point's capture gained no strategic advantage for the Colonists. In fact, Washington had to order the fort abandoned three days later. The second point, of real significance, was that the Continentals, properly led, could accomplish anything expected of the finest European troops.

And for once Congress acted with dispatch to reward proven merit. Wayne was voted official thanks and a gold medal. Silver medals went to Fleury and Stewart while Lieutenants Knox and Gibbons were given brevet promotions.

As for the dangers, frustrations, and uncertainties that confronted Wayne and his corps, it is evident that they were not only formidable but would have been overwhelming had they not been countered by something more formidable.

It was a rare combination of physical courage, discipline, and training that can provide a model for any army in any time or place. The Light Infantry Corps could have been brought to the Stony Point operation in the highest state of readiness, but it would not have succeeded in doing what it did without that cool courage shown at all levels. From Anthony Wayne to the three sergeants who charged into the citadel with Fleury and Knox, courageous leadership was the common denominator. And because we have seen the main attack through the eyes of key leaders in those scenes it would be unjust to overlook the same high standards of leadership in Colonel Butler's secondary attack. His men suffered heavier losses than did Wayne's column. For example, Lieutenant Gibbons, leading the other forlorn hope, lost seventeen men killed or wounded out of his twenty!

All that has been said about the physical courage that

made possible the victory at Stony Point is not to gainsay the importance of moral courage that must have contributed to the success of the American corps. That kind of courage is the subject of the next section. Stony Point deserves to be remembered because it highlights so brilliantly the physical aspects of courage.

Moral Courage

FIELD MARSHAL MONTGOMERY, writing in his *History of Warfare,* got at once to the heart of the subject when he said: "Many qualities go to make a leader, but two are vital—the ability to make the right decisions, *and the courage to act on the decisions. . . . Above all, he must have that moral courage, that resolution and that determination which will enable him to stand firm when the issue hangs in the balance. . . .* A battle is, in effect, a contest between two wills—his own and that of the enemy commander. If his heart begins to fail him when the issue hangs in the balance, his opponent will probably win."[14]

Because certain of those words bring out the essence of moral courage I have repeated them here in italics. They show us the other face of courage. We have seen the physical in action at Stony Point, now here is its counterpart and, in a sense, the other end of a spectrum.

In the opening of this chapter I stated that there were wide differences between the two kinds of courage. What are the essential differences?

In the first place physical courage is courage in action. It is *visible* bravery, usually exhibited at some critical point in time or place during battle: the youthful British lieutenant at the Somme in 1916 who stood on the parapet of the trench in full view of the enemy, pointing his swagger stick at the Germans, and saying "we had better be going now"; the twenty-six-year-old Bonaparte placing himself in front of his grenadiers to lead their column onto the fire-swept bridge at Lodi. Anyone who has known war or studied military history could add a dozen examples of this kind of courage under fire, all distinguished by visibility.

The moral sort is the quiet resolution and calm determination that Montgomery speaks of—the kind of courage seldom if ever observed by the troops. It exists and operates only in the mind—and heart, if you will. It strengthens the will against the uncertainties and frustrations that constantly beat upon the commander in every battle. It provides the strength that makes the strong-minded appear that way. It enables the commander to stand resolutely against anything his opponent can throw at him. There are times too when the same kind of firmness is demanded of him in knowing when to disregard the orders of his superiors. This, of course, requires judgment as well, but that judgment—once decision has been made—has to be supported by moral courage.

It would be shortsighted indeed if one were to associate moral courage solely with one quality such as resolution, for as the perception of the distance between the moral and the physical widens the more apparent becomes the idea of responsibility. This idea should not be confined to the dry terms of regulations (e.g., the commander is responsible for all that his command does or fails to do), rather it is the idea of the leader being responsible for the lives and welfare of those in his charge. It is the most sobering thought that can weigh upon a leader, one that causes lesser men to hesitate—"With this regard their thoughts turn awry,/ And lose the name of action." Thus is presented the enigma that so often confronts a leader—it takes moral courage to assume the responsibility for men's lives, yet moral courage is even more in demand when the situation calls for the commander to order men to take an action that clearly puts their lives at risk. Unhappily this is part of the loneliness of command, and there is nothing in anyone's writing (including The Regulations) that "teaches" a leader how to get through this traumatic experience. It is something that must be faced—alone; the decisions made—alone; the decision stuck to—alone. It is one of the high costs of command.

The final consideration to be borne in mind about any kind of courage, however essential an attribute courage may be, is that it cannot, *in itself,* foster a tactical art, an art of leadership; nor can any of the other attributes we will be examining. They must be linked together as appropriate, so that a balanced view may be sustained.

There is nothing novel about the idea of balancing courage with other qualities. Pericles in his great funeral oration, cited by Thucydides in *The History of the Peloponnesian War,* refers to such a balance.

> Again, in our [Athenian] enterprises we present the singular spectacle of daring and deliberation, each carried to its highest point, and both united in the same persons; although decision is usually the fruit of ignorance, hesitation of reflection. But the palm of courage will surely be adjudged most justly to those who best know the difference between hardship and pleasure and yet are never tempted to shrink from danger."[15]

And Napoleon, writing in his Maxims twenty-two centuries later, advises us that

> It is exceptional and difficult to find in one man all the qualities necessary for a great general. That which is most desirable, and which instantly sets a man apart, is that his intelligence or talent, are balanced by his character or courage. If his courage is the greater, a general heedlessly undertakes things beyond his ability. If on the contrary, his character or courage is less than his intelligence he does not dare carry out his plans."[16]

In the next battle scene we will see "a man of balance," a leader whose moral courage was great enough to match his superb tactical skill in the face of adverse odds.

Auerstadt—the Victory That Amazed an Emperor But Failed to Please Him

The two marshals were alone in the great dining hall of the schloss that had once housed the margraves who centuries before had made Naumburg their stronghold. Two Frenchmen more opposite would have been hard to conceive: Davout, short, stocky, balding, direct in manner to the point of bluntness; Bernadotte, the tall Gascon famous for his charm, whose ringlets of jet-black hair framed a handsome face with its beak of a hooked nose.

They stared at each other across the flicker of candles on the long table that separated them. Bernadotte was the first to look down at the map unrolled between the candelabra. The mass of thick hair fell over his forehead, shielding his eyes from Davout's searching glance.

"Then you will march on Apolda by way of Hassenhausen and Auerstadt?" Bernadotte asked without looking up.

"As you've seen in the Emperor's order of ten o'clock last night, that is the most direct route for me. And I have already alerted my division commanders to march at four this morning, hardly a half-hour from now," Davout said.

"So, your IIIrd Corps has its orders, and you've handed me mine for Ist Corps. It all seems clear enough to me, for both of us."

"Do you think that I, a Marshal of France, would come here as courier, just to hand you an operation order? For the last time I will point out the two things that change the intent—the spirit—of my orders and yours. First, I read to you the postscript of my orders, written in Marshal Berthier's own hand: 'If Marshal Bernadotte is with you, you may both march together, but the Emperor hopes that he will be in the position indicated at Dornburg.' My second point: I have personally questioned the Prussian cavalrymen made prisoner by my outposts near Hassenhausen only six hours ago. That interrogation, plus the reports of my patrols, confirms enough reliable intelligence to convince me that the Prussian main army, estimated at seventy thousand, is retreating from the threat of the Emperor's concentration near Jena. The Prussians are probably moving northward toward Halle or Leipzig. All of which means that you should follow Berthier's orders and move to support my IIIrd Corps as I march across the Saale toward Hassenhausen and block the Prussians' withdrawal," Davout's formal tone carried clearly the coolness between the two commanders.

"I read no spirit, as you call it, in either set of orders. Ist Corps will march this morning, when I am ready, for Dornburg via Camburg," Bernadotte said, raising his eyes from the map.

Davout didn't miss the sudden glint in the other's eyes, recalling how Frenchmen joked, only half in jest, about the combination of Gascon cunning and caution.

"Perhaps you don't choose to see, that by marching south, you will put two rivers—the Saale and the Ilm—between us. And that you will be obeying to the letter an order that has lost its validity, an order overtaken by events," Davout said.

"My dear Louis, you have your judgment. Be kind enough to leave me to mine. Now, if you have nothing further—"

"I do," Davout cut in, "to remind you that you will be turning your back on III Corps, with its strength of only twenty-six thousand to face an army of seventy thousand Prussians."

"Your estimate of seventy thousand—not mine. Now, have you finished?" Bernadotte asked, looking up again from the map. He found he was looking at Davout's back. The IIIrd Corps Commander was halfway to the hall door, the clack of his jackboot heels echoing between the stone floor and the vaulted ceiling.

Davout's staff and three division commanders were at his headquarters awaiting his return from the meeting with Bernadotte. As he entered the hotel foyer that served as a conference room the officers rose to their feet. Davout handed his hat and saber to an aide, and stood silent for a moment, his attention fixed on the corps operations map propped on its easel in front of the group. The map differed from Bernadotte's in the situation posted on it by the IIIrd Corps topographical officer. Davout studied the array of crayoned symbols—the enemy's units in blood red, the French in black—until he was satisfied with what he saw. He turned his attention to the waiting group.

"Listen carefully. We have little time. To sum up operations, the six corps of the Army debouched from the Thüringer Wald on October 9, five days ago. Since then the Army has moved northward in a *bataillon carré** to execute the Emperor's plan to bring the Prussian armies to battle on his terms.

"Two days ago, four corps of the *carré*—IVth, Vth, VIth, and VIIth—were turned westward toward Weimar and Erfurt where the Emperor has expected to pin down the main Prussian army. Meanwhile, our IIIrd Corps in conjunction with Marshal Bernadotte's Ist Corps was prepared to march to the southwest to strike the Prussians in flank or rear as the opportunity should arise.

"Now, as some of you know, I received orders from GQG**

Bataillon carré—Napoleon's flexible, wide-flung method of controlling the maneuver of the corps of the *Grande Armée*. See Appendix A for a detailed description of this "grand tactic."
**GQG—*Grand-Quartier-Général*, Napoleon's General Headquarters.

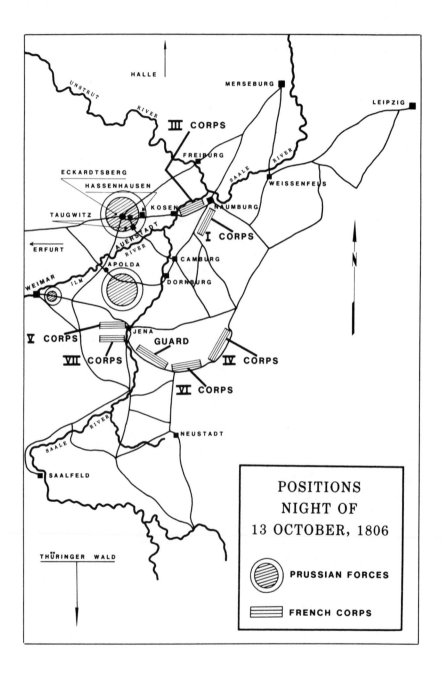

POSITIONS
NIGHT OF
13 OCTOBER, 1806

PRUSSIAN FORCES

FRENCH CORPS

at three o'clock this morning to march to Apolda—here—by the most direct route, that is via Kosen-Hassenhausen-Auerstadt. Our mission, as I have indicated, is to attack the Prussian army's flank or rear. However, the latest intelligence I have interpreted convinces me that the Prussian main army under the Duke of Brunswick has not been fixed and forced to fight by the four Corps now being concentrated under the Emperor's hand. Instead the Prussian army, which I estimate to number seventy thousand with over two hundred guns, is retiring northward headed for Halle or Leipzig—as you see here."

The Marshal paused long enough to scan the upturned faces of his staff and commanders. Some registered the surprise he had anticipated, others, such as the veteran Friant, remained impassive.

"I see some surprise, as well there might be, but save your questions until I have finished. Now, we will march as ordered, and as I conceive the situation to develop we will be prepared to strike the Prussian advance elements as soon as we find them. If our advance guard should be heavily outnumbered, it must be ready to assume the defense until it can be reinforced. What happens after that will depend upon my assessments and decisions.

"I have already directed General Gudin to dispatch a battalion, reinforced by a cavalry squadron, to secure the bridge over the Saale at Kosen. The corps strength in round numbers totals twenty-six thousand which includes forty-four guns and General Vialannes' Corps Cavalry Brigade with one thousand sabers. The Corps will march as soon as I dismiss this conference. The order of march will be with divisions moving out in reverse numerical order. That is, beginning with General Gudin's 3rd Division, eight thousand men. Following at one hour's march will be General Friant's 2nd Division, seven thousand men. Last, following as closely as time permits, General Morand's 1st Division, ten thousand men. My orders to the Corps Cavalry and Artillery will be given to their commanders by my staff after this conference. One final point: our outposts and patrols around Taugwitz—up here—report dense fog closing in over the whole area with visibility restricted to less than fifty meters. Now, gentlemen, I have but a short time for questions."

General of Division Friant spoke first.

"I don't question the Marshal's estimate of enemy strength,

but if we are forced on the defensive, what reinforcement can the Corps expect?"

"As you well know," Davout said, "the maneuver of the *bataillon carré* is based upon any corps being able to take on and hold against superior enemy numbers. How soon we'll be supported by another corps depends upon the Emperor—and God and the situation. At this time I can promise no one anything, except that we will support one another as I see the operation proceeding."

"Granted," Friant said, "but what about Ist Corps? Can't we expect them to support us, since its divisions are bivouacked along the road between Naumburg and Camburg?"

"Marshal Bernadotte is carrying out an order to march on Apolda via Dornburg. With Ist Corps moving in that direction, we can't expect it to help us at this time. What future developments might bring Ist Corps to our support will depend on factors I've already mentioned."

Thirty-five-year-old General Morand's face showed a puzzled smile, as he shook his head in seeming wonder. Davout looked at him with a trace of annoyance.

"I can see you are looking doubtful, Louis. If you have a question, let us hear it," Davout said.

"I don't know if I can put it in one question. What I mean is—if I understand what is happening—can it be possible that the Emperor with something over ninety thousand men has *not* brought to bay the Prussian main body, and because of that we must fight it?"

"That's true only in part," Davout replied. "We have no way of knowing the exact strength of any force the Prussian high command has positioned between the Emperor and the Prussian army moving in our direction. As I see it, I have no alternative but to maneuver against and fight that enemy force. Do I make that clear?"

Davout's grim glare was not directly solely at Morand, it took in the whole group. Heads nodded assent; the room became silent.

"Very well then, I and my key staff will march with General Gudin's advance guard. Messages will reach me there. This conference is dismissed." Davout turned, reaching for his hat and saber.

Davout and Gudin rode at the rear of Gudin's 25th Regiment as it cleared Hassenhausen village at seven in the morning. The fog had closed around them hours before, when they had crossed Kosen Bridge, and had continued to envelop the marching column for the three kilometers between the bridge and the village.

The last houses of the village were fading mistily away on Davout's right when Gudin brought the two staff groups to a halt to meet a cavalry courier riding out of the fog. It was young Captain Surcoupe who had been dispatched by the commander of the cavalry screen.

"Sir," the captain reported to Gudin, "Colonel Burke reports that we have run into an estimated four squadrons of Prussian cavalry, reinforced by an artillery battery, between Taugwitz and Poppel and—"

"Ah, so I was right when I thought I'd heard firing about a half-hour ago. Only pistol shots I suppose, Captain?"

"And carbines, Sir. They didn't have time to unlimber their artillery. There were no casualties, but we took three prisoners," Captain Surcoupe said.

Gudin's tone was that of a veteran infantry officer addressing a young cavalryman:

"So this bloody engagement *did* produce a result. And the prisoners confirm the Prussian units, right?"

"That's correct, General."

"Very well, get back to Colonel Burke and tell him I am deploying my two leading battalions to the north and south of this road. We will continue to advance. I want both flanks screened, as well as my front," Gudin ordered.

Leaving Gudin to give his next orders to the colonel of the 25th, Davout took the cart path to his right, trusting it would lead northward to the crest of the Ranzen-Hugel, the low ridge that paralleled the high road and overlooked Hassenhausen and Taugwitz.

As Davout and his staff officers walked their horses along the rutted path, the fields and their walls on either side began to emerge from the fog that had begun to drift away in thick patches. The path did ascend as Davout had hoped, and turned to bear to the northwest. In minutes they had reached the flat top of the ridge and Davout could see the rooftops of Hassenhausen and Taugwitz above the receding fog. He put on his special spectacles that he had had designed for wear in battle. They were ordinary eyeglasses, modified with double ear pieces, two of which were attached to a length of flexible ribbon that fastened in a catch at the back of his head,

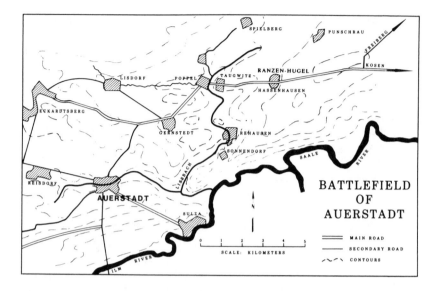

securing the glasses so that hard galloping could not budge them. Their commander's nearsightedness was common knowledge among IIIrd Corps staff, but when they saw their Marshal doff his cocked hat and slip his battle-spectacles over his balding head they knew that things were about to happen.

Things did begin to happen in the valley south of Davout's temporary observation post. As he looked to the south he could see Gudin's line of battle advancing westward toward Taugwitz. The 25th of the Line had deployed in the *ordre mixte*,* its two flank battalions marching in massed battalion columns while the third in the center advanced in three-rank line. Davout looked toward Taugwitz and saw Prussian cavalry appear out of the mist less than a thousand meters from Gudin's advancing regiment. As he watched the French line, the battery of Gudin's divisional artillery unlimbered and went into action. The gunners opened up, ranging in with round shot on the Prussian cavalry. Horses and men went down as the eight-pound iron balls plowed bloody furrows through the ranks of the enemy squadrons. The artillerymen set to work with a will, shifting to ricochet fire so that every thirty seconds each of the battery's six guns was throwing a skipping round shot ripping through the cavalry.

*Ordre mixte—a tactical formation wherein combinations of battalions in line and column moved into action, the column used for rapid cross-country movement and the line for immediate fire action.

The enemy cavalry's deployment into line ceased as suddenly as it had begun. The French artillery fire was more than horses and men could stand, and the double ranks dissolved into scattered horsemen fleeing to escape. Davout watched a moment longer before he turned with an order to the first officer in the line of aides at his left.

"To General Gudin—you may deploy the rest of your division, but do not advance farther than the Lissbach stream to your front. You will have to stand alone until I can bring up Friant and Morand to support you."

The hussar major was off at a gallop down the ridge toward the little cluster of mounted men behind the line of the 25th. Now Davout could focus his attention again on Gudin's infantry. The fog had broken up under the early morning sun, and he could see the dark blue blocks that were battalion columns fanning out across the gold and green of the fields. Gudin's other three regiments were moving up toward the flanks and rear of the 25th. The heads of the two battalion columns of the 25th seemed suddenly to explode as the tiny figures of the *tirailleurs** swarmed out to the front of the regiment.

Davout thought as he watched: *Those battalions all seem to march well enough, and at this distance it's impossible to tell that half of those men are conscripts going into their first battle. Still, they've been soldiering alongside veterans in every company, so the mixture should work as it has before.*

Davout watched the 25th's attack, noting that Gudin had had the good sense to halt its impetuous advance—for a far greater threat had materialized. Dense columns of Prussian infantry jammed the high road from Gernstedt to Poppel, and closer bodies of infantry were deploying in the fields on both sides of Taugwitz. Davout's experienced eye told him that at least a division of the enemy would soon be thrown against Gudin. Worse, his other observations showed that the menacing infantry attack was not the only threat.

Yes, there they are, he thought, *more cavalry massing around Spielberg, and they've learned to stay out of range of Gudin's artillery until they're ready to attack. There are at least a dozen squadrons, perhaps under old Blücher himself. At any rate that cavalry could turn Gudin's right flank, even attack his rear. And my corps cavalry*

---

*Tirailleurs—skirmishers whose role was to attack and soften the defending force in order to assist the main attacking force.

brigade still an hour away—as well as Friant's division and the corps artillery. Gudin is not in position to see it all as I have. I'm wasting time up here on this ridge.

The aide who had returned from Gudin led the way to the division commander's post at the northwest corner of Hassenhausen.

Charles Étienne César Gudin, at thirty-eight, was two years older than his corps commander, and he knew that chances were that he had gone as far as he was destined in high command. Yet he was loyal to a fault—though Davout was never a charismatic figure—as well as battle-hardened, full of grace under pressure, and content to be one of the "three immortals" whose fame as Davout's division commanders had spread through the *Grande Armée*. And he knew his chief well enough to come right to the point. Davout never interfered with his subordinates' operations, but he demanded concise reports on them. Gudin's handsome face was lit by a grin as he took off his gold-laced hat and took his sheaf of notes from it.

"As you see," he told Davout, "I'm pulling back the 85th to base a defense on Hassenhausen and the walls and hedges south of it. My other regiments will be positioned—the 21st and 25th on line north of the village, the 12th in rear of the last two as division reserve."

"I approve of your dispositions, but are you aware of the cavalry threat to your right?" Davout said.

"Only those I took care of with my artillery a half-hour ago."

"I estimate between two and three thousand sabers concentrating just now on this side of Spielberg," Davout said, pausing to gauge Gudin's reaction.

He had no need to wait. Gudin was giving orders to two aides.

"To brigade commanders—major Prussian cavalry attack developing against our right. The 85th continues to defend Hassenhausen. The 21st and 25th form battalion squares. The 12th forms in regimental square."

Davout and Gudin rode together toward the area where the 21st and 25th Regiments would be redeploying. It was 8:20 A.M. and still no messages from Friant or Vialannes with the corps cavalry. But Davout had no time to reflect on his dire need for news from the rest of his corps. He could look northward as he rode and see the long columns of enemy cavalry crossing the skyline of the Ranzen-Hugel, not over a kilometer away from the 25th Regiment on the division right. The regiment's three battalions were in the act of forming square, and there was no time to lose. Davout called over to Gudin:

"There are too many of us to get inside one square. Take your staff into the center battalion. I'll take post in the square this side of it."

Gudin waved a salute in acknowledgement, and spurred ahead, trailed by a half-dozen staff officers. Davout trotted his horse to the nearest corner of the square he had selected, coming to a walk as a company commander backed three files aside to let the horsemen enter. The *chef de bataillon* ran up to report to the Marshal, but Davout waved him back to his duties. Here there was nothing for a Marshal and his staff to do except cluster together in the center of the square and stay out of the way of battalion officers who were about to spend some of the busiest moments they might ever know in their trade.

Since a Marshal of France wouldn't be able to practice his trade for the next few minutes, Davout could turn his mind, with its accustomed precision, to matters like calculating the combat power of the Prussian cavalry vis-à-vis the firepower of the French square. Because of his cavalry background—he had been commissioned and trained in the Royal-Champagne Regiment of the old Royal Army—Davout was well aware of the futility of unsupported cavalry charges against steady infantry in square. He could recall such actions as the Battle of the Pyramids, eight years before, when he had witnessed six thousand splendid Mameluke horsemen battered to bloody bits by the fire of Bonaparte's squares.

His mind turned to calculation: *Now, counting files I can see that this 2nd Battalion of the 25th Regiment averages about 120 muskets per company, and the* chef de bataillon *has formed a square in a logical manner with a little over two companies making up each side. With all companies in three ranks that will average about 240 muskets for each side of the square. Then the most horsemen any cavalry unit can bring against each square side can be assumed to be 80, figuring the cavalry squadrons attacking in the usual two ranks, that is, with about 40 horses in each rank. Thus an attacking cavalry unit will be opposing 80 sabers against 240 muskets, and the infantry will be doing all the firing, since a charging cavalryman cannot be expected to fire anything, not even his pistol. But all this figuring is for naught if this is not steady infantry—infantry that will act under strict fire discipline, delivering or reserving volley fire on command. Now we'll see if months of training and a heavy leavening of veterans will pay off.*

From his vantage point in the saddle Davout could see over the ranks of the square and observe the other battalion squares of the 25th and 21st. The tactical skill of the two regimental commanders showed clearly in the way the six squares had been aligned to provide mutual support as well as clear fields of fire for the "killing grounds" in front of each square's face.

Davout turned to look over the side facing the advancing cavalry. The squadrons had wheeled into double-ranked lines, and were coming on at a walk three hundred meters away. A hundred meters closer, leaders' sabers flashed overhead, and the lines broke into a trot.

Fusilier Jean Daborde was on the side facing the oncoming cavalry. His company's deployment had placed him in the center rank where his platoon stood at order arms except for the front rank, which knelt with muskets grounded and slanted forward to present a solid line of bayonets to the enemy. Jean's youthful eye could not perceive the "line of squadron columns" as could his Marshal. To Jean, the front rank of cavalry was the leading wave in a sea of horsemen. As that wave came out of a fold of ground a hundred meters distant he saw the flash of sun on brass helmets and steel breastplates. They were tall men on big horses, seeming to tower to awful heights. Behind Jean, Sergeant Bruit was bellowing at the platoon.

"They are cuirassiers in armor. Aim low—at the horses!"

The thunder of hooves grew until it drowned out every other sound in the world. Jean couldn't look around him, but he knew that every new *fantassin** must be clutching his musket, as he did, with whitened knuckles. This was not like facing the measured advance of infantry as they had a half-hour ago. Now they were fixed in place, having to confront a charging horde of monsters that would crash down upon them and trample them into the ground. If only he could turn and—

"Present! Take aim!"

It was their captain shouting the commands. Jean looked down the barrel of his musket and brought the muzzle down until it was pointing at the chest of a charging horse.

"Fire!"

Fantassin—French soldier slang for an infantryman, a GI.

The kick of the musket's recoil turned Jean into an automaton that seemed to be going through the loading drill all by itself. When the platoon returned its muskets to the Order, Jean was astounded to see that the platoon on his right was still standing at the Present, a triple tier of bayoneted muskets. Why didn't they fire? Then Jean saw the answer. Forty meters in front of the square, wounded horses—their riders thrown clear—threshed and tossed on the ground, a few uttering high pitched screams that chilled the blood of the French conscripts. But what had happend to the sea of horsemen that had threatened to engulf them? The realization ran through the infantry like an electric shock: the following waves of cavalry had shied back from the slaughter in front of them and had veered off to either flank to pass around the square. But the veering off had only brought them into the killing grounds of the adjoining faces of the square, as another litter of dead and wounded horses and riders attested.

That shock of surprise was succeeded by elation that turned into backslapping and handshaking, sweeping through the companies that had fired. There was laughter, too, when a dismounted cuirassier, clumsy as a drunk in his heavy gear, took off on a waddling run to the rear, then turned and fired his pistol at the square. It was not a gallant act, it was simply a foolish gesture to the infantrymen.

Officers and sergeants were barking order back into the confusion, for fresh cavalry squadrons were forming to renew the attack. The next attack came on as had the first: columns of squadrons in line, starting from a walk, and, as the distance closed, going into a trot, then a canter, and finally a full gallop over the last fifty meters. Again the square's volleys were withheld until the cavalry's front rank reached the swath of dead and wounded horses forty meters from the square. Again the volleys crashed into them, and again the leading wave went down in slaughter while succeeding waves broke and flowed around the square, only to lose more dead and wounded to the fire from the other sides of the squares.

Incredibly, the Prussians reformed at a distance and repeated the attack. The result was the same, except that the swath of carcasses had grown to become a grisly barrier that brought the horses to a quivering standstill, resisting all efforts of their riders to spur them forward against the bristling rows of steel.

There were four charges in all, and all were disasters for

the Prussian cavalry. In the French squares the men were allowed to stand down, and a chorus of cheers ran from battalion to battalion. Even Davout's stern face had cracked into a smile, though he was heard to say to his nearest aide: "Let them cheer while they can. Poor devils. Their trials for this day have only begun."

After congratulating the *chef de bataillon* and his men, Davout rode out to join Gudin on the little hilltop halfway between Hassenhausen and Punschrau. Together they observed with growing anxiety the long lines of enemy infantry that now extended beyond either flank of Gudin's division. Since the Prussian cavalry had withdrawn in disorder toward Lisdorf, the infantry threat had become paramount. Davout and Gudin compared estimates and agreed that they were already faced with the elements of at least three divisions. Though it was not Davout's custom to express fears to subordinates it was essential that both commanders share freely their observations at their critical hour of 9:00 A.M.

"Still no word from Friant. It looks like you'll have to hold here. It appears that the enemy's next big effort will be directed again at your right flank. I believe they intend to keep their road open to Freiberg, and at the same time cut us off from Kosen and our reinforcement," Davout said.

"I'll extend as far as I can to the north and keep the 12th ready for counterattack in that direction. If our luck continues we'll hold until Friant makes it here," Gudin said.

"What luck continuing? What do you mean?"

"We've been twice lucky so far. First, not one of those cavalry attacks was supported by artillery. And now the Prussians seem to be taking their good time organizing their attack, so they are wasting minutes that are valuable to us."

"Right on both counts," Davout said, mounting his horse and looking toward the high road that disappeared over the crest of the hill east of Hassenhausen. A high, thin dust cloud was rising over the road, and Davout's spirits rose as he recognized the column of his corps cavalry followed by the guns of the corps artillery. He put spurs to his horse and galloped toward the head of the column.

By 9:15 he had sent Vialannes' squadrons trotting off to take position covering Gudin's right flank, and had sent an aide galloping ahead to select a firing position for the 12-pounders north of the village. Gudin would position the guns in single battery as Davout had directed, in order to cover his division's right and front with massed fires.

At 9:30 Friant arrived and Davout lost no time in having him deploy his division on the double on Gudin's right.

With Friant committed, as well as my cavalry and artillery, I can organize a stable defense, he thought, *until I can get Morand up. Yet, according to the latest report from him, he is still four kilometers away. It will take him another hour and a half to get here. It's 9:30 now, so he should be arriving at 11:00. The question is, what kind of a defense can I manage with my two divisions against the Prussians' five? There must be three divisions deployed against me now and two more to come. If the luck that Gudin spoke of holds, the worst I have to fear is a coordinated attack instead of the piecemeal efforts the Prussian command has been mounting.*

The worst of Davout's fears was only fifteen minutes in becoming a reality. At 9:45 the Prussian main attack began—and as Davout had estimated from reports and his own observations—with two divisions attacking frontally and a third appearing to divide its strength by sending a brigade to reinforce each flank of the Prussian attack. At 10:00 Davout's two divisions were in a critical situation. Friant on the north was taking a battering from the enemy's infantry and artillery while Gudin was just managing to hold firm in his center. There the Prussian preponderance in artillery had become all too evident as the French casualties were reported to Davout. He was certain now that his intelligence estimate of two hundred Prussian guns had been accurate. Two hundred guns against the forty-four in the whole of IIIrd Corps! Yet Gudin was still holding on to Hassenhausen, and here it was possible that luck was still looking over Davout's shoulder. The Prussian infantry of Schmettau's division (now a confirmed identity to Davout) was being handled ineptly in its attack on the village. The enemy battalions, lacking the experience of the French in fighting in built-up areas, were held in line, delivering ineffective volleys against the French, who were using the protective cover of houses, field walls, and hedges with skill in their defense.

Yet it was in the south, on Gudin's left flank, where Davout's worst fears were realized. The Prussian division attacking south of Hassenhausen was overpowering Gudin's 85th Regiment. The aide who brought that report was unable to inform Davout of Gudin's present location, only that he had ridden northward, presumably to coordinate operations with Friant. Davout saw that there was no time to search for Gudin. The situation called for immediate action and he was the one who must start it. He galloped off with an aide who knew the position of Gudin's 12th Regiment. He found Colonel Vergès with his staff and battalion commanders at the corner of the regimental square. Davout cut short the colonel's formal report with:

"Form your regiment for an immediate advance in line of battalion columns, and direct your center battalion to follow me. You will ride with me and I'll give you your mission as we march."

Behind Davout and the colonel the blue-white-red of the regimental tricolor streamed in the wind beneath its eagle. Drums were beating the quick march at the heads of the three battalions as they dressed their front ranks on the color. Davout had finished giving Colonel Vergès the mission of counterattacking to restore the situation on the corps left flank, south of Hassenhausen, and now the two rode side by side, guiding on a hedge corner south of the village. To their front the gravity of the situation was becoming all too clear. Groups of fugitives appeared in the open, first in twos and threes, then in large disordered bodies of fleeing men. Some were hatless, some few had even discarded their muskets and sidearms. The blue coats and white breeches of straggling infantry were showing more and more against the green of the farm fields. Davout motioned the colonel closer.

"You can't allow this mob to affect your men. Get your *tirailleurs* out now and clear the way," Davout growled at him.

The men of the *voltigeur* companies leapt into action, dashing through the intervals to fan out into a dense screen two hundred meters ahead of their battalions. Davout turned to the aide at his left.

"Major, take two officers from this regimental staff and set up a rallying point to collect those stragglers. We'll send any of their officers we can find back to you."

While he was turned in the saddle Davout glanced back at the regiment marching behind him. No soldier had to be told how to behave when he was being led into battle by a Marshal of France. The ranks were dressed in parade order, keeping their alignment in spite of the rough ground.

Davout turned the command back to the colonel as it became time for his battalions to deploy into line. He halted with three aides in a battalion interval until the rear ranks of the regiment had passed.

There it goes, he thought, *the last reserve of IIIrd Corps, and Morand must still be a half-hour away! If that 12th Regiment can only restore order on the left, there is nothing left to do in both my divisions but to fight these Prussians to a standstill.*

He gave his order to the nearest aide.

"I will take post over there," he pointed to the knoll on the ridge a half-kilometer southeast of Hassenhausen. "Ride to General Morand, tell him that the mission—yes, the survival—of the corps depends on the arrival of his division. He must push forward with all dispatch. Then direct General Morand to join me at my post."

From his post on the knoll Davout had an overall view of his battle. The irregular front of his two divisions stretched for four kilometers from Friant's right flank, at a point midway between Spielberg and Punschrau, through Gudin's division to its left where the 12th Regiment was restoring the line south of Hassenhausen. The fronts of the French regiments were now locked into their defensive positions. All the maneuver of large units was now the prerogative of the Prussians. Davout noted that their major efforts were being directed toward frontal assaults on Hassenhausen. If only the defenders of the village and the farms around it could hold, the whole of the corps line might hold. The battle for the village commanded his attention while the enemy threw no less than four assaults against it. Not one succeeded in penetrating the defenses; all were thrown back, leaving windrows of casaulties in the fields west of the village. The French infantry, firing from the cover of houses and field walls, supported by artillery firing canister, took such a toll that it was unnecessary to counterattack in order to hold their positions.

Davout felt something more than relief when he could break off his surveillance and greet Morand, who rode up at 10:45. The head of his division column was only fifteen minutes behind him as Davout pointed out the situation and assigned him his mission.

"You will deploy and advance to a line extending from the left of the 12th Regiment, directly south until your left flank reaches the Saale River. Prepare to attack to the west to seize Rehausen and Sonnendorf as initial objectives. You will note heavy concentrations of enemy cavalry apparently moving to attack our left, south of Hassenhausen," Davout said.

"Understood," Morand said. "I will deploy in line of battalion columns behind a screeening force made up of my light cavalry and the 13th Light Infantry."

"That is your affair, and you've no time to lose," Davout said.

In minutes Davout could watch Morand's cavalry, followed by the infantry skirmishers, moving past his post, advancing westward to clear the Prussian reconnaissance cavalry and infantry from the ridge running southwest from Hassenhausen. Behind Morand's screening force his battalions were deploying at the double, south of the Kosen road. Davout felt the huge burden of anxiety fall away as Morand's columns came up into line and moved westward in a coordinated advance. Another form of relief came with an aide-courier from Friant who reported that he had weighted the right of his line to attack Spielberg, and was moving west in spite of heavy losses from Prussian artillery.

Davout's relief was short-lived when he again turned attention to the situation in the south. The masses of enemy cavalry had increased in numbers far beyond those in the attacks on Gudin's squares. Those earlier attacks had employed around 2,500 sabers, while the masses moving against Morand must number five times more—as many as 12,000 to 15,000. It was obvious that Brunswick was mounting an all-out cavalry effort to overwhelm Morand. The latter's battalions were changing formation again, this time from column into firing line, and were engaged in fire fights with the Prussian infantry.

Morand can't withstand those masses of cavalry with his units in line, Davout thought, *but he knows as well as I that he will have to form squares. And he can see the situation even better than I, because he is closer to it. Yet, I've got to go down there, even if it's only to show myself to his troops.*

While Davout was riding to join Morand the battalions in the south were already redeploying into squares. Morand hurriedly briefed Davout on his plan to receive the cavalry attack. His battalions on the right would remain in line, they could easily fend off cavalry attacks since they had taken cover behind hedges and walls. Davout had scarcely voiced his approval when it was evident that he and Morand must seek cover in the squares just as he and Gudin had earlier.

The Prussian cavalry attacks were repeat performances of the morning's debacle, though on a massive scale never before experienced by Davout or his veterans. Yet Morand's *amalgame* of recruits and veterans—in much the same proportion as those in Gudin's units—behaved like solid formations of old hands, loading and firing at ranges as close as thirty meters. The bloody effects of their volleys were in direct proportion to the numbers of horsemen thrown against them. Yet squadrons were replaced or reformed and the waves of horsemen—cuirassiers, uhlans, dragoons—came on, were decimated as their waves broke around the rocks of the squares, came on again and were slaughtered until their squadrons were broken and scattered. The French repulsed with ease the succession of cavalry charges because the Prussian command failed to support the attacks with artillery.

Finally, the clouds of horsemen drifted off to the west, a beaten rabble. Davout left the square to reassume his post on the hill, leaving Morand to redeploy again and attack to the west to reach the Lissbach and take Rehausen and Sonnendorf.

Back on his hill Davout was amazed to see a development in the battle that was unforeseeable, but was to prove as favorable to him as it would be fatal to the Prussians. In their zeal to get around Haussenhausen—following the failure of their repeated assaults on the village—both Prussian flanks, north and south, had turned inward toward the village. It was a sudden opportunity for Davout, as golden as it was fleeting.

Battle of Auerstadt

Davout sent aides flying with orders to his three division commanders: Gudin to hold fast in order to provide a *point d'appui,* the base for a corps counterattack; Friant and Morand to push forward aggressively with their division artillery and use it to enfilade the Prussian lines.

While Davout's orders were on the way Morand's division was attacked by the elite of the enemy's infantry, the Prussian Guard. The attack was defeated by Morand's inspired infantry and artillery who resumed their advance. The interrogation of Prussian prisoners taken during this action revealed that the Duke of Brunswick had been seriously wounded as he had led forward a grenadier regiment in an attack on Hassenhausen. There were conflicting reports regarding Brunswick's successor in command; some said it was the chief of staff, Scharnhorst; others said the King himself had assumed command.

It was noon and at the zenith of the day there was a pause, a brief lull, while Davout's 1st and 2nd Divisions maneuvered to counterattack. Davout felt that surge of "second wind" that comes to a champion runner when he realizes that a final, vital effort will win. Now everything would depend on Friant's and Morand's skill and aggressiveness to exploit that second wind.

Davout knew that he need not worry about those qualities in his division commanders. Friant drove on, the axis of his advance aimed at Taugwitz and Poppel, while his artillery was pushed forward to positions from which it was pounding the Prussians with short range fires. In the south Morand's leading units reached the Lissbach after taking Rehausen and Sonnendorf. Morand had gotten his artillery into position on the Sonnenkuppe, the western end of the ridge above Sonnendorf. From there his guns were battering the flank and rear of the Prussian division on the south.

Caught in the murderous crossfire of Friant's and Morand's artillery, the Prussian flank units began to disintegrate. Davout watched fresh enemy infantry—he estimated them to be the major elements of a new division—thrown into the battle in desperate counterattacks, obviously meant to free the shattered flanks and restore the Prussian situation across their front. These attacks crumbled under the same deadly crossfire while Prussian units in the center were being hammered by Gudin's infantry. "Very soon a large number of Prussian troops were trapped in a narrow gully and a murderous close-quarter scrimmage ensued. Davout later paid tribute to his adversaries in his *Journal:* 'We were within pistol range, and the cannonade tore gaps in their ranks which immediately closed up. Each move of the [Prussian] 61st Regiment was indicated on the ground by the brave men they left there.' . . . By 12:30 the pride of the Prussian army was streaming away to the west and north. . . ."[17]

Davout's seizure of the initiative at the critical moment was paying off. While Morand was continuing his attack across the Lissbach, Friant had taken Spielberg, had gone on to take Poppel, lost it, retook it, and continued his attack toward Lisdorf.

Again Davout saw a critical phase open for him if he continued to take the initiative. He recognized it and made his decision. It was time to throw everything into a coordinated corps attack. He directed the axis of his corps attack on Gernstadt-Eckartsberg and ordered Gudin forward. Gudin stormed Taugwitz and drove on toward Gernstadt. "Davout's three divisions bore down on the Prussian army in a menacing crescent-shaped formation, horns pushed aggressively forward."[18]

A pattern was set which was to characterize the battle for the rest of the afternoon. Each time Prussian rear guards were deployed in the attempt to halt the triumphant French, Gudin would thrust forward frontally while Friant and Morand worked battalions and guns around the Prussian flanks and renewed their lethal crossfire.

As the enemy lines crumbled away before him Davout never ceased to wonder at the masses of Prussian reserves that he saw withdrawing, reserves that were never committed to battle. But he had little time to ponder over that observation. He was too deeply engaged in driving forward every element of infantry, cavalry, and artillery in his corps. His hat lost, the gold lace of his uniform as powder-blackened as his face, he continued to gallop from division to division, pushing to the last degree every element that could keep up the momentum of the advance. It was no longer an attack—it was a pursuit. He drove his exhausted units until those in the van collapsed on the crest of the Eckartsberg. Flesh and blood could endure no more, and with the greatest reluctance of his career, the Iron Marshal had to call a halt for his divisions. One can imagine this stern soldier as close to tears as such a man could come.

But he was not through. He ordered forward the only force he had left: three regiments of cavalry and a single infantry battalion. He flung them in pursuit, knowing that the tiny force—in terms of the numbers of Prussians they were chasing—could only harass, not destroy. Nevertheless he ordered them to drive as many Prussians as possible to the south and west in order to push the fugitives into the path of the other corps of the *Grande Armée*.

It was at 4:30 that Davout's divisions had been forced to halt, an hour before sundown on that October Tuesday. "The weary but triumphant soldiers of IIIrd Corps turned to the task of rounding up prisoners and caring for their wounded before taking a well-earned rest."[19] Then came the other unmistakable evidence of the exhaustion of Davout's combat power: the near tragic toll of French casualties. "Of the 26,000 men he had succeeded in bringing on the field, no less than 258 officers and 6,794 men, viz., $25\frac{1}{2}$ percent, had fallen, and the 3rd Division, Gudin, with 41 percent, is perhaps the heaviest loss as borne by victorious troops in so large a unit as a division."[20] In comparison Davout had caused Prussian losses of 10,000 casualties, 3,000 prisoners, and 115 guns captured.

While IIIrd Corps soldiers were going about their grim afteraction tasks, Davout's courier, Colonel Falcon, was carrying the Marshal's report to Napoleon stating that he had defeated the Duke of Brunswick's army and driven it toward Weimar in a rout. The colonel arrived at Napoleon's headquarters at an inn in Jena where, as he awaited the Emperor, he watched aides decorating the walls with captured Prussian regimental colors. In time the Emperor arrived and allowed Falcon to deliver his report. Napoleon read it with growing scepticism and a certain lack of enthusiasm. Here, incredibly, it told him that: "Davout claimed to have fought and defeated the Prussian main body near Auerstadt, ten miles away. 'Your marshal must be seeing double,' he somewhat ungraciously snapped at the emissary. Little by little, however, he came to realize that in fact he—the Emperor with 96,000 men—had been engaging only the Prussian flank forces, jointly 55,000 strong, while Davout—the subordinate, a mere 26,000 troops under his command—had been locked in mortal conflict with Brunswick's main body. Napoleon found it hard to swallow the magnitude of the calculational error under which he had labored, but next day he awarded Davout the unstinted praise he richly deserved."[21]

There is another aspect of the vanity of emperors and the manner in which awards are disbursed by them. Davout was created Duke of Auerstadt, but it should be noted that an emperor who was capable of awarding a marshal's baton on the battlefield took two years to appoint Davout to that dukedom.

What then of Bernadotte's actions and their consequences? "When Napoleon demanded an explanation of his amazing conduct, Bernadotte tried to justify himself by describing the difficulties (largely imaginary) which he encountered along the road. The Emperor replied to this in no uncertain terms on October 23: 'According to a very precise order you ought to have been at Dornburg. . . . In case you had failed to execute these orders, I informed you during the night that if you were still at Naumburg when this order arrived you should march with Marshal Davout and support him. You were at Naumburg when this order arrived; it was communicated to you; this notwithstanding, you preferred to execute a false march in order to make for Dornburg, and in consequence you took no part in the battle and Marshal Davout bore the principal efforts of the enemy's army.' "[22]

If one studies Davout's life and military career it is not difficult to understand his display of moral courage at Auerstädt—courage that not only opposed the dynamics of battle, but overcame each as it arose.

Davout comes through as a stern, uncompromising figure, never a charismatic one to his soldiers or anyone else. He had the lasting reputation of being as incorruptible as he was exacting in enforcing discipline—two traits not common among Napoleon's marshals. He worshipped duty first and last, no doubt a quality inherited from his martial and aristocratic background. There was a saying in Burgundy that when a male Davout was born a sword was drawn from the scabbard. Hence it is not surprising that he became the most dependable of the marshals. "His troops were always the best trained, equipped, and disciplined in the *Grande Armée*, and usually got the hardest assignments."[23] Thus the Iron Marshal, who his soldiers also called "the just," was respected but not loved—except perhaps on one occasion, the evening after Auerstadt.

Part Two

WILL

Hernan Cortes at
Cempoalla, 1520

John R. M. Chard with Gonville
Bromhead at **Rorke's Drift**, 1879

WILL

> Why is the will of the military commander deemed more decisive of success than the will of leadership in any other calling? Clearly it is because the inertia, frictions, and confusions of the forces of the battlefield make all positive action more difficult.
>
> —S. L. A. Marshall, *Men Against Fire*

If Thucydides had interviewed the Athenian oarsmen and marine infantrymen as they were disembarking from their fighting ships following their victories over the Spartans at Naupactus, he might have been the first to profit from firsthand insight into the minds of men fresh from battle. We will never know whether the historian of the Peloponnesian War might have conceived such a system, but if he had he might well have been S. L. A. Marshall's historical harbinger. In any case we believe that Marshall stands alone in this regard, as the record shows.

Why then could Marshall have made the positive statement just quoted, and at the same time pull back with apparent skepticism saying, ". . . this whole subject of the will of the commander cries out for a modern resurvey and better understanding."[1] I imagine he saw the problem clearly enough, but realized in that small book of his—dedicated to finding clear-cut solutions to the problem of better command in future war—he could only point the way toward "better understanding" the influence of the leader's will. For he did light the way to understanding with two beacons that serve to keep us out of the byways and heading in the right direction.

Essentially he was able to open the heart of the matter and reveal a fundamental fact: in battle things don't get done simply because a leader wills, or wants to will an outcome. "They are done because they are doable," because a sensible leader sees what is possible and weighs that against the things that his men are capable of doing. In actuality Marshall had not uncovered anything startling. His was a simple way of pointing out what Napoleon had recognized, writing at St. Helena a century and a quarter earlier:

> The first thing for a commander to determine is what he is going to do, to see if he has the means to overcome the obstacles which the enemy can oppose to him and, when he has decided, do all he can to surmount them.[2]

86

To determine what he is going to do, to get things done because they are do-able—this means simply that if a leader wants to exercise his will, he first must know its limits in the situation in which he finds himself. Yet like most simple truths it continues to suffer obscurity because men hide it somewhere between wars. Un-oddly enough it has always been a truth as Thucydides learned 2,373 years before Marshall wrote his book; learned it the hard way by underestimating the capabilities of his opponent and, as a consequence, was not only relieved of his command but was exiled for twenty years.

Marshall's other way of shedding light on the development of the leader's will was to perceive another simple truth, namely that the concept of the strength of a commander's will has appeared, in the common and popular view, to be the peculiar property of generals; and the generals have done nothing to discourage the idea. Yet Marshall was to observe that "the good general is simply the good company commander in his post-graduate course." He pursued that truth until he found in the end that the ultimate test of the combat leader's will comes when he must be capable of making his men accomplish their mission in spite of their inherent human frailties—all this in what John Keegan has called "the face of battle." Marshall further concludes that a leader cannot *fully* know how to exercise his will until he has learned to do it in the crucible of "the small fight," that is, in combats where the leader develops his will through battle experience alongside the men he will lead later from higher levels of command. One— at least this one—finds that conclusion well-nigh impossible to deny.

Yet, though I find Marshall's conclusion an invaluable piece of guidance, it cannot be relied on as the single means of understanding the exercise of the leader's will in war. This might be seen as an unfortunate shortfall, but it also can be considered a blessing because it reminds one that one is seeking to examine a leader's attributes *without having to do it on the battlefield*. It will be recalled that a similar concept of Marshall's had to be held in abeyance because it could only be tested in battle. Accordingly, we may follow the path that Marshall's insights have lighted, though our main reliance continues to be on the lessons of history—and on trustworthy commentaries on them.

In extending the search for exemplary cases of the leader applying his will to win battles, I have re-scanned a number of battles to find a pattern emerging. The pattern took the form of a spectrum with two qualities outstanding at opposite ends. At one end there is *boldness* which, in its military sense, may be expressed as reflective intelligence undertaking a daring action; another way of saying it is that the will directs the effort to attain an intellectual aim.

At the other end of the spectrum one finds *tenacity* which, in this context, means that the will enables the leader—and hence his men—to hold out until the mission has been accomplished, no matter how adverse the odds or conditions. More about tenacity later.

Boldness

ONE QUOTE MOST frequently attributed to the wrong
source is that made by poor old Georges Jacques Danton. I
have seen his ringing words ascribed to sources ranging anywhere from Napoleon to Betsy Ross; therefore I'd like to give
Danton credit for the conclusion of his stirring speech to the
Legislative Assembly on the occasion of its facing the alliance
threatening revolutionary France. He said: "Boldness, again
boldness, and always boldness—and France is saved!"

There can be little doubt that Danton, the politician, delivered those words with flair, and boldness, employed by an
intelligent military commander, has usually carried off victory with flair. Yet it is all too easy to get carried away with
the idea of boldness as impetuous action. To reasonable men
there is always an underlying awareness that boldness unrestrained by careful forethought equals rashness. The thought
of the pratfall of boldness gone awry has been the chief de-
terrent to many a commander's action. The fear of failure
has always haunted ordinary men, but the fear of ridiculous
failure is more than haunting, it is damning to positive action.
It is the same fear implicit in Hamlet's question as he tries to
face whatever it is that ". . . puzzles the will,/ And makes us
rather bear those ills we have/Than fly to others that we know
not of?"

Hence there is a corollary question in the back of the
reasoning leader's mind: When is the time for boldness and

when the time for caution? If that leader is well-grounded in history he will recall that, with the rare exception of a commander like Charles XII of Sweden (who stuck his neck out once too often when he stretched it over a trench parapet in time to stop a Danish bullet), no successful leader has made a career of being consistently bold. This reminder was put nicely to our airmen in World War II in the adage: There are old pilots, and there are bold pilots; but there are no old, bold pilots.

With these admonitions in mind, how does the good leader go about deciding where and how to be bold? Let us see what great soldiers and thinkers have concluded in this regard. We have already heard what Napoleon had to say about a commander's first step in planning—to determine what needs to be done. He added to that another piece of advice that is ageless in applicability.

> The first quality for a commander is a cool head, which receives a correct impression of things. He should not allow himself to be confused by either good or bad news. The impressions which he receives in the course of a day should classify themselves in his mind in such a way as to occupy the place which they merit, for reason and judgment are the result of the comparison of impressions taken into just consideration.[3]

Which, in today's terms, says that the cool guy sorts out the facts before he acts.

Napoleon has been quoted as asking before appointing a general: "Is he lucky?" Now only the unthinking would conclude that the Emperor put his trust in commanders who seemed to come out well no matter how their battles were fought. David Chandler, the British military historian, saw what was really being asked: "Is he [the appointee] competent at taking calculated risks?"[4] Chandler went on to clinch his evaluation in another work in which he cites the British General Wavell, who had looked deeply into the matter: "Further qualities demanded of a good general by Wavell included boldness, which he stressed was what Napoleon really meant by luck: 'A bold general may be lucky, but no general can be lucky unless he is bold.'"[5]

The old *maitre* Clausewitz also thought boldness an important enough quality to devote a major chapter to it in his *On War,* but he is careful to place it following his remarks on foresight and prudence. Though he deems boldness an essential element—even "a creative power"—he points out repeatedly that "the higher the rank the more necessary it is that boldness should be accompanied by a reflective mind." He further observes, however, that boldness, in the light of history, becomes rarer as the commander attains higher levels of command.

To add proof to this latter point Clausewitz looks on the reverse of the coin to note that most of the generals in European history who have been rated mediocre in their performance in independent command were men renowned earlier in their careers (that is, while serving as subordinate commanders) for their boldness and power of decision. From this and other reflections he concluded:

> The higher we rise in a position of command, the more of the mind, understanding, and penetration predominate in activity, the more therefore is boldness, which is a property of the feelings, kept in subjection, and for that reason we find it so rarely in the highest positions, but then, so much the more should it be admired. *Boldness, directed by an overruling intelligence, is the stamp of the hero** . . . We think then that it is impossible to imagine a distinguished general without boldness, that is to say, that no man can become one who is not born with this power of the soul, and we therefore look upon it as the first requisite for such a career. . . .

Finally, one can scarcely overemphasize the thought that boldness, as an element of the will, must be developed from within before it can be exercised upon the leader's men. If he is made of the stuff that clearly sizes up the situation, sees what should *and can be done,* then gives his orders, his decisions and subsequent bold actions will lead to success in battle.

At this point it would be easy to turn to famous battles like Austerlitz or El Alamein for examples of contesting wills. It would be equally less rewarding to add to so much that has already been written. Instead, let us watch a bold leader stake his life, his army, and an empire on a night attack against a better-armed force which outnumbered his by three to one.

*Italics added.

Conquistadors, Cannon, and Cocuyos

> "That which I have myself seen and the fighting. . . . And the
> word came up there were ships hove-to in the offing:
>
> And we knew well the governor's men had the wind of us . . ."
> —Archibald MacLeish, "Conquistador"

Indeed fat Diego Velasquez, the Governor of Cuba, did "have
the wind" of Cortes' expedition, even though the scent was
more than a year old in this spring of 1520. And Velasquez had every reason, in his way of thinking, to follow that
scent. He had not forgotten a single detail of his public humiliation when Cortes had given his governor the slip by sailing
out of Santiago harbor in defiance of Velasquez's last-minute
attempt to countermand the expedition's sailing orders.

Cortes had had word of the governor's "secret" decision
to replace him as the captain-general of the expedition to
Mexico, and had weighed anchor with his half-prepared fleet
to slip out of the harbor. When the enraged Velasquez—half-
dressed in his haste to stop Cortes—had shouted from the
quay "Is this the way you part from me!" Cortes had replied
with something to the effect that "time presses, and there are
some things that must be done—has your Excellency any
commands?" The mortified governor, helpless and frus-
trated, could only watch Cortes' longboat pull away towards
his ship, quite unable to think of a proper command that would
bring back the expedition's commander, who was politely
waving his farewell.

Now the ships that had "hove-to in the offing" were truly
the fleet that carried the governor's punitive expedition. It
was commanded by the Castilian hidalgo, Pánfilo de Narvaez,
who had orders to displace Cortes and "establish the governor's jurisdiction over the conquered territories in Mexico."
Narvaez had landed on the same beaches at San Juan de Ulua
where Cortes and his tiny "army" had disembarked the year
before. The punitive expedition outnumbered Cortes' original force more than two to one, totaling nine hundred soldiers including eighty horsemen, eighty arquebusiers,* and
eighteen field cannon, and stores of ammunition with other

*The infantry armed with the unwieldly matchlock (arquebus) of sixteenth-century Spanish arm-
ies.

supplies to match. There were even one thousand Indians to do the menial chores.

This gallant armada anchored off San Juan de Ulua, on April 23, 1520, and began disembarking. Narvaez waded ashore and proclaimed his intention to march against Cortes in the name of the Governor of Cuba.

It was the news of this expedition that had been carried secretly to the Emperor Montezuma, the captive-guest of Hernan Cortes in Tenochtitlan, the Aztec capital. Montezuma had savored the intelligence for three days, tasting the sweetness of the surprise he would pull on Cortes and his conquistadors. Now it was time to receive his captor and his captains; they were being ushered down the halls toward his chambers in response to his invitation to an audience.

Montezuma heard the clink of armor and the sound of Spanish voices behind the green-plumed escort of Aztec noblemen before he caught sight of Cortes. When the ushers stepped aside he saw the familiar figure of his conqueror, wearing his three-quarter armor blackened against the tropical weather. Cortes was bare-headed, his casque carried by his page, Orteguilla. The Captain-General's face was pale as usual, in spite of much campaigning, a paleness seeming to belie the broad shoulders and deep chest that were the outstanding features of his muscular frame. Cortes bowed slightly, his dark eyes looking into Montezuma's.

Cortes saw a slight man of forty with shoulder-length black hair, staring back at him with Indian eyes under his miniature golden crown. Seated on his gold-mounted throne the Emperor seemed anything but a prisoner as he waved Cortes to the chair beside him. Montezuma waited until Doña Marina, Cortes' interpreter—and, as all knew, his mistress—took her place, standing behind Cortes' chair. When the three captains—Olid, Alvarado, and Marin—had ranked themselves to Cortes left, Montezuma spoke in carefully spaced passages so that Doña Marina had time to interpret between pauses.

"Malinche, we waste no time on formal things today. I have great news, received only moments ago, news that will change all your plans here in Tenochtitlan and at Villa Rica." Montezuma's guttural tones were as flat as his expressionless face.

Cortes' smile was quick, though his dark eyes were grave as he returned Montezuma's gaze. He nodded politely, almost carelessly, as though great news purporting to change his plans arrived every morning.

"I am grateful for your consideration, and I know that any news you have should be important," Cortes said.

Montezuma motioned to an aide whose gold lip plug showed him to rank high in the warrior caste. He knelt and extended a cotton-cloth roll to his emperor who took it and unrolled a series of picture writings which he began to read off to Cortes.

"Eighteen of your great high ships are landing an army on the beaches at the place you call San Juan De Ulua. They were men of your nation, numbering nine hundred, with eighty horses and eighteen cannon. Their leader is called Narvaez and he has said that he comes to march against you."

Cortes' eyes never shifted, and in his turn his face showed only polite interest.

"Surely you mean 'march to join me' not against me. And you must be aware that in the prophecies of your god Quetzalcoatl, there will come more men with white skin, bearded and in armor."

Montezuma continued to tick off the accounting of Narvaez's force to the last detail of men, equipment, and supplies as though he had not heard the Spanish leader's words.

His cursed couriers have outrun ours again, Cortes thought, *so I'll have to put my best face on the matter and get all I can out of this heathen bastard.*

"Your highness is well-informed as always," Cortes continued to smile, "so you must realize that my King has sent me reinforcements—as I had expected."

"Well then, Malinche, if these are indeed your reinforcements, you can stop building those ships at Villa Rica.* You now have plenty of ships to take you and your soldiers to your homeland. Am I not right?" Montezuma said, his face no longer expressionless, its stoniness replaced by a sly smile.

"You are right, highness, and that is why I am delighted to extend you the greatest honor that my King can bestow."

The three captains looked at one another in scarcely concealed and puzzled surprise as Doña Marina finished translating.

"I do not understand what you are saying—what is this

---

*Villa Rica de la Vera Cruz, Cortes' first settlement, near the modern port of Vera Cruz.

honor?" Montezuma's smile had faded as his gaze became a question.

"It is a thing as simple as it is great. You must come with us so that you will meet our ruler, our gracious King," Cortes said, rising to his feet while making a half-bow.

Doña Marina's words struck home like a bolt from a crossbow. "I? Come with *you*? I?"

"As I said—truly our greatest honor, both to extend and to be honored with your highness' presence—as my king's guest."

Montezuma's face was that of a man just sentenced to be executed. The hand that covered his lower face trembled before he lowered it.

That will teach the dog to play at trading intelligence with me. Now I'll leave him quickly so he can wrestle with the thought of being exhibited like a captive animal in a Spanish general's Roman triumph.

Cortes bowed again, and without waiting for the imperial gesture of dismissal, strode from the room, trailed by his staff.

Once inside the council chamber in his own compound Cortes was no longer the smiling courtier, but the Captain-General addressing his conquistadors.

"Already you've let the word slip to the troops. Diaz, be kind enough to stop at once those salute firings of the cannon. We'll have need of that powder before long," Cortes said.

Across the room the burly Alvarado's laugh died away. He had been describing the look on Montezuma's face to the other captains who had not been at the audience. The room became silent as Cortes looked around him.

"I am astonished at my senior officers. Haven't any of you bothered to reflect on the meaning of this so-called reinforcement? I thought not. Now listen to a little reasoning. In the first place, if those ships came directly from Spain, why did they not put in at Villa Rica, our headquarters on the coast, instead of San Juan de Ulua? And why was it not Narvaez's first action to send a messenger galloping to me here in Tenochtitlan—or to Sandoval at Villa Rica? No, my friends, those ships come from Cuba, not from Spain, and they carry anything but reinforcements."

The captains looked uneasily around the chamber; this was a Cortes few of them had ever seen. His jaw was set, his angry mouth a thin line.

"Now you can see what has happened if only you will

open your eyes. Something or someone has alarmed Velasquez in Cuba. Maybe Puertocarrero or Montejo did land there in spite of my orders. Perhaps they were trapped and our gold seized. In any case, the bull is loose in the farmyard, and those eighteen ships are truly debarking nine hundred of the *governor's* men. God in heaven, here we've conquered an empire that could boast warriors in the tens of thousands—all this we did with less than half a thousand of our soldiers! And now we must face an expedition—brother Spaniards outnumbering us by three times—who come to dash all our hopes and all our conquests in the dust. How many are with me in this fight to come?"

Cortes unhooked his baldric, drew out his sheathed sword, and slammed it down on the table in front of him. Alvarado was the first to rise to his feet. He looked around the room, then faced the table.

"We have been with you all this way, Hernan, but what of this next fight, as you say?"

"What of it, indeed! Are you captains so dense that you cannot see the choice? Perhaps there are among you some who would join Panfilo de Narvaez on the coast. Surely that's the easy way to guard your gold. The hard way to keep it might be to stand behind me. But then how many of you still know how to soldier the hard way?"

That has got to do it, Cortes thought, *these conquistadors are all gamblers at heart, or they wouldn't be here.*

The reaction of the captains came as quickly as Cortes' thoughts, and they reacted as one man. Swords flashed out of scabbards and were laid in a line of steel, their hilts facing Cortes' sword on the long table.

"You see your answer, Hernan," Alvarado bellowed, "what say you now?"

Cortes picked up his sword, drew the blade from its scabbard, and laid it down with its hilt alongside the others.

"Then, señores, we are for it. Pick up your blades and give me time to collect my thoughts. There is much that must be done—and now. Be ready to assemble on the terrace where I will join you in good time."

Cortes was left alone to agonize over his challenges and his scanty means of countering them—

Here, three score leagues from the coast, surrounded by potential armies of a hundred thousand Aztec warriors, what ways are open to me?

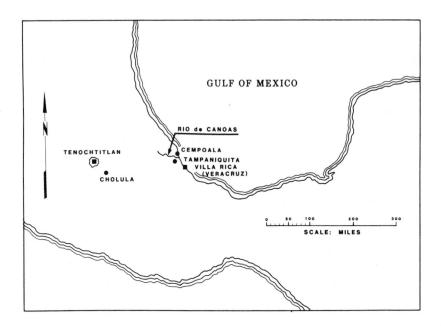

I see three. First, I can stay here, mobilize my Indian allies, and negotiate with Narvaez. I reject that, for it surrenders the initiative to Narvaez.

Second, I can take all of my force and some Indian allies, and march against Narvaez. But if I do that I abandon all that I have conquered and leave a hostile Montezuma in my rear as well, an emperor then free to assemble his warriors against me.

Or lastly, I can leave a garrison here that will keep Montezuma subdued. That would be a terrible risk—splitting my force—and that will be complicated by finding a way to attack Narvaez's army with all its horses, cannon, and muskets, outnumbering us with fearful odds.

Yet this third way is the one I must take. Risky and dangerous as it is, there will be two compensations. Velasquez de Leon and his 150 men can fall back and join my march at Cholula. I must take the chance on his remaining loyal, even though he is the Governor's kinsman. My other compensation may be the two thousand reliable warriors in Chinantla province. They are hostile to Montezuma, and may heed my summons—if they can be assembled in time!

Yes, this is the course I will follow, and I will need God's help to succeed.

His mind made up, Cortes called for his page to pass the order for assembling his captains.

From the terrace where they had assembled—it was actually a broad, flat roof surmounting the great temple-pyramid—Cortes and his officers could view the magnificent expanse of Tenochtitlan laid out before them on that sunny spring morning. The city with its teeming thousands, its myriad rooftops, wide avenues, and lines of canals extending to the great lake of Tezcuco, all seemed to sparkle in the sunlight that lit up flowered terraces and green gardens. It was all serene in its widespread beauty, encircled by its green environs and the deep blue of its surrounding lake. Yet each officer could never forget that the peaceful, charming scene was underlaid with the savage terror of the Aztec priesthood with its human sacrifices and bloody ceremonial feasts. There still remained the racks displaying thousands of human skulls outside the teocallis, the temple-pyramids, to remind the most careless cavalier.

Cortes, looking around before he spoke, sensed with his ever-present insight the feelings that dominated the group. He took advantage of the moment to make a sweeping gesture across the view.

"To think that a year ago we were struggling to survive beyond the beaches of San Juan de Ulua, facing a hostile land extending we knew not where. Yet look what we have done, four hundred of us conquering a vast empire that no white man dreamed existed."

He paused, knowing they would remember the body-racking marches, the fierce battles—victories and defeats—against incredible odds, the conquest of the Tlascalans and the alliance with them, the ascent of the towering mountain ranges, and finally the taking of Montezuma and the domination of his empire, which had accepted them as demigods. Neither was there need to remind them that there was a growing and seething restlessness throughout the capital, an unrest that could put these foreign god-warriors to the extreme test.

"Now all this," Cortes went on, "is going to be yours to rule, my friend, Pedro de Alvarado."

He ignored Alvarado's startled stare.

"I march, as soon as preparations permit, with 70 men. I'll give you the list of them by the end of day. I leave you all the artillery, all but 5 horses, and all but 8 arquebusiers. That gives you two-thirds of our force, 140 men. I will charge you with detailed, written orders to carry out your mission here, Pedro, as soon as time permits. For now, know that my command will march lightly-armed and with only the minimum of baggage."

Cortes' upraised hand silenced the murmurs of surprise and protest running through the group.

"The time for discussion has passed, *caballeros*. You will receive your assignments in my second set of orders. Return to your commands, and let your men know only that I await confirmation of the movements and destructions of the governor's force at San Juan de Ulua. Pedro, you and Cristobal de Olid will remain with me as well as my pages, Burguillos and Orteguilla. Cristobal, be kind enough to send also for Father Olmedo. All others are dismissed."

As Cortes led the four men back to his council chamber his mind was occupied with the writing of orders and letters. He had already decided that the letters must take first priority. There were things to be done with words and gold that his captains did not always understand. He looked at Alvarado and Olid as he took his seat at the table.

"I will detain you only enough to let you know about the letters I am going to write. First, those to Velasquez de Leon and Rangal to direct them to withdraw their detachments to Cholula and await my coming there. Also, to alert Sandoval at Villa Rica to march to meet me."

Cortes paused to allow Fray Bartolemé de Olmedo to take a seat on his left. As he watched the stout friar in his habit of the Order of Mercy take his place, the Captain-General's pale face took on the look of the fox, the look that never failed to set Alvarado and Olid on their guard.

"Now, Father," Cortes said, "we will draft a most conciliatory letter to friend Panfilo de Narvaez assuring him of our readiness to share the fruits of conquest. Oh, we will make him most welcome as our comrade-in-arms and make him know that our strength lies in the union of our forces. All this based, of course, on his producing the royal commission which will show us the requirement to submit to his authority—"

"But, my son," Olmedo broke in, "if Narvaez comes as an expedition from the Governor of Cuba he cannot be bearing a royal commission like that."

"Ah, Father, that must be the other key to Narvaez's understanding our situations—and that will throw him off balance," Cortes said, turning his courtier's smile on Olmedo.

"But the *other* key?" the friar asked.

"Certain articles of gold that you will carry, along with my letter. We will discuss later their distribution to Narvaez—and certain of his followers. This governor's cavalier will have to learn that campaigns are not always won with simple arms like swords and cannon."

On a mid-May morning the troops of Cortes and Alvarado were ranked, facing each other across the wide courtyard of Cortes' compound. In the open area between them Cortes was making his farewell to Montezuma. The emperor, seated in his gold-encrusted litter, embraced Cortes while Doña Marina interpreted their adieus.

When Cortes had mounted his horse, El Molinero, he reined up alongside Alvarado who was obviously ill at ease.

"Montezuma wants to accompany you to the great causeway. I don't think it wise to let him go that far—at least not fully attended," Alvarado said.

"You are seeing things as a master should, my old friend. Use your judgement as to the escort and the distance. We both know how far he can be trusted without our guards," Cortes tapped the hilt of his sword, "about the length of this blade."

Alvarado grinned and nodded his assent, while waving to his trumpeter to sound. The drums rolled, Cortes' troops wheeled into column, and the march began through the opening gates of the courtyard.

Outside Tampaniquita, the Indian town designated for the rendezvous, the barren volanic rock of the countryside begins to contrast with the fertile plain of the *tierra caliente* with its tall cottonwoods mingling with the lower stands of green bamboo and banana. Cortes had selected an open, rock-strewn field outside the town for the inspection of his army, if such an assemblage could be called an army. The Captain-General, while not a man subject to lingering doubts, did have mixed feelings about his force as he dismounted from El Molinero to make the review on foot. He had reason to feel relieved about the growing numbers of his force since he had left Tenochtitlan. At Cholula he had been joined by Velasquez de Leon with his detachment, and only yesterday Sandoval had arrived from Villa Rica with his sixty effectives. Today, after discounting the sick and others sent back to Alvarado, Cortes was ready to take stock of his 266 veterans. So while his total strength had increased about four-fold there was reason for despondency at what Cortes saw when he and his captains strolled down the ranks. They were looking at an infantry force, for only Cortes and 4 of his captains were mounted, hardly a cavalry to match against Narvaez's 80 horsemen! To make matters worse the comparison of fire-power with Narvaez's potential was almost laughable: Cortes' 15 arquebusiers against Narvaez's 80; Cortes' 14 crossbow-men against Narvaez's 150.

The armor of the infantrymen also might have raised laughter among Narvaez's men. With the exception of a handful of battered brigandines, the universal armor for pikemen, arquebusiers, and swordsmen was the tattered native *escapuil*, the cotton quilted armor which could stop an Indian arrow but not a Spanish bullet. Months of campaigning in tropical heat had caused the infantrymen to barter off their steel armor and adopt the *escaupil*. Their heavy leather boots had also disappeared, worn out long ago and replaced by local hemp sandals. Yet they all hung on to their helmets, clearly as precious to the men as the heavy gold chains which the common soldier wore around his neck, his only way of securing his portable wealth.

When the men had been dismissed to march back to camp, Cortes faced a downcast half-circle of officers. It was evident to all that the inspection had done little to raise their hopes of defeating Narvaez in a pitched battle. Yet their confidence in Cortes had not diminished; he had pulled them through too many impossible situations for doubt to take hold now. As usual he was able to sense their feelings.

"A motley array of companies, yes. But did you look in the eyes of those men and note their bearing? These are veterans with confidence in us and themselves, veterans of the wars under the great Cordoba and here in Mexico. They have been unbeatable because they *know* they are unbeatable," Cortes said.

Gonzalo de Sandoval was quick to expand on that note.

"You could see too that their weapons are all in order, swords sharpened and bucklers shining," he said.

"Yes, but what good are the swords and bucklers against Narvaez's horsemen?" asked Diego de Ordas, who often played the part of the skeptic.

"It is fitting that you have asked, Captain Ordas, for that brings me to the next step in training these men to contend with Narvaez's cavalry—and infantry if need be. Father Olmedo is coming just now with Tobillos, the master pikeman, and you'll see for yourselves that we are going to become an army ready to take on Burgundians or Swiss, let alone Narvaez's men," Cortes said, pointing out the approaching friar and his companion, a helmeted infantryman who carried a twenty-foot spear over his shoulder.

Cortes had Tobillos demonstrate the employment of the weapon as a pike, after pointing out the deadly double head fashioned by Chinantec smiths out of native copper.

"Tobillos has brought three hundred of these from Chinantla," Cortes explained. "I had ordered them made in a letter written before we left Tenochtitlan. Now Master Pikeman Tobillos here, a veteran of the Italian wars and an expert at arms, will train a cadre who will, in turn, see that every foot soldier becomes proficient in the use of this pike, especially against cavalry. Are there other questions about dealing with Narvaez's cavalry?" Cortes said looking at Ordas.

Cortes let the silence sink in before leading the officers back toward the camp. Sandoval, anxious to channel conversation into other subjects, spoke up as the group started back across the rocky fields.

"I have heard talk while in Villa Rica of Father Olmedo's mission to Narvaez's headquarters, but all I have learned was that the father here was dispatched with a letter and some trinkets," Sandoval said.

"Far more than mere trinkets, Captain Sandoval. But Father Olmedo, why don't you tell him yourself about your mission and what you learned in Narvaez's camp," Cortes said.

The stout friar, living up to his notoriety for eloquence, was delighted to regale the captains—some for the third time—with the tale of his success as an emissary and intelligence agent. He told how Narvaez had moved his army to Cempoalla, which he now occupied. There Father Olmedo had delivered Cortes' letter to an enraged Narvaez whose first reaction was to clap the friar in irons, next to expel him from Cempoalla. He was easily dissuaded when he was presented with the gift of golden "trinkets." Olmedo had, however, held back similar presents which he later gave in secret to some of the more apparent malcontents in Narvaez's service.

Olmedo went on to describe Narvaez himself as a cap-tain-general overawed by his own importance and, at the same time, one who was careless in his operations because of his overconfidence in the size of his force and the comparative weakness of Cortes' command. Narvaez, it seemed, was surrounded by captains who acted more like courtiers than officers. One, Salvatierra, a blusterer, had even declared his intention of slicing off Cortes' ears and having them broiled for his breakfast! Then too Olmedo had noted that many of the troops in Cempoalla held no love for their commander. Their loyalty was questionable at best, especially since these men had no stomach for fighting fellow soldiers. They had shown much interest in the stories about Cortes and his ex-ploits, and their eyes had reflected gleams of gold when they saw some of the gold Olmedo had quietly distributed. Ol-medo concluded with his final dismissal by Narvaez who gave him a letter, in reply to Cortes, ordering Cortes to submit to his authority and threatening him and his command with dire and deserved punishment. Thus, though Olmedo had been expelled, the poison of his intrigues was left behind to work on the least loyal of Narvaez's officers and soldiers.

When Olmedo had finished, the group had already en-tered the camp, and Cortes gave his orders for the next day.

"We march at the first hour, our destination a ford on the Rio de Canoas, a stream most of you have crossed before. We will make camp on this side of the river at this point about a league south of Cempoalla. From there I make a final re-connaissance, and after that I will give my final orders," Cortes said in dismissing the group.

The last stage of the march to the Rio de Canoas was the most wearing, not only because the men were tired, but also because the spells of torrential rain were at their worst as the afternoon lengthened. Late in the day the sun broke through, the clouds drifted off, and the heat plagued the marching men as much as had the rainstorms. When they reached the stream they found it had become a real river swollen from the rains. At the selected sites Cortes ordered the companies to fall out and rest before making camp for the night. After leaving orders that the camp should be made in quiet and without fires, Cortes, accompanied by Olid and Sandoval, rode off to reconnoiter the best place to ford the river. While they rode Cortes broke the news of his decision to carry out the operation that night.

"Nombre de Dios!" Sandoval could not restrain himself. "This may be madness, but it is the kind of madness that will catch Narvaez with his armor off. I like it."

"I know the men feel the effects of our last march, but they'll warm to their work once they understand fully what is happening," Cortes said.

"And how do you propose to let them know that?" Olid asked.

"As soon as we get back we'll dispense with the captains' assembly. I'll talk to one and all at this time," Cortes said.

Prescott said it well in his *Conquest of Mexico:* "Before disclosing his design, he [Cortes] addressed his men in one of those stirring, soldierly harangues, to which he had recourse in emergencies of great moment, as if to sound the depths of their hearts, and, where any faltered, to reanimate them, with his own heroic spirit. . . ." Bernal Diaz del Castillo, one of Cortes' captains, one not always animated with unrestrained admiration of his captain-general, says in *The Discovery and Conquest of Mexico* that Cortes ". . . began a speech in such charming style, with sentences so neatly turned, that I assuredly am unable to write the like, so delightful was it and so full of promise, in which he at once reminded us of all that had happened to us since we set out from the Island of Cuba . . ."

Delightful or not, honeyed words or not, Cortes did recapitulate the battles and campaigns, reminded them of the dangers and incredible odds they had overcome to attain victories, and, not the least, the wealth they had all gained. But now, they were about to lose it all to an adventurer who came in force *but with no commission from the Crown of Spain,* only a dispatch from a greedy governor who would *punish them* for their hard-won conquests. Their claims, based on their service to his majesty, were to be dishonored and they had already been branded as traitors by Diego Velasquez and Narvaez. "But now the time had come for vengeance and God would not desert his soldiers of the True Cross. And, if they should fail [in their coming attack on Narvaez], better to die like brave men on the field of battle, than, with fame and fortune cast away, to perish ignominiously like slaves on the gibbet. This last point he urged home upon his hearers; well knowing there was not one among them so dull as not be touched by it. . . ."

It is said they all "responded with hearty acclamations,"

Spanish light cannon

and when the shouting died two captains, Velasquez de Leon and De Lugo, spoke for all the rest, saying,

"We are ready to follow where you lead!"

Cortes looked around at them in the falling light of the day, knowing that it would no longer be necessary to raise their spirits; he needed only to guide them in the right direction.

"Gather closer now and hear my orders to your captains. The first objective I assign to Gonzalo de Sandoval who, as *alguacil mayor*, will seize Panfilo de Narvaez as prisoner. If he resists he will be killed. Captain Sandoval, you will have your chosen sixty men to accomplish this mission.

"Captain de Olid, as *maestro de campo*, you with sixty men must first capture and secure Narvaez's artillery. Then you will assist Sandoval by keeping any enemy from going to the aid of Narvaez.

"Captains Velasquez de Leon and De Ordas, with sixty

men each, will arrest the other officers of Narvaez that I shall designate, and prepare to assist my other captains on order.

"Lastly, I will keep under my own command the remaining twenty men to act as general reserve for our attack.

"A final word to all—I propose these awards from my war chest: To the soldier who first lays hands on Narvaez I will award three thousand gold pesos, to the second soldier, two thousand pesos, and to the third, one thousand.

"Our battle cry and watchword—because this is the eve of Whitsunday—will be *Espiritu Santo*. Captains, you may assemble your companies."

Cortes had marched with Sandoval at the head of the lead company in the column. It had started raining again as they had entered the ford and it had been rough going as officers and men had slipped time and again on the smooth stones of the river bed. Their twenty-foot pikes had turned out to be their mainstay as they used the long shafts to brace themselves and find their footing. Cortes had stood by on the far bank until the last dripping files had emerged from the river before he went up the halted column to rejoin Sandoval and give the order to continue the march. Already the night had become a vicious combination of torrential rain and buffeting wind.

"Hernan, this weather is no friend of ours," Sandoval said as they stumbled along in the howling darkness.

"You are wrong, Gonzalo. On the contrary, this storm has been sent by the Savior himself, for it will keep the enemy under cover in his stone quarters—no better aid for us in surprising him," Cortes said, his last words ending almost in a shout.

Sandoval's answering shrug was lost on Cortes in the dark, but his next movement was to reach out and place his gauntleted hand on the Captain-General's shoulder, bringing them both to a halt. As the files following them thumped into their backs Cortes realized that Sandoval had just encountered three of his scouts who were dragging a prisoner toward them. The two officers thrust their faces close to that of the soldier who led the scouts.

"Captain Sandoval, there were two of Narvaez's sentinels. We have here Gonzalo Carrasco, but his companion has escaped. Surely he has run to warn Narvaez," the scout reported.

"Did the other one see you or any other scouts?" Cortes asked.

"We think not. This prisoner says his companion ran when he heard us grabbing him."

"That much may be good. But here now, Carrasco, if you want to live, tell us of the locations of Narvaez and his artillery," Cortes said, shoving his face into the prisoner's.

The quick interrogation that followed ended in stubborn silence after the prisoner had confirmed that Narvaez occupied the great teocalli outside of which his artillery had been posted to cover the main avenues leading into the plaza. Carrasco would not—or could not—reveal more, and Cortes could waste no more time on him.

"Have him bound to a tree there, Gonzalo. We'll need these scouts out in front again. What the prisoner has told us confirms the intelligence of Olmedo and Duero who learned far more than this soldier seems to know. Come, we must be moving on. Every minute counts," Cortes said to Sandoval and the lead files.

Miraculously the rain slackened as the wind began to die down. For brief seconds the moon peered through a break in the clouds and was gone again. In that short spell of moonlight Cortes could make out the distant outline of the stone pyramids that marked the center of Cempoalla.

"Look, Hernan, see that light on one of the teocalli's towers?" Sandoval said.

"I see, I see. It's on the tallest one, and that has to be Narvaez's. That's our guiding beacon, Gonzalo," Cortes replied, and stepped up the pace.

In minutes the head of the column was passing the outlying Indian huts and in no time Cortes and the others began to feel the stone flagging of streets underfoot.

"For God's sake, Gonzalo, have your men split their column to both sides of the street. Have them stick close to the walls. If Narvaez's artillery should open up on us we don't want men slaughtered like cattle in a pen. Keep up the pace, I'm going to bring up my reserve to follow Olid's party as they go after the artillery," Cortes said, giving Sandoval a parting clap on the shoulder.

When Cortes had stepped aside to let Sandoval's men pass he had time to look around and orient himself. The rain had died away completely and the moon shone through the rapidly breaking cloud masses. Cortes stared in astonishment at the sight beyond the files of rushing men. Rising from the sodden fields, up between the huts and stone walls, all across his field of vision, Cortes watched the display of brilliant flashes winking on and off as hundreds of sparks seemed to rise from the earth. He was about to cross himself when he remembered his first night march, months before, when he had led another column through the *tierra caliente* in this same area. These winking lights were carried by the *cocuyos,* the huge firefly-beetles whose bodies emitted such an intense light that— so their Totonac guides had said—it was strong enough to enable one to make out picture writings by it.

God willing, Cortes thought, *this is an omen, a good sign sent by the True Cross.*

He stopped a passing pikeman long enough to find that Olid was only a few paces behind him.

"Follow me, Cristobal," he ordered Olid, "we're on the right street and now you can see your way to the plaza."

Olid had already followed Sandoval's example and deployed his men along the sides of the street as they began to dash forward. Cortes' order to Sandoval paid off within the next minute. The entire street was lit by the sudden flashes of cannon fire from the plaza. The crash of the artillery volley blasted their ears and downed three soldiers while sending other of Olid's men staggering against the walls. The air overhead was ripped with the passing balls and stones of langridge* some of which were ricocheting off the stone walls.

"In the name of God, get on, get on!" Cortes was shouting at the men who had stopped in their tracks. "Get on the gunners before they can reload—and we've got them and the guns!"

Olid had the coolness to direct a file of pikemen to take on a half-dozen horsemen who had loomed out of the night to the left of the artillery battery. He sent the next file to the right and in a flash the sword-and-buckler men were darting among a troop of cavalrymen who were still trying to mount their horses. The swordsmen were using their swords and daggers to slash the saddle girths before they turned their weapons on the cavalrymen.

In the same flash of time the rest of Olid's men were overrunning the gunners, doing deadly work, first with the

*Langridge—a kind of case-shot made up of irregular chunks of metal or, in some cases, stones; used for close-range fires against infantry or cavalry.

pike and then the sword. In the time it would have taken Olid to report it to Cortes the main battery was silenced, and Cortes had to order a halt to the slaughter.

"Stop them, Cristobal," Cortes shouted, "we'll have need of these guns and crews soon enough. We'll make these gunners part of us—as you can see they are crying out to do."

As Cortes started to leave and locate his captain of the reserve, Sandoval's messenger came dashing up to report.

"Captain-General, we fought Narvaez and his guards and have driven them up the great stairs of their teocalli. But they fight well and we are losing men to their arquebuses and crossbows."

"I will be taking my men to your captain's aid, but you go on—in that direction—and give Captain De Ordas my order to come to your captain's support as soon as he can," Cortes ordered.

Cortes found Olid reorganizing his company, having detached his swordsmen and their officers to supervise the gunners in preparing the guns for towing to a new position.

"A magnificent piece of work, Cristobal! Now send all the men you can spare to reinforce Sandoval. I'll see that the guns get in position to fire on all three of the main buildings," Cortes said.

He paused long enough to collect his thoughts, trying to picture the whole of the situation from his observations and the fragments of reports that were coming in.

We've got all the artillery but that is still only half the battle. I've got to have Narvaez, alive or dead, before we can get his officers—then his men—to lay down their arms. After all, if I can overcome Narvaez's army I want to take it as intact as possible. Dead and wounded men are of no use to my cause. Now, in case Olid does not find Sandoval at once, I'll send a messenger to tell him the guns are on the way. Then I can go on ahead while my men assist Olid's with the cannon.

He waited only long enough to send his page, Orteguilla, speeding off with the message to Sandoval. Then Cortes was off toward the great teocalli, after giving directions to his captain of the reserve for bringing up the artillery.

He found Sandoval and Olid at the foot of the great stairs amid a swirl of pikemen and swordsmen who were being reformed into their units while the wounded were being carried away.

"Hernan," Sandoval reported, "we've battled them up and

down these stairs, losing men to their bullets and crossbow bolts, but now we have driven them into the sanctuary at the top. So far, Narvaez and his men have been able to hold that narrow entrance against us."

"The artillery can batter our way in, but that's going to use up too much time because the guns are being pulled by hand. There's no other way in, other than that door?" Cortes asked.

"None, We've already checked that out," Sandoval said.

"And the roof—no way through that?"

"Wait—oh, mother of God, why haven't I seen it? Look, the roof," Sandoval was pointing at the top of the pyramid.

Cortes saw in a flash what was meant. He looked around him.

"Pass up the nearest arquebusier," he called out. In a moment a soldier was at his side.

"Let me see your match. Good, you've kept it burning," Cortes said, "now where is a man with a good right arm, a man who is a great thrower?".

A tall soldier pushed his way through the press of men; Olid recognized him.

"Martin Lopez, the shipbuilder, just your man. But what will you have of him?" Olid asked.

It was the work of seconds for Cortes to have the arquebusier set fire to an improvised torch. Lopez sprang up the stairs, stopped halfway, and threw the blazing torch onto a corner of the thatched roof of the sanctuary. As the blaze mounted, lighting up the sides and stairs of the teocalli, Cortes gave the order to Sandoval and Olid.

"They'll be popping out of there soon enough now. They're not going to stay in there and be roasted alive. As soon as they start to come out—up you go! Rush them, and remember the awards for the soldiers who capture Narvaez!" These last words were shouted at the waiting men, and grins broke out on faces gleaming with sweat in the light of the blazing thatch.

As if they had been prompted by Cortes' order the first of Narvaez's men came staggering out of the door onto the stairs. Sandoval and Olid led the dash up at them, pikemen and swordsmen at their heels. Cortes saw a figure in their midst, helmeted and clad in bright armor. As he watched he could see a tall, husky soldier drop his pike and grapple with the cavalier.

"It's Pedro Farfan, and he's got Narvaez. Look, it is him, Narvaez. He was wounded in the eye when we first rushed the stairs," Sandoval's aide was telling Cortes.

Two other soldiers had pinned Narvaez, dragging him to the ground and down the stairs where he was clapped into irons. Cortes was off again, leaving his two captains to take the surrender of the rest of Narvaez's headquarters men. The guns were being dragged up, and their new positions must be selected so that their fire would be directed on the other two teocallis which the remainder of Narvaez's force was defending against Cortes' units, now in the act of surrounding of the buildings.

Cortes stood in the interval between two batteries—his men had now brought up all eighteen guns—waiting for his messengers to return. He had dispatched them to deliver the summons of surrender to Narvaez's leaders, who were holding out in the two buildings. Both messengers returned with reports of arrogant refusals to surrender. Cortes turned to his captain acting as master of the ordnance.

"Very well, fire one volley over the roofs of the teocallis, and let us see what happens."

When the smoke from the volley drifted aside Cortes got his answer in the form of white cloths waving from pike staffs atop both pyramids.

"It would seem that the cannon are better at delivering proclamations than my messengers. Take your men, Velasquez de Leon, and seize the officers, then have their men come to the plaza with their arms," Cortes commanded.

In the full light of the morning Cortes, a richly embroidered orange robe draped over his shoulders and upper armor, was seated in the center of the plaza surrounded by the trappings of state—an awning under which his staff had placed his throne-like chair.

From his chair he had watched Narvaez's soldiers file by to stack their arms in the plaza, and he had made sure that four of his captains supervised a careful accounting so that the weapons could be returned to their owners after they had taken the oath to serve under Cortes' banner. After the mass swearing-in of Narvaez's men he had dismissed Narvaez himself, sending him off in chains to be taken to Villa Rica. The humiliation of the defeated commander had been carried out in true Spanish cavalier style. Narvaez, standing fettered in front of his conqueror, his ruined eye covered with a bloody bandage, had sought to depart gracefully with a knightly acknowledgement of Cortes' victory.

"Señor Cortes, you may hold high the good fortune you have had, and the great achievement of securing my person," Narvaez said.

Cortes smiled his courtier's smile as he looked down at his captive.

"Señor Narvaez, many deeds have I performed since coming to Mexico, but the least of them all has been to capture you."

After Narvaez had been led away, Cortes started to turn his attention to the matter of securing the ships of Narvaez's armada. He was distracted by loud laughter coming from a group of officers and soldiers in a corner of the plaza. They were grouped around Sandoval, who had always been a popular figure with the men. The tall, black-bearded captain had them guffawing at some tale he was spinning. Cortes motioned a page to his side.

"Ask Captain Sandoval to share his joke with us," he said.

Sandoval was brushing tears of laughter from his eyes as he approached Cortes.

"It's not one joke but two, Hernan," Sandoval said.

"So much the better. Let's hear them then."

"You saw them take away Salvatierra, the captain who was going to have your ears broiled for his breakfast. Well, it seems that he was standing under the roof of his teocalli when you had the artillery fire over that roof. His soldiers say that Salvatierra became suddenly ill, so violently ill in fact that he fell on the floor and cried that he could no longer stand to fight, his stomach was tied in such a knot."

"And that is the big joke?" Cortes asked.

"Not just that, Hernan. His soldiers said that they could not come to his aid. It seems that his stomach trouble had extended to his bowels, loosening them in a most explosive way so that no man would approach him."

"That can truly be said to be a sound reason for his solitude. But what of your other tale, how does it relate to Salvatierra?"

"It doesn't. It concerns the sentries Narvaez's captains had stationed in the towers, the ones who gave the alarm that tumbled Narvaez's men from their beds when we were first entering the streets in our attack. Do you recall then the cloud of *cocuyos* that rose from the fields and streets around us, just after the rain stopped?"

"Yes, for a moment I knew not what to think of it. Then, seeing what was happening, I remember counting it as heaven-sent."

"That *you* may have done, my general, but not Narvaez's sentries and the soldiers they aroused. One sentry, seeing the moving flashes of light, took them to be hundreds of arque-busier's matches, the matches of an advancing army. That one called out his fears and the word spread as though carried on the wind—to be taken up by the already confused troops who had just been shaken from their beds into the dark. But as you say, Hernan, it must have been our good fortune— yes, sent from heaven," Sandoval said.

"Not exactly, Gonzalo. One day when you are in high command, you will find that all good fortune does not come from heaven."

If Cempoalla were to be compared with other battles that led to the overthrow of empires—Arbela or Waterloo, for ex-ample—it would indeed seem a piddling affair: a night action lasting less than an hour and involving fewer than 1,200 men. Yet Cempoalla assured that Cortes' past and future con-quests, subduing the mightiest empire in the New World, would open two continents to European colonization. When threat-ened by Narvaez's "counterinvasion" Cortes had stood to lose everything. Was it desperation then that made him bold? The question appears to be answerable in the affirmative, but less so when one looks into the character of Cortes. What sort of man was he really?

At first glance an obvious facet shows the daring con-quistador, the brave warrior. Certainly he was that or he would not have been able to lead that rough crew of his for longer than a week under the best of conditions; the record shows him leading them under the worst. A second look reveals a scheming, plotting Machiavellian type to whom the end sought was worth any means to gain it. Let us remember that Ma-chiavelli and Cortes *were* contemporaries, though worlds apart in certain senses.

A third observation of the man shows him to be the con-summate politician, an actor of a higher order, and a per-suader who could have run a night school for LBJ. A fourth and final aspect discloses the meticulous planner, the kind who never overlooks a critical detail.

Plainly Hernan Cortes was not made up of any *one* of these outward faces of character. He was a combination of them, showing only the face he wanted on the occasion he thought demanded it. He had all the courtly graces, employing them where needed. At other times he was the bluff, good-humored soldier, but never the hearty, backslapping kind, for he always maintained a cool reserve. Truly a complicated man, but a product of his times.

This attempt to look inside Cortes, brief as it has been, is enough to demonstrate that this was not a man forced to take the bold actions he did out of desperation. There are too many signs of an iron will guided by a subtle intellect throughout his operations. There was nothing of the impetuous in the planning and conduct of his campaign, from the time he first gained intelligence of Narvaez's expedition (later confirmed in several ways through his own reliable sources) until he led the night attack on Cempoalla.

There is enough evidence to permit one to view Cortes' actions from yet another viewpoint—from that of a reversed image, looking at them from the mirror provided by Narvaez himself. From beginning to end Narvaez never set himself a clear objective, one that he should have had to succeed in his mission. Hence he was never able to make a clear evaluation of his problems and come up with a workable plan. Conversely, Cortes saw from the outset what had to be done and how to muster the means to do it.

His critical shortcoming left Narvaez to be governed by events which he could not control. On the other hand, Cortes had set clearly-defined goals toward which he advanced with step-by-step actions. Lastly, Narvaez never got a clear conception of his opponent's character and, most important, his capabilities. Cortes employed every means available to assess the character of Narvaez and determine what his opponent could do with the means at his command—and to find the weakness of his enemy's seemingly powerful force.

Thus Cortes was able to direct that will of his in a way that allowed him to adopt bold measures, calculated measures that prepared him and his men to deal with the dynamic forces he knew would threaten his plans, and to capture intact a force three and a half times the size of his own.

Remembering the dynamics described in the introduction, one should have little trouble detecting their presence in the Cempoalla campaign. The danger to Cortes' command threatens at the very outset with the news of Narvaez's landing in Mexico. The other dynamics appear in the marches from Tenochtitlan to the coast, the approach march to Cempoalla, and in the night attack.

It may be argued that Cortes got two good breaks: in the weather and in the matter of the *cocuyos*. Yet Cortes had to be advancing to the attack or he would not have been able to turn either factor to his advantage. Finally, if the miracle of giant fireflies strains the credibility, there is some comfort in Byron's aphorism in *Don Juan*—

> " 'Tis strange but true; for truth is always strange;
> Stranger than fiction; if it could be told."

Tenacity

At last the Persians, finding that all their efforts to gain the pass [of Thermopylae] availed nothing, and that, whether they attacked by divisions or in any other way, it was to no purpose, withdrew to their own quarters. During these assaults, it is said that Xerxes, who was watching the battle, thrice leaped from the throne on which he sat, in terror for his army.

Next day the combat was renewed, but with no better success on the part of the barbarians. The Greeks were so few that the barbarians hoped to find them disabled, by reason of their wounds, from offering any further resistance; and so once more attacked them. But the Greeks were drawn up in detachments according to their cities, and bore the brunt in turns. . . . So when the Persians found no difference between that day and the preceding, they again retired to their quarters.
—Herodotus, VII, 211–212.

The Persians had ample reason to "retire to their quarters." For three days running Leonidas and his Greeks held their ground against truly overwhelming odds (twenty-eight-to-one: two hundred thousand Persians against seven thousand Greeks) until the tragic end. Behind the story of one of the most heroic defensive actions in history stands the cold fact that Leonidas accomplished his mission of buying time for the Greek states. This in spite of the leader sacrificing himself and his three hundred Spartans in an epic rear-guard action. What made Leonidas do it?

115

He was a Spartan king and the well qualified leader of an allied force; however, do those facts supply the answer? Only in part. Was the famed Spartan discipline sufficient cause? Again, only in part because their discipline, while it enabled the Spartans to fight more effectively than their enemies, was not the underlying cause. The real reason was that Leonidas made the decision to hold out, to accomplish his mission as he saw it. He was able to make the decision and to see it carried out because of his sense of duty. A strong will guided by cool reasoning directed the course he would follow to fulfill his responsibility to the state. Leonidas' decision and its outcome speak for themselves in the famous epitaph on the tomb of the Spartan leader and his soldiers: "Go, stranger, and tell the Lacedaemonians that we lie here in obedience to their laws."

Before looking further into the idea of duty it will be remembered that, earlier in this chapter, we observed that *effective* boldness was an extension of the intellect; additionally that boldness when employed without reason becomes rashness. There is a parallel case here in linking the sense of duty to tenacity. A rational sense of duty provides a sound base for tenacious action; however, tenacity without basis in reason becomes mere obstinacy in its worst sense—commonly referred to as being bullheaded or "stubborn as a mule," hardly what we look for in a leader.

What is meant by a sense of duty as a mainstay of tenacity? It would be as easy as it would be unrewarding if one were to duck behind the idea of duty as something required by a regulation or as a quality learned in some academic setting. If our inquiry goes, as it should, beyond such patent cop-outs we will find eventually that duty is essentially a constitutent of morality. Marcus Aurelius, no mean leader by anyone's lights, said in *The Meditations:* "It is thy duty to order thy life well in every single act; and if every act does its duty, as far as is possible, be content. . . ." The Emperor went on to point out that man's only good will is a dutiful will—the sort of thinking that puts him on our side.

Coming down to a less lofty plane the whole thing can be reduced, for our purposes, to a straightforward progression:

Reason governs a sound sense of duty.
Duty provides a sound base for tenacious action.
Tenacity becomes a function of the will.

Tenacity implies hanging on, sticking with it, but here a word of caution: time is not the only measure of tenacity, or else sieges would be our prime gauge for tenacious action. The intensity of combat can become a major—if not on occasion the chief—determinant of what tenacity can accomplish. It is with this thought in mind that we should watch this next action, one of the epic stands of all time.

Rorke's Drift

This is the story of not one leader but two, both lieutenants in Queen Victoria's army in South Africa in January 1879. Their story begins not with them, rather at the top of their chain of command.

Lt.-Gen. Sir Frederic Augustus Thesiger, Second Baron Chelmsford, KCB, Commander-in-Chief British Forces in South Africa, was not a soldier given to yielding to—or even expressing—his emotions. Yet this morning his stricken face showed every sign of the shock and horror that had overcome him. At first he had put up a front of cheerful incredulity; this had grown into grave disbelief as more reports had reached him, and now he was forced to believe his own eyes as he rode out in the rising mists of the African dawn.

He and his staff had ridden up to the foot of Isandhlwana Mountain at the head of the returning half of his center column, but it had been in pitch-black darkness and they had had to wait for daylight to ride over the rocky fields around the site of the massacre. Now he was seeing the ruin of his base camp for what it really was, no longer a battlefield but the scene of massacre. His horse, moving at a slow walk, picked his way cautiously to avoid the hundreds of bodies lying singly or in lines and heaps across the plain. Many of the slain soldiers had been stripped of their red jackets, but clothed or not most of the corpses were lying face up; many were horribly mutilated and all had been disemboweled by stabbing assegais, the heavy, broad-bladed thrusting spear of the Zulu warrior. Lord Chelmsford had heard his share of the stories about the slitting open of bellies of slain Zulu enemies, done, it was said, in accordance with Zulu belief, to prevent the bodies from becoming the abode of evil spirits.

Here, at a stroke—in less than three hours—the Commander-in-Chief had lost half of the center column that he

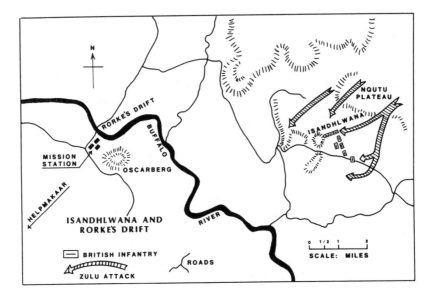

ISANDHLWANA AND
RORKE'S DRIFT

had led to invade Zululand only eleven days before. He was
to learn, when all accounts were in and casualties counted,
that out of the 1,774-man force he had left in the base camp
at Isandhlwana 1,329 lay dead on the field—the Zulus took
no prisoners. The dead British soldiers and the bodies of the
native contingent soldiers were not alone on the rocky plain
around Isandhlwana Mountain and Stoney Hill. Two thousand Zulu bodies were counted, these left by an army of 20,000
warriors. But that was of small consolation to Lord Chelmsford. No count of Zulu casualties could make up for the disaster that now confronted him.

He had ordered out half of his center column—the other
two columns were several days march away to his north and
south—to support the reconnaissance in force that he had
sent out the day before. He had ridden with the center column's force to observe what he had hoped to be the first major encounter with Zulus in strength. Major Dartnell, the
reconnaissance force commander, had called for support saying that the enemy was appearing in far greater numbers than
he had anticipated. But Lord Chelmsford's supporting strike
had fallen on empty air ten miles from Isandhlwana. The
clouds of Zulu scouts and their supports had melted away
before British attempts to engage them. Their retreat was to
Chelmsford "nothing less than cowardly." Too late the Com-

mander-in-Chief was to realize that his supporting force was chasing a decoy. There had been no Zulu impi* in front of him, instead a Zulu army of twenty thousand had been hiding five miles north of Isandhlwana screened by the Nqutu Plateau. And too late he had received the reports of the disastrous battle at his base camp, after the Zulu army had made its bloody counterstrike.

Back in his tent at Isandhlwana, Chelmsford was recalling lines from the letter he had written two weeks before to his commander in London, the Duke of Cambridge: "It is impossible to speculate what tactics the Zulus will pursue. . . . Our movements will all be made in the most deliberate manner. . . . Your Royal Highness, however, may rest assured that I shall do my best to bring it [the war in Zululand] to a speedy close, so that I may be enabled to send back to England some of the regiments now under my command."[6]

Never were words to come home to roost so woefully on a writer's shoulders! Yet they were not one of Chelmsford's immediate cares, for the Zulu victory had not only wiped out half his central column, it had also destroyed or captured all his supplies, including his command's reserve of ammunition. In a predominantly infantry force the only ammunition remaining was the seventy rounds each rifleman carried in his pouches.

No longer was the Commander-in-Chief forced to cope with the problem of deciding whether to advance, fight, or maneuver. Clearly his only recourse was to withdraw the remainder of his force back into Natal over the route by which it had advanced. That meant marching out, as soon as possible, over the ten miles of rough road back to Rorke's Drift where he could re-cross the Buffalo River. But even that inevitable course of action was overcast with a foreboding shadow. Scouting parties on the road back to Natal had sighted clouds of black smoke rising from behind the Oscarberg, the hill behind which lay the post of Rorke's Drift. Was that base lost too, gone up in flames from Zulu torches?

The afternoon of the same day that Lord Chelmsford's force had left Isandhlwana to support Major Dartnell's reconnaissance in force, a Lieutenant of Royal Engineers was supervising the securing of ferry cables at the drift, the ford named after the trader Jim Rorke. He was Lt. John Rouse

---

*Equivalent of a large regiment, an organized Zulu tactical unit.

Merriott Chard, R.E., and he was still concerned with the impression he had gotten that morning while visiting the base camp at Isandhlwana. He had ridden back to Rorke's Drift with the disturbing but unconfirmed news that a large Zulu force might have bypassed Lord Chelmsford's base camp on its north side and was still unaccounted for in the vast expanse of rugged country north and west of Isandhlwana.

Although Chard was temporarily in command of the post at Rorke's Drift, his official duties were limited to the completion of the ferry crossing, a task that he felt he could well have, by this time, left to Sergeant Milne and his work party of six natives. Chard's real interest—the one he wanted to get back to—was the laying out of earthworks at the former Swedish mission, now the military supply depot and hospital. He had already sketched out the work, now he was anxious to complete his plans in the hope that a company of Royal Engineers would arrive one day to do the work, though right now that remained only a hope. But there *was* the company of British infantry—Lieutenant Bromhead's B Company, 2nd Battalion, 24th Foot—now garrisoning the station, and Chard had work plans in mind for the company that would surely have failed to delight any of the infantrymen—from Bromhead to the latest-joined private.

Chard was a fine military figure standing there on the river bank. He was of medium height, his tanned face half-hidden by his dark beard and mustache under his white tropical helmet. He wore his scarlet uniform jacket, crossed by a leather shoulder belt, and instead of his sword he carried his sketch-case attached to his sword belt. He was thirty-two with eleven years of service before his recent arrival in Africa, and he had the good sense to listen to advice from Bromhead who had completed a tour of field service in South Africa. He had to smile under his mustache at the thought of his being "temporarily in command" and, as such, being Bromhead's commanding officer. Only an hour ago Major Spalding had left Rorkes's Drift after finishing his lunch and leaving Chard in command of the post. Spalding was officially the officer in command of two posts, Rorke's Drift and the depot at Helpmakaar ten miles to the southwest. The major had been annoyed enough to ride off to Helpmakaar for the purpose of personally seeing to it that a company of infantry from that garrison was moved up to reinforce Rorke's Drift. He had already sent orders for a company at Help-

Zulus rallying to renew an attack

makaar to move up, and now it was long overdue. Spalding's departure had been prompted by reports of large bodies of Zulus that had been sighted moving on Isandhlwana, the Spalding's two depots existed only to provide stations on the line of communications* for Lord Chelmsford's base camp and center column.

Chard had not been overwhelmed at the idea of his command responsibility since he expected Spalding to return in a few hours. Nor was he concerned over the odd command relationship between him and Bromhead. The infantry lieutenant, although two years older than Chard and with a year and a half more service, was actually the junior. The reason was the Queen's Regulations which allowed graduates of the Royal Military Academy like Chard to be commissioned directly as lieutenants** in the Royal Engineers or Royal Artillery. Bromhead, as an infantry officer, had to serve four years as a second lieutenant before his promotion to lieutenant. Fortunately for Chard and Bromhead, this state of affairs remained only a matter of the regulations. Their personal relationship was a cordial one with no professional jealousies or friction.

*For practical purposes this term denotes a major resupply route for a force in the field.
**The equivalent of first lieutenants in the U.S. Army.

Chard was making up his mind to ride back to the post when his thoughts were interrupted by the sound of galloping horses approaching the opposite bank of the river. He saw two horsemen ride down the slope to the ford and start swimming their horses across the hundred yard stretch of chest-deep, yellow-brown water. The one in the lead, evidently an officer, was shouting something but Chard could not make out the words. As they got closer Chard recognized the two as Lieutenants Adendorff and Vane of the Natal Native Contingent. Both their horses were streaming with sweat and river water. The officers wore the khaki slouch hats of the N.N.C., but the rest of their uniforms were in anything but parade order. Adendorff's jacket and shirt front flapped in the wind while Vane was in rolled shirtsleeves. Their faces were caked with dust that had been creased by rivulets of sweat. Adendorff had to catch his breath before he could pant out his news.

"The camp has been butchered to the last man. It's gone. Everything is lost—"

"Hold on now," Chard broke in, "I was up there earlier this morning and the only Zulus sighted were scouts—and they were two or three thousand yards away."

"Yes, but when did you start back from Isandhlwana?" Vane asked.

"I would say about midmorning. I was back here by noon," Chard said.

"There you are then. The whole affair started in late morning and it was all over by one o'clock," Adendorff said.

"We're wasting valuable time. Why don't you give him the rest of the news?" Vane said.

"You're right. What he means is that there's an impi—estimated to be four thousand strong—moving toward Rorke's Drift, and on your side of the river," Adendorff blurted out.

"My God, man, and we stand here talking. How far away are they?" Chard said.

"Might be only a matter of minutes. We can't be sure because we lost sight of them in getting away from them."

Chard didn't wait for Adendorff to finish. He was shouting for Sergeant Milne and his six men to report on the double. He had hardly got an acknowledging salute from his sergeant when he saw another galloper coming toward him, this one coming down the road from the post. Chard recognized him to be one of Bromhead's lance-corporals astride Bromhead's horse.

"Sir, Lieutenant Bromhead reports sightings of large numbers of Zulus coming from the east and northeast. He says to tell you that he has struck tents and is preparing to march or fight—whichever you will decide."

"Very well," Chard said, turning back to Adendorff and Vane, "both of you ride on to the post. Follow this lance-corporal. And Lieutenant Adendorff, inform Lieutenant Bromhead that I'll be close behind you. Then you can go on to Helpmakaar to alert the garrison there. I'll stay here only long enough to see that Sergeant Milne's men have secured the punts,* then I'll be there as fast as I can," Chard ordered.

After Chard had left at two o'clock to oversee the ferry construction, Bromhead was one of the two line officers left at the post. The other was Capt. George Stephenson, who commanded a hundred-man Natal Native Contingent which supplemented Bromhead's garrison. Since Stephenson was a colonial officer his captaincy did not outrank Chard's regular commission, so there was no question that Chard was in command.

A few minutes after the departure of Spalding and Chard, Lieutenant Bromhead was walking through the street of white conical tents that sheltered the eighty-five men of his company. He was not making an inspection though the thought had occurred to him to use that as a pretext for avoiding Stephenson. He held the colonial officer in the same low esteem as B Company's soldiers held Stephenson's natives—a scruffy, untrained lot as undisciplined as they were unreliable. But to Bromhead and Chard the native contingent could furnish an additional hundred badly-needed rifles for a defense.

As he strode down the company street he presented no less a military figure than Chard: good height, handsome features adorned with full muttonchop whiskers and a mustache that hid a small mouth. He also wore his scarlet jacket topped by his white tropical helmet. The only part of his dress that was not faultless were his leather riding boots, covered with the dust that layered the rocky ground of the area.

Twice since noon his sergeants had reported hearing cannon fire to the east, and each time Bromhead had had to accept the reports without question. This was not laxness on

---

*Flat-bottomed, iron ferry boats built to carry about eighty men. There were two in operation at the ferry.

his part; his deafness was common knowledge though no one of his company dared show that knowledge to his face. The reports had concerned him enough to consent to Surgeon-Major Reynolds' request to take the two clerics and ride to the crest of the Oscarberg, the hill called Itchiane by the natives, just to the east of the post. Bromhead's thoughts were on the three men on the Oscarberg as he turned back up the street, his boots scuffing up little whorls of dust in the hot African sun.

Four men were dismounting from their horses in front of the hospital verandah. Bromhead started to step up his pace, then saw that he need not have hurried. The four men, led by his colour-sergeant, were running to meet him. The sergeant brought them to a halt and saluted.

"Sir, these men come from the Isandhlwana Camp with a message and—"

The hatless corporal behind the sergeant interrupted before he could be stopped.

"Lieutenant, the base camp has been taken and all our men in it massacred. No power can stand against those thousands of Zulus," he gasped out.

Bromhead held up his hand to slow down the rush of the corporal's words. For a matter of seconds his gesture was useless. All four of the frightened men wanted to talk at once. Bromhead and his sergeant finally brought order out of the garbled reports. The corporal had calmed down enough to fumble in his shirt pocket and produce a pencilled message. He handed it to Bromhead who read snatches of it half-aloud.

"Captain Essex, 75th Foot, transport officer with center column . . . escaped on my horse . . . got to the drift four miles downstream from Rorke's Drift . . . hillsides black with trotting Zulus . . . some pursue fugitives across the drift, others heading north following the river . . . at least an impi made up of thousands . . ."

Bromhead stuffed the message in his jacket pocket. There was no sense in questioning these men further, he'd get only babble to add to the confusion. But he knew enough now to act without hesitating.

"Sergeant, let these men ride on to Helpmakaar. I don't want them alarming the native contingent and men in hospital. Then assemble the company—here, at once," Bromhead ordered.

Must get my kit from my tent, he thought, *I'll need my note-*

pads and case. After I've assigned company parties to tasks, there's that damned N.N.C. company of Stephenson's to put to work somewhere . . . Good lord, what is Reynolds doing back here—in the devil's own hurry like everyone else all of a sudden.

The tall surgeon-major had dismounted and was leading his horse as he called out to Bromhead.

"I saw the four of them riding up. Thought I'd ride down and report," he said.

"Report what?" Bromhead stopped in his tracks.

"Good visibility toward Isandhlwana Mountain. Good enough to see clouds of natives coming around the mountain this way. Occasionally saw groups—large groups—poking into dongas* and Kraals for stragglers. What's the matter, Bromhead, why look at me like that? I'm only reporting what I saw."

"What you saw, Surgeon-Major, were natives all right— the tall kind that come from the north around Ulundi. And I don't have time to discuss their origin and intentions."

"Good heavens, man! You mean Zulus, do you?"

"Quite. Now please stay with me while I assign tasks to my NCO's. I'll be sending a party to help with what needs to be done at the hospital."

Bromhead hid a grin under his thick mustache. The Surgeon-Major's face was a red study in amazement.

Chard met Bromhead and James Dalton on the verandah of the storehouse. Dalton, a retired sergeant-major living in Natal when the war broke out, was now serving as a volunteer at the drift in the capacity of Commissariat Officer. Both Chard and Bromhead valued his African service experience and good common sense. Dalton's dust-brown civilian jacket was in odd contrast to the scarlet of the two officers, but Dalton had never lost his sergeant-major's bearing, and it showed now as he stood listening to Chard, who was summing up his courses of action.

"And there's still time to get the wounded on the wagons, form column, and get across the drift and on the road to Helpmakaar," he concluded, looking at Dalton.

"Sir, since you're asking my opinion, I think that's the worst thing we could do. As far as we know the Zulus are

---

*Gullies or dry watercourses.

scouring the whole countryside, and I've known their warriors to trot as much as fifty miles in a day. We'd be tied down to the pace of the wagon teams, then caught in the open to be surrounded and slaughtered like that big force at Isandhlwana. What chance then of our hundred-odd men—we know we can discount the natives here standing and fighting in the open—against thousands of Zulus under those conditions?" Dalton said.

Chard and Bromhead looked at each other. The infantry officer pointed to the orderly knots of red jackets grouped along the road from the drift. His company, already assembled in work parties, was waiting.

"Dalton is right," Bromhead said, "and we know that we do stand a chance here—if we'll just use all the materials we've got. There are hundreds of mealie bags*, then the wooden hundred-weight biscuit boxes, as well as the boxes of tinned meat—all will serve to make barricades. We also have another asset that will buy time for us."

"What asset?" Chard asked.

"Mr. Dalton, as you know, was qualified in laying out field fortifications. He has already been marking out lines for barricades, and he can supervise the laying out of whatever other walls you may direct."

"That settles it," Chard said, "we'll waste no more time talking. We will make our stand here. Assign what NCO's you think necessary to work under Mr. Dalton. After your companies' work parties are started, see what you can do to fortify the hospital. I'll be in the area sketching out the perimeter walls. Mr. Dalton, you'd better start first by building a wall running from the northwest corner of the storehouse here to the nearest corner of the hospital. You can use those two wagons there to form a section of the wall."

In seconds Chard found himself at the center of an anthill of activity. Parties of soldiers, their jackets discarded, sweated under the blazing African sun, dragging and lugging mealie bags and crates from the storehouse out to lines where sergeants and corporals were having them stacked into four-foot high walls. Dust rose from the rocky ground, settling on sweat-streaming faces, amid a din made by the scraping of dragged boxes, grunts, and the rolling mutter of curses that the British soldier always managed under stress. In spite of

*Sturdy bags of native corn weighing over one hundred pounds.

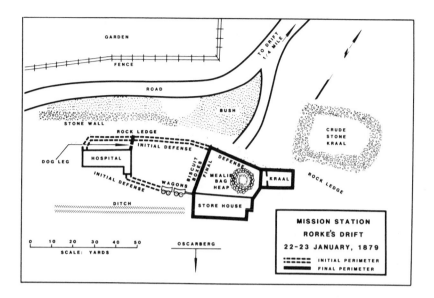

the heat and the noise there was order in the seemingly cha-
otic coming and going of the work parties.

For the moment Chard was the only stationary figure in
the bustling scene. He had taken post in the middle of the
forming compound, standing with his notebook in his right
hand, his left resting on the hilt of his sword.

Strange, he thought. *Don't remember at all picking up my sword
and the rest of my kit. Now that I've given my sketches to Dalton and
my list of priorities to Bromhead there is the problem of fields of fire
from these walls we're making. God save us, there couldn't be a worse
spot in all Africa less suited for building a fort than this place. Two
small buildings forty yards apart commanded by a hill rising five
hundred feet above them.*

He looked up at the crest of the Oscarberg, then at its
terraces sloping down to the rear of the storehouse and hospital.

*Any Zulus with guns taking cover up there can pot shot our
men defending the north wall that we're building from the front of
the hospital to the kraal adjoining the storehouse. But if what I've
heard is true only a few older warriors have guns—muzzle-loading
"Birmingham gas pipes" and maybe a few Sniders*—and they are
known to be very bad marksmen. What this fight will amount to surely*

---

*The former, old trade muskets as dangerous to the firer as to the enemy; the latter, the single-
shot, converted breech-loader that had been the standard British infantry rifle until replaced
by the Martini-Henry Model 1871.

will be the Zulus' light-throwing assegais and heavy-stabbing assegais against the Martini-Henry rifle and its bayonet. But Rorke's Drift being a supply point we will have plenty of ammunition, which reminds me to get some men opening those sealed crates of ammunition. Yet worst of all is the matter of the men in the hospital. I've been forced to include that building in the perimeter because there's no place to evacuate the sick—and everyone of those who can stand will have to handle a rifle. As soon as time—and the enemy—will permit I must get the men out of there and abandon that building and the whole perimeter between there and the storehouse. And there's the matter of the brush and the stone wall and the fruit trees, all on the north side. They will all give good close-in cover to the Zulus, but where will I get the men and the time to level all that cover? I see that Bromhead has had the good sense to strike his company tents. At least they won't be furnishing cover to screen an enemy advance and the tangle of guy ropes and tents will make a fine obstacle to a Zulu attack.

The whirl of thoughts that were making up Chard's dilemma came to a spinning halt when he heard shouting that sounded like cheers coming from Bromhead's men working on the north wall. Chard ran over to the half-completed barricade of mealie bags to see a sight that brought relief from his gloomy dilemma. It was Lieutenant Vause riding up the road at the head of his troop of Sikali Horse, a column of a hundred native horsemen equipped with Martini-Henry carbines. Chard leaned over the parapet.

"Are you coming in to join us?" he called down to Vause.

"Right you are, but let me ask two conditions," Vause shouted back as he reined in his horse and halted his troop.

"What are they? I've no time for discussions now."

"First, issue us rations—my men haven't eaten since last night. Then I ask you to use us on a cavalry mission; you don't want a hundred horses milling around in there."

"Send a party to Mr. Dalton and he'll see they get rations. Yes, I do need you to get your men deployed to screen the post—on the Oscarberg there, at the drift, and with vedettes posted between."

"Is that all?"

"No, of course not. You'll have to delay the main Zulu advance, and then fall back here to join the defense. You'll have to get going as soon as you've drawn your rations."

Chard didn't wait to return Vause's wave of a salute. He was on his way to give his news to Dalton and Bromhead, his elation bubbling up in him. Vause's troop would bring the total of defenders to over 350 men, which would allow—he calculated quickly—one modern rifle to about every six feet of the walls. This should give them the firepower they needed for a fighting chance to repel the Zulu assaults.

Many of the same thoughts had occurred to Bromhead as he made his rounds checking on dozens of tasks that had to be seen to. He saw that the loopholing had been completed in the storehouse, that ammunition had been issued all around, and that the necessary doors and windows in the hospital had been barricaded. The layout of the one-story hospital was a nightmarish crazyquilt of tiny rooms, and a centrally controlled defense was out of the question. Bromhead picked six of his men and assigned them, two to each of the three rooms with seriously ill patients, and sent runners to bring back haversacks full of cartridges. He also saw to it that the hospital defenders were issued pickaxes to loophole the walls.

As he came across the hospital verandah he caught sight of Dalton supervising the finishing of the mealie-bag wall in front of the building.

"Lieutenant, if you could spare the men I could start clearing some of those things to give us a better field of fire along here," Dalton said, pointing at Reverend Witt's old stone wall and the bush between the perimeter wall and the road.

"There's nothing I'd rather do, but I'll have to stand with Lieutenant Chard on the matter of not being able to spare a man until we've finished all work on the walls," Bromhead said.

The afternoon sun continued to beat down through the dust-filled air throwing a pale amber sheen over the toiling men. Bromhead could have prayed for a sudden shower to lay the dust and wash the stink of sweat from the air. He was too sensible a man to dwell on such wishful thinking, so he crossed the open area between the two buildings to encounter Chard and learn that his reply to Dalton had been a sound one.

"I know that your men need to rest and that there are a dozen other jobs to be finished, but I'm going to need a special work party, the strongest men you can find," Chard said.

Bromhead took off his helmet and mopped his forehead with a dirty grey handkerchief.

"What and where?"

"Here and now. We've got to have an inner defensive wall to run straight north—right across here—from that northwest corner of the storehouse, extending to the north wall. I've measured it—seventy feet," Chard said.

"More mealie bags?"

They grinned at each other, feeling that singular kinship born out of sharing danger.

"No, we'll be different this time. Use those hundred-weight biscuit boxes stacked in this end of the storehouse. Actually they're easier to handle than mealie bags," Chard said.

Bromhead started off to find his colour-sergeant, then turned back toward Chard as though he had overlooked something.

"I daresay we've hit on something of great import here," Bromhead said.

"And what is that?"

"You know, this is not the finest fort that was ever built by the British Army, but it does have one great distinction."

"Again—what?" Chard asked.

"I'm willing to wager that it will be the only edible one ever on record."

It was after four o'clock when the last biscuit box had been heaved in place, and Bromhead could start the posting of his riflemen around the walls. This task was complicated by the necessity to spread the rifles of Stephenson's native contingent in a way that would ensure control over their firing—or to make sure the native soldiery fired at all.

Bromhead solved this by first assigning each of his NCO's a section of wall, then giving each a share of B Company men and a share of natives armed with Martinis. When a post had been assigned to each man Bromhead, accompanied by Chard, repeated the round of the perimeter, checking each man's sector and field of fire. They also checked to see that each had a full water bottle, full ammunition pouches, and that an additional stack of cartridges was placed beside each man for his first firing. When that was done Bromhead made one final posting. He selected Pvt. Frederick Hitch from a handful of volunteers, and pointed to the roof of the hospital.

"All right, up with you to the ridge pole. I want a sharp lookout all around. Sing out when you sight Zulus in numbers," Bromhead ordered.

Hitch went scrambling up as fast as he could make it, feeling the stares of the grinning privates of B Company.

Bromhead gave his last formal command to his company.

"Fix bayonets!"

The steely ring of bayonets drawn from the scabbards was followed by the snapping of bayonet sockets on rifle muzzles. The garrison was ready.

Chard and Bromhead were still standing in the middle of the open area between the hospital and the storehouse when Hitch called out his first sighting.

"Mounted men coming down the Oscarberg and on the road."

The two officers dashed to the north wall and climbed up on the parapet for a better view. It was a wasted effort. The sight of the fleeing Sikali Horse could be observed from anywhere around the perimeter. Vause's horsemen were streaming down the flanks of the Oscarberg and flying down the road past the post in a disorderly rout. Following the last flurry of his fleeing troop was Lieutenant Vause, hatless, waving his saber, and shouting curses at the fast disappearing troopers. He reined in his horse opposite the wall long enough to shout.

"They've disobeyed my every order, but when they slow down I may be able to rally them."

"What about the enemy? What about a report?" Chard's rage carried clearly as he yelled at Vause.

"Maybe five thousand. Maybe more. They're approaching the Oscarberg from the east," Vause called back, and he was gone galloping after his men.

Chard jumped down and was joined by Bromhead. Chard was still trying to control his anger.

"In full sight of the garrison. What a show! And we've lost a hundred carbines just when we need them most," Chard almost snarled at Bromhead, but the other officer hadn't heard the rasp of Chard's voice. He was staring wide-eyed at the south wall and east end of the perimeter. It had started happening while the fleeing Sikali Horse were still galloping down the road.

The first of Stephenson's company to desert were his natives, armed only with assegais, who had huddled in the kraal near the storehouse. They were over the stone walls and gone before the men of B Company had noticed their flight. They were joined in seconds by the rest of the native contingent who simply vaulted over the north wall, dashed across the road, and ran through the garden and across the open fields. This part of the natives' desertion went on under the astonished eyes of B Company men stationed along the walls, but their astonishment had not checked their reaction. Someone shouted, "Come back here!" and before Chard and Bromhead could stop them infantrymen had opened up on the backs of the running blacks. Pent-up resentment exploded as men fired off a round before Bromhead's shouted "Cease fire!" could take effect. During the sudden affair—over as quickly as the natives had disappeared—it had not escaped Chard's notice that Captain Stephenson had joined in the flight of his company.

Chard and Bromhead faced each other, too stunned to really see one another. The shock of two mass defections in five minutes was too much for mere words. In the time it would take to relate it 60 percent of his garrison had vanished before Chard's eyes. There remained only 140 men of the 350 he had counted on, and over 30 of the 140 were incapacitated in one way or another. Bromhead's B Company, with 81 effectives, was now the garrison's only organized and reliable unit.

And with those 140 men, Chard thought, *we are supposed to defend nearly 300 yards of perimeter! Now the hospital has to be evacuated so that we can pull back and defend only the inner perimeter. Thank God we finished that last wall. But do we have time? Time, always time, nothing can buy it now with the enemy almost on us.*

There was no time. Before Chard could think more about the enemy, the alarm was sounded. Chaplain Smith and Reverend Witt had descended the Oscarberg at a run, and as they neared the south wall Smith could be heard yelling—

"Here they come, black as Hell and thick as grass!"

Private Hitch slid down the thatched roof of the hospital to hit the ground running to join his section at the wall. Bromhead took station near the middle of the south wall just in time to see the attack come on. A massive column of Zulus charged around the western end of the Oscarberg and broke into a dead run along the lower terraces, as if to parallel the south wall, then wheeled in a flash to charge the wall. The whole maneuver was being executed in silence and with precision.

Chard at his post behind the wall was seeing Zulu warriors for the first time. They were the tallest black men he had ever seen, seeming even taller under their nodding ostrich plumes, their glistening black heads bobbing up and down over the tops of their long cowhide shields with the gleaming assegai blades showing around the sides. There was no time to estimate, let alone count, the massed ranks coming toward Chard, but he knew they had to number in the hundreds. His impressions of the charge were blotted out by the first volley and the rapid fire taken up by the defenders. The trigger-guard levers of the Martinis were jerked up and down as the men ejected empty cartridge cases and reloaded the single-shot rifles.

Chard recalled the figures Bromhead had briefed him on regarding the rifle—a well-trained infantryman could get off twelve rounds a minute in aimed rapid fire and each heavy 480 grain bullet he was pumping out could knock a running man flat at 500 yards. Now he was seeing Bromhead's words coming to life. The flaming rapid fire of B Company's rifles was taking a fearsome toll of charging Zulus right before his eyes. It was more than even a Zulu regiment could stand. The mass swerved to its left leaving scores of warriors strewn so thickly in its wake that every move of the force could be traced by the bodies left behind. Some survivors jumped into the shelter of the ditch west of the storehouse, others took cover among the rocks and folds in the ground on the lower terraces of the Oscarberg. The roar of climactic rapid fire slackened down to an intermittent banging that was sufficient to pin down the Zulus who were still facing the wall.

Bromhead, watching the repulse of the first attack, saw the next stage taking shape. The bulk of the regiment making the initial attack was swerving around the west end of the hospital to link up with the main attack coming at the post from the north and northwest. Bromhead ran to a spot near the northeast corner of the hospital. The sight he watched from his new post would have alarmed the toughest veteran of colonial wars. To his front, extending from the rock ledge, over Witt's stone wall, through the bush and the garden beyond, surged black masses of the attacking impi. This was no silent attack, the hordes came on screaming, beating their assegais against their shields to keep up a rattling roar. The Zulu ranks poured forward until the earth seemed covered with a black flood that swept up the rock ledge and beat like breakers of surf against the barricade above. The leading wave hacked and stabbed at the soldiers manning the wall, then at the mealie bags of the barricade itself when they could not reach the defenders. There were knots of hand-to-hand combat when the soldiers were too rushed to reload. Zulus mounting the parapet were met with thrusts of the two-foot bayonets while other soldiers dropped back a pace or two to blast the Zulus off the barricade at point blank range. Such close combats came in spurts and the Zulus could not maintain the crest of their assault waves for long at the top of the barricade.

Bromhead saw this climax of the assault drop back, but this was by no means to mark the end of the attack. Hundreds of Zulus clung to the slopes of the rock ledge, springing upward from time to time to jump on the heaped bodies of their dead at the foot of the wall in desperate surges to mount the barricade and get at the defenders. When they could the soldiers didn't wait for the Zulus to climb the barricade and thus developed an on-the-spot tactic to thwart the constant rushes. A soldier would fire, reload and fire—leaning through the embrasures between bags—until the attackers were literally at bayonet point, then he would brace himself to lean forward and thrust his bayonet into face or neck of his enemy.

When the first series of surges began to subside, Bromhead saw a strange sequel to the leading assaults take form. Hundreds of warriors continued to swarm through the brush and the garden, and from these masses groups would suddenly detach themselves and charge furiously at the wall. Whether these separate charges were a Zulu tactical device or the effects of fanatical exhortations Bromhead had no way of knowing. Regardless of the cause, the uncoordinated assaults were to prove the salvation of the defenders during the later phases of the attack; this form of assault enabled the soldiers to concentrate their fire on a rushing group and repulse it after inflicting unendurable casualties. If the Zulu impi had continued to press its initial attacks en masse it might well have broken over the wall and overwhelmed the thinly spread garrison.

As it was, the battle for the north wall continued without let-up for over an hour, the Zulus constantly renewing fresh rushes of howling warriors. The Zulu mass attacks and rushes were not led by "suicide squads"—every man, every company, even the entire impi seemed to be inflamed with the same suicidal madness. The British soldiers had heard tales

of it; now they were seeing it for fact. Yet the screaming warriors still had the presence of mind to find their own counter-
tactic to oppose the defenders' point-blank firing and bayonet
thrusts. The Zulus scrambling up the barricades snatched and
clawed at the bayoneted rifles trying to wrest them away from
the soldiers, even trying to wrench the bayonet from the rifle.
The soldiers countered by stuffing a fresh cartridge in the
chamber and blasting the Zulu with the muzzle shoved against
his body. Often a soldier was rescued by his nearest comrade
who did away with the attacker with clubbed rifle or bayonet
thrust.

Bromhead, rifle in hand to assist in backing up the wall,
watched an amazing performance by Cpl. Friederich Schiess,
a Swiss who had enlisted in a native contingent and had chosen to stick with the garrison. The man was raging with a
blood lust that would have done credit to a Zulu—in spite of
a wound in the lower leg. He had sprung on top of a mealie
bag to get at a Zulu below. The warrior, crouching against
the bottom of the wall, rose and fired at Schiess, missing him
so closely that the muzzle blast blew off the corporal's hat.
Schiess bayoneted him, jumped back down and retrieved his
hat, and put it back on his head just in time to shoot another
Zulu who had scrambled up over his companion's body. Schiess
had no time to reload when a third warrior's head and shoulders appeared on the parapet and Schiess sprang at him and
killed him with his bayonet.

Chard had also picked up a rifle, dropped by young
Byrne, Dalton's commissary assistant, who had been shot
through the head. He stood back several paces from the south
wall, firing at Zulus who showed themselves on the parapet.
He kept his eye, however, on the fight as a whole, from time
to time resuming his back-up firing. When he ran out of cartridges—he had no belt pouch to carry spares—he was re-
supplied by wounded Corporal Scammell, a hospital patient
who crawled over to Chard and handed him his packets of
ammunition. Even Chaplain Smith had entered into the fight
as far as he thought his cloth allowed. The tall, red-bearded
cleric kept up a constant patrol around the barricades re-
plenishing the men's ammunition from the haversacks of cartridges slung from his big shoulders. When he ran out he
refilled the sacks from the ammunition boxes that Chard had
ordered opened and placed in front of the storehouse verandah.

When the mass attacks had slackened off into series of

uncoordinated assaults, Chard took time to confer with Bromhead.

"Two things must be done at once," Chard said; "you must take care of the first. I don't care how you do it, but you must clear the hospital, then the wall in front of it. That's got to be done so we can withdraw everyone into the inner perimeter."

"And the other thing?" Bromhead asked.

"Send me your colour-sergeant, so he can pick out a dozen of your best marksmen. I've got to stop that Zulu fire from the Oscarberg. They've already killed or wounded seven of those men along the south wall. The damned savages have got a clear field of fire to get at our men along that wall."

When Bromhead took stock of the situation at the front (north side) of the hospital he calculated the order of tasks to be done.

First, I've got to get a new barricade, a dogleg to run from the northeast corner of the hospital to join the barricade. When that's done I can start pulling away the eighteen men from the wall in front of the hospital. Next, I can repost those men in the perimeter, assigning six to posts behind the dogleg. Their fire must keep the Zulus who come over the abandoned wall away from the verandah and the front doors. Then we can get the men out of the hospital some way, even if we have to breach the walls.

The first two steps in Bromhead's plan were carried out without a hitch. With a corporal and four privates he hastily threw together the dogleg using mealie bags and boxes. He was able then to repost the men from the wall in front of the hospital. The latter step was by far the hardest since Bromhead had to lead two counterattacks, rifle in hand, to clear Zulus from the hospital front until rifle fire from the dogleg could take over.

But the evacuation of the hospital was a different story. It was not possible for the fire from the dogleg to keep the Zulus from assaulting the west and south sides of the hospital. Because Bromhead's duties kept him with his company, he was unable to learn until later—until the last survivor emerged through an east window of the hospital—of the heroic defense that had been made by the men assigned to defend and evacuate the patients. The battle inside the hospital became a nightmare of an epic defense in itself. That nightmarish defense posed a dilemma to the minds of both Bromhead and Chard. The former had to carry out his plans to accomplish the mission assigned him—as well as exercising the command of his company. The latter had to maintain overall control of all the post's defense. All of which meant that neither leader could become involved in the struggle within the hospital; in any case they could not have led anyone in that hand-to-hand, room-to-room battle through the rooms of the mud brick walled hospital.

Hundreds of Zulus stormed at doors and loopholes of the south and west sides of the building, snatching at rifle muzzles, battering in doors, while thrusting and throwing assegais at any opening. The six B Company soldiers assigned to the defense of the patients not only had to fight off scores of Zulus at every step but had to use their pickaxes to knock holes in the inner walls through which they had to pull the patients from room to room. The savagery of the Zulu attacks and the heroism of the defenders was acknowledged in the after-action awards: out of the eleven Victoria Crosses awarded to the defenders of Rorke's Drift, four went to soldiers who distinguished themselves in the defense and evacuation of the hospital. On the other side of the coin—the frightful side—was the fate of Joseph Williams, the Welshman who sacrificed himself in taking on the Zulus single-handed in order that his comrades could escape to the room behind him. The Zulus broke through and surrounded Joseph Williams, while his comrade, John Williams, "flat on the floor, peered through the opening and the horrified men in the room watched, [while] the Zulus spread-eagled Joseph Williams on his back, pulled away his belt and tore his tunic open. An assegai ripped down through his exposed belly, a dozen blades plunged into his body, and the maddened warriors quartered him and tore the corpse to bloody shreds."[7] Such was the ferocity typifying the room-to-room fight. Toward its end the Zulus had managed to set fire to the damp thatch of the hospital roof and pen the fourteen surviving defenders and patients in the center rear room. From there, after a series of struggles, the group managed to get through two more rooms and jump down into the perimeter from an east window.

As the savage fight raged within the hospital, Chard had started the general withdrawal to the final perimeter, the inner defensive area consisting of the storehouse and the walled enclosure attached to it. A step-at-a-time retreat was made by B Company and the other defenders, picking up each man along the north and south walls as they moved toward the biscuit box wall by the storehouse. Now the thirty-yard gauntlet between the hospital and the storehouse had to be crossed by the survivors who had escaped through the hospital east window. Not all the surviving eleven patients made it safely; one took a bullet wound in the leg as he was being carried, another was not so fortunate. Trooper Hunter of the Natal Mounted Police was too crippled to walk and as he was crawling across the yard a Zulu darted down and plunged an assegai into his back.

By now the hospital roof was fully ablaze. Darkness had already fallen and the blazing roof became a godsend to the garrison now lining the walls of the inner—and final—perimeter. The burning hospital lit up the entire area so that Zulu attackers swarming over the abandoned walls became easy targets for the defense. But the abandonment of the hospital and the original perimeter between it and the storehouse brought reinforcements to the Zulus. Scores came down from the Oscarberg—no longer having exposed targets—while the hundreds who had surrounded the hospital were released to join others in encircling the last defensive perimeter.

Chard was well aware of these developments, but far too occupied to give them his attention. He left the reorganization within the new enclosure to Bromhead while he looked after other urgent demands. His engineer's mind turned to them.

There are the wounded, he thought, *and I must see that Surgeon-Major Reynolds gets his aid station working on the verandah of the storehouse. Then there's the matter of getting men on the roof of the building to take the Zulus under fire when they're coming at the enclosure from north and south; also one or two up there can take care of the danger to the thatch of the roof. The devils have already started to throw assegais with burning straw onto the roof. With those things attended to I must get to my never-ending problem—that of constantly building up inner defenses. Even an innermost fort must have its citadel, its donjon-keep. And the means for ours is here in front of my eyes—those two remaining piles of mealie bags in front of the storehouse. I'll get a work party—that will be easy now with the perimeter so reduced—and make the bags into one great heap with the top hollowed out to form a breastwork. We can put the worst of the wounded up there and still have room for fifteen or twenty riflemen who will have an all-around field of fire at the Zulus assaulting the walls and the storehouse.*

As Chard set about his tasks the Zulus' pressure was renewed around the new perimeter. This began with a series of night attacks, the strongest of which was concentrated on the stone kraal at the east end of the perimeter. The savage rushes began again, this time coming out of the dark shadows to emerge in the light cast by the burning hospital. Charge after charge was beaten back at the side and top of the stone walls. Supporting Zulu forces took shelter in the circle of boulders that made up a low kraal outside the permanent one linked to the storehouse. From there the charges were organized and launched again and again. Finally the roof of the hospital caved in and the firelight began to die out. The soldiers gave up the kraal, withdrawing step by step and leaving the bloody straw of the kraal floor covered with Zulu bodies. At last the kraal was abandoned and its western wall had now become the eastern barricade of the final enclosure. The Zulus poured into the kraal, and as they launched new rushes from there, new assaults came against the front wall up the rock ledge from the south, then from the west around the ruined hospital and across the open yard and along the abandoned walls.

By 10 P.M. Chard and Bromhead had to face each other for the last time that night. They were, like the rest of the garrison, beaten into bone-tiredness. Their once-scarlet tunics were patchworks of grimy powder stains, dust, and darker stains of blood. They had discarded their helmets, and, as they sank down to rest on the ammunition boxes by the storehouse, Chard managed a grin at Bromhead's powder-blackened features above his tangle of dirty sidewhiskers. Bromhead stared back realizing what the other was thinking.

"You're not exactly a music-hall dandy yourself," Bromhead said.

"Never gave much thought to beauty lately. Do you realize that these men have been at this without rest for over six hours?" Chard said.

"There has been some slackening off by the Zulus in the last quarter hour. What do you say we try some sort of a stand-down?"

"We can try. Why not let every other man stand down— sort of sit down in place. God knows the men won't be able to sleep anyhow with this tension and din all around. Do give it a try."

"Very well," Bromhead said, "but there's the matter of inspecting the rifles. You've never seen such overheated barrels, hundreds of rounds fired through most, burnt hands from them and that's not the worst of it. Some of those barrels were hot enough to soften cartridge cases in the chambers, so that extractors have pulled the heads off cases—and that means the men had to dig out the empties with knives or whatever they could lay hands on. Hell of a state to be caught in during a Zulu charge."

"Quite right. So now while you're getting around the walls arranging the stand-down I'll get Dalton and a couple of your NCO's to work replacing the worst rifles with others we salvaged after the withdrawal. Get going like a good chap," Chard said.

After Chard had gotten the rifle inspection and exchange under way he had paused, halted in place by the moaning of the wounded outside the storehouse.

"Here," he said to the sergeant beside him, "pull six men off that mealie bag work and have them follow me—with loaded rifles and fixed bayonets."

When the party had followed him to the biscuit box wall Chard stopped and peered out into the semi-darkness lit now by sporadic showers of sparks thrown up by crumbling timbers in the hospital. He could see the bodies of Zulus all across the area, then he could make out the dim outline of the two-wheeled water cart halfway across the yard.

"All right, lads, over you go! Follow me and let's get that cart back here to the wall," Chard ordered.

The seven dashed across the fifteen yards of the open area, the men opening fire to right and left at Zulus along the walls. Two warriors who dared to rush them were bayoneted while four of the party got the cart moving. Pushing and tugging, they got it back to the outer side of the wall where they were covered by the fire of the garrison.

"There's no chance of getting the cart through the wall. Corporal, take that leather hose and lead it over the wall. Now, the rest of you, back over the wall!"

Chard turned on the valve on the cart end of the hose and scrambled back over the wall, almost deafened by the muzzle blast of Martinis two feet from his head. In a matter of seconds, water was running through the hose and the sergeant was having helmets filled and carried to the wounded.

Just after midnight the first relay of men who had stood down had just replaced the others when another series of all-around charges was launched out of the dark. The hand-to-hand combats across the barricades were renewed, neither side lacking in ferocity. Bromhead's head ached as though under a trip hammer, and he knew in his heart—though he would never say it aloud—that the exhausted men in his company had fought on beyond human endurance. Now they were existing in a dazed never-never land made up of ceaseless explosions, thrustings, stabbings, and blood—their own and the enemy's.

They can't go on. Yet they must. Even if relief were coming it couldn't come in the dark. And how does anyone know there is such a thing as a relief? You can't tell the men that and you can't let them think about it, let alone talk about it. Now I've got to see that the ammunition party gets around to this end. That, and the water bottles need to be collected and filled. . . .

He stumbled back to the storehouse, glad for once of his deafness. The firing party atop Chard's mealie-bag citadel had opened fire over his head as he passed beneath the mound.

It was almost 2:30 A.M. when the last of the Zulu attacks had subsided. The second relay of men was allowed to stand down and this time the stupefied men were allowed to fall asleep as they sank down. Their comrades, however, had to collapse across the barricades to strain reddened eyes into the darkness. They had lost all track of time, all count of the ceaseless charges against the walls. Even as they strained their eyes at the dark, they could still see in their minds the savage black faces that had lunged at them over the wall, before seeing them blasted out of sight.

By four o'clock the last of the Zulu sniping fire had died away, though the garrison knew that thousands of their enemies were hiding out there in the darkness waiting to gather strength for a new charge. The last sparks from the hospital's fires had gone out and the velvet black of the African darkness closed in on the men behind the walls. The reek of powder smoke was carried away on the night wind. Aching bodies relaxed and aching heads drooped, but the watch was maintained. Chard, who had taken the most strain of all, could not allow himself to relax. He marvelled at the working of his tired mind. How could it marshal all those thoughts that were staggering through it?

Thank God many of them have gotten some rest—if you can call that resting. What dangers still face us God alone knows. And our losses! It is well that only I count them now—fifteen dead and two dying, Dalton and seven others badly wounded, and of the eighty men who can fire a rifle half of them suffer burns and lesser wounds. I don't know if those eighty can beat off another mass attack like those this afternoon. Good God, eighty against how many? Even if we've given them five hundred casualties, there are still thousands of them squatting out there in the dark. And what about this post being relieved, where would such a column come from? I can't speak to those men about relief, and there'd be no sense in lying. They'd know better. We've got to go on fighting. Now I'll have to tell Bromhead how low our ammunition reserves are.

Dawn was slow in coming at first. The early morning breezes carried the stench of bloody bodies and burned thatch across the post. When it was light enough to see the crest of the Oscarberg, the grey light began to reveal the outlines of more distant hills. Chard and Bromhead realized with a start that the only sounds outside the walls were the quiet stirrings of the opening day. There were no other. At five o'clock the exhausted men on watch were straining to see the battlefield out in front of them. When the light came up suddenly, as it does once day breaks in Africa, the soldiers could see only the litter of battle—cowhide shields, assegais, and the heaps of dead. The only living things that moved were straggles of wounded warriors making their way around the distant east end of the Oscarberg. The Zulu regiments were gone.

Chard sent out cautious patrols after five o'clock to probe the dead and start collecting weapons. The rest of the men stood to at the walls covering the patrols in case Zulus sprang from the ground. But all the warriors who might have sprung to the attack had disappeared.

At seven a whole impi was sighted, this time loping slowly from behind the cover of the Oscarberg, headed down river. They were soon out of sight.

Chard sent a party out to clear the Zulu bodies from the cookhouse. It was time to heat up the water for tea.

An hour later Chard's lookouts sighted men moving from the hills across the river and down toward the drift. In minutes the men on the roof were shouting and waving a flag. There were mounted infantry—British troops—moving up the road toward the post. It was the advance party of Chelmsford's center column moving back into Natal.

Some have said that Rorke's Drift deserves a place of honor alongside Thermopylae and the Alamo. A later writer has asserted that the military significance of the herioc defense of Rorke's Drift was deliberately exaggerated by the British government in order to draw the public's attention away from its mismanagement of colonial affairs and army reform—as well as the disaster at Isandhlwana, the severest defeat ever inflicted on a modern army by untrained natives.

Our purpose in observing the things that happened at Rorke's Drift would not be served by taking sides on the question of whether the action was an epic or a political plum. The fact remains that 140 British soldiers successfully repulsed repeated attacks by an enemy who committed 4,000 highly motivated warriors to a twelve-hour battle. Since those are facts the question concerning us is: if the British soldier was so effective at Rorke's Drift, what enabled him to endure his twelve-hour ordeal and defeat his enemy?

Before evaluating moral factors, it might be wise to look first through the cold eye of the military-operations analyst at the comparison of the effectiveness of weapons systems in the kind of battle we have been examining. In so doing one should look at *both* Isandhlwana and Rorke's Drift. If one does not consider both, then the latter can be rejected out of hand as a simple victory of a modern rifle over spears. Such simplistic responses, however, usually lack substance on close scrutiny.

One of the most obvious measures of effectiveness is the number of casualties inflicted by the opposing weapons systems. This is a summary of such effects in the two engagements.

	Isandhlwana		Rorke's Drift	
	British	Zulu	British	Zulu
Total Casualties	1,320	2,000	25	470
Percent of Force	75%	10%	18%	8.5%
Caused by	Assegais and obsolete muskets/ rifles[1]	Martini-Henry Rifles[3]	Obsolete muskets/ rifles assegais[2]	Martini-Henry Rifles[3]

Notes: 1. Great majority caused by assegais.
       2. Majority caused by obsolete muskets/rifles.
       3. Includes casualties inflicted by the 24″ bayonet on the rifle, though the bayonet was a minor factor in causing casualties.

Note that there is a significant dissimilarity in the cause of the British casualties in the two engagements as indicated by Notes 1 and 2. That difference is a key factor in understanding what happened. The basic difference between the British (modern European) and Zulu (African natives) weapons and tactics lay in the ability of British firepower to hold at a distance the assegai-bearing warriors until the latter broke and withdrew; conversely, the Zulus to succeed had to bring a massive numerical superiority into close combat (hand-to-hand fighting) with their enemy so that their stabbing/thrusting assegais could attain their maximum effectiveness. A simpler way of saying it: it was a contest between two break points. If the British could keep on killing Zulus at a safe distance until the Zulus gave up, the British would win. On the other hand, if enough Zulus could crash through the hail of British bullets and use their assegais, they would win. That was the difference between the two battles.

Two things happened at Isandhlwana to bring on the British disaster. First, their rifle companies (the basic firepower units) were committed piecemeal and subsequently deployed in a manner to leave wide gaps between several companies, with the result that the Zulus could break through the gaps and exploit their success with their assegais. Second, when the British ammunition resupply faltered* causing a slackening in their firepower (an event quickly discerned by the Zulu leaders) the Zulu impis closed in and broke through the gaps and around the British flanks. The result we know.

At Rorke's Drift British infantry was protected by improvised barricades and blessed with an on-hand resupply of ammunition. Hence British firepower kept inflicting enough Zulu casualties to keep their *massive* force at a distance, though as we have seen, the rifle fire could never reach the intensity

---

*There was a plentiful supply of ammunition with the wagons in the camp behind the deployed British force. Two unfortunate factors made the resupply start to break down. The ammunition wagons were hundreds of yards from the fighting companies and there was no provision for moving a continuous resupply over those distances. Next, the ammunition wagons were under the direct control of battalion quartermasters (a set of bureaucratic supply officers with more rank than brains) who could not or would not see the tactical urgency for resupply. Finally, the heavy wooden ammunition boxes were sealed with copper bands, each held securely in place by nine large screws—and the only screwdrivers were in the hands of the quartermasters. All for want of a horseshoe nail!

needed to keep the defenders secure from hand-to-hand combat. In any case, rifle fire was the decisive *material* cause of the successful British stand.

Was firepower then sufficient cause for the British success? I think not. The soldiers of B Company, like the rest of their regiment and the other regular regiments in Africa, were disciplined and well trained. They were the rightful heirs of the tradition of the steadfastness of British infantry on the defensive: "As General Reille told Napoleon on the morning of Waterloo, 'British infantry in position are impregnable because of their quiet steadiness and their excellent fire discipline.' Napoleon had not believed him but Napoleon had been wrong."[8]

Given that the men of Rorke's Drift were sustained by their tradition and training, was that sustenance sufficient cause? Again I think not. From the beginning, it must be recognized that one company of infantry (the main source of defensive firepower at Rorke's Drift) could not have withstood 4,000 Zulus fighting in the open. The company would have been surrounded and overwhelmed on open ground in a matter of minutes *in spite of their firepower*. It was the protection of their improvised fort, and hence the assurance of an adequate resupply of ammunition, that made the difference. And those fortifications would never have been built had it not been for provident and active leadership by leaders who converted a highly vulnerable supply base into a defensible base for firepower.

Yet firepower, even with an adequate resupply of ammunition, was not self-sustaining. It took leadership of a high order not only to make the preparations for defense but to ensure that the defense held out until the enemy reached his break point—and the Zulu withdrawal was the uncontestable proof of that break point. Therefore, mere preparation was not enough. Leadership had to be maintained in order that the garrison put up a tenacious defense. In order to avoid misunderstanding or argument regarding the meaning of a tenacious defense I would rely on a respected semanticist, S. I. Hayakawa, when he says: "Tenacious has the implication of hanging on, refusing to let go no matter what the odds against eventual victory."[9]

Lastly, Chard and Bromhead could not have led a tenacious defense without a commonly shared and inbred sense of duty. It is fitting to point out here that Lieutenants Chard and Bromhead have been referred to in some accounts as "two young officers." This has been unfortunate because it leaves the reader to infer that perhaps the two "striplings" were leaders by the accident of their being there at the time and had probably been carried along by the discipline of the NCO's and soldiers. Nothing could be further from the truth. At the time of Rorke's Drift, Lieutenant Chard was thirty-two with eleven years of continuous service. Bromhead was thirty-three with over twelve years of service. Compare those ages and lengths of service with officers in today's American army and you would be talking about majors and lieutenant-colonels.

So, we have been looking at two mature leaders, winners of Britain's highest military award, the Victoria Cross. Leaders who had to contend with all the dynamic forces of battle and who overcame them through sheer force of will.

Part Three

INTELLECT

Scipio Africanus
at **Ilipa**, 206 B. C.

Henry Bouquet at
Bushy Run, 1763

George Custer at
Little Big Horn, 1876

INTELLECT

There are three classes of intellects: one which comprehends by itself; another which appreciates what others com-
prehend; and a third which neither comprehends by itself nor
by the showing of others; the first is the most excellent, the
second is good, the third is useless.

—Machiavelli, *The Prince* (XXII)

Since we are considering intellect in the light of its value as an attribute
of the leader we can dismiss the third class out of hand and reject the
second as not good enough. Concentration on the "most excellent," however, demands a definition of intellect that is centered on our purposes.

Without going into the processes of arriving at a definition, my best
guideline seemed to be: keep it clear and straightforward. In trying to stick
to that rule this is what I have found: *Intellect*, as used herein, *is the power
of thought as the first cause of effective action.*

Armed with this intellectual probe I stirred through my historical spec-
imens until I had uncovered three possibilities, staying always within the
limits of the practicable. These fell into three areas each of which could
be considered a quality that contributes to the attribute, intellect. They can
be identified as *imagination, flexibility of mind,* and *judgment.* They may be
thought of as making up a triangle, any side of which represents a practical
application of intellect.

The diagram is not intended to suggest the dependency of its elements. Any single quality contributes to this attribute of leadership, and
though the three might occur in combination in a leader, it can be said
that any one by itself is enough to show intellect as a power to produce
action.

Imagination

THIS QUALITY should be thought of as including innovation, for imagination operating in its own vacuum produces nothing but images in the mind of their originator. Thus imagination, unless it leads to innovation in a practical way, is useless. "Leaps of the imagination" can produce innovative and effective methods as long as the leaps are constrained by reality.

Keeping within the bounds of reality, let us see what a superior order of imaginative intellect could accomplish where reliance on force of arms could have failed. The time: the spring of a year two centuries before the birth of Christ. The place: a hilltop overlooking the valley of the River Baetis (the modern Quadalquivir) in southern Spain. The man: thirty-year-old Publius Cornelius Scipio who holds the Roman supreme command in Spain and who in four years time will defeat Hannibal, conquer Carthage, and gain a resounding fourth name—Africanus. Now, however, Hannibal is still tying up Roman armies in Italy while Scipio marches against another Carthaginian army that is spoiling for an all out fight, and the prize that will go to the victor is no less than the whole of Spain.

The Things That Happened at Ilipa

Here, even in the spring, one could see only brown hills backed
by brown mountains—very different from the green hills and
blue mountains of Italy. This was a hard land bearing a hard
race of men who respected only two things: force and guile.
Scipio's father and uncle had lost their last battles, and their
lives, here in Spain because they had relied solely on force.
Treachery and trickery had betrayed them. Scipio respected
both Spanish toughness and trickery, and did not fear them.

From his hilltop Scipio watched the long column of his
Roman and allied legions strung out in their march down the
river valley road that ran southwestward toward Ilipa. There
the army of his Carthaginian enemies was reported to be encamped, and if Scipio's intelligence was as reliable as it had
been in his other Spanish campaigns, the odds had been set
against him from the start. Against him, that is, if he were to
base the odds on numbers alone: 70,000 Carthaginian infantry—Libyan and Spanish—4,000 African cavalry, and 32 elephants. To match that strength Scipio had been able to raise
only 45,000 infantry and 3,000 cavalry.

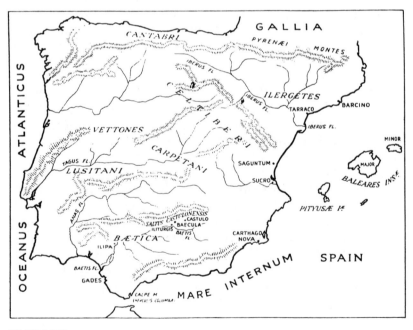

SPAIN 206 B.C.

Scipio was not the man to be dismayed by numbers. He had led those Roman legions through four years of the Spanish wars, and no one knew better the quality of those troops, infantry that could not be matched anywhere in the Mediterranean world. Behind them lay their victories—battles like Carthago Nova and Baecula—and he smiled as he thought of Baecula.

It was there that I gave the Carthaginians a sound thrashing, and that crowned my reputation for tactical genius. I handed those Carthaginians a rough leaf right out of Hannibal's book, pinning down their main body with my light troops, then smashing in their flanks with my heavy infantry. Yet now I will face this other Hasdrubal with my new and untried Spanish infantry, which means that the decisive stroke will have to be made by my Roman legions. I can make the show of force I need with my Spanish, but that tactical stroke I seek will only be disclosed to me when I see the enemy's array.

He mounted and rode down the rocky slope toward the marching columns. Days of marching lay ahead of the Roman army as it followed the north bank of the Baetis. Scipio's strategy called for placing his army between Hasdrubal's camp at Ilipa and the Carthaginian coastal base at Gades. Then if the Romans were victorious they would be in position to cut off any aid from Carthage. Following that course of action would then leave Scipio and his allies free to follow up the victory since there would be no other Carthaginian armies left in Spain.

At this point let Scipio take up his own story.

Seventy-two days have passed since I set out from Tarraco to launch this campaign. Seventy-two days of marching, all the while recruiting and training Spaniards as we marched. Now here in my destined spot I've made the last camp we will use before battle. This last one would have been finished and occupied a day earlier had it not been for Mago's "surprise" cavalry attack which I and Gaius agree was really a blessing in disguise. We were talking about it the following evening in my tent after we had led the legions and allies back into camp after their first—and uneventful—confrontation with Hasdrubal's whole army.

"There was an element of surprise in Mago's attack after all," I said.

"Surprise? If anyone were surprised it had to be Mago's Numidians—unless I'm not tracking your thought," Gaius said.

"I have been obscure, haven't I? No, I meant that I was surprised at Carthaginian aggressiveness so early in the game, though their whole approach to the action was rather clumsy, even a bit amateurish, right?"

"Right, I agree, especially when Mago must have thought a sudden cavalry strike against legionairies in the act of entrenching a camp would have caught them defenseless. Not very bright, considering that we're in our fifth year of operations in Spain," Gaius said.

"Granted, but he was taken in by failing to discover our cavalry that I'd posted out of sight behind that hill. Until they charged over the hill and smashed into his flank he had thought he was master of the situation."

"A truly smashing sight if you'll forgive the word, and a more than satisfying one when our lads were tumbling those African cavalrymen* off their horses, right and left. It was one of the finest calvary counter-attacks I've ever seen—and a successful one since not an enemy trooper ever reached the legionaries working on the ramparts."

"Yes, but remember that we did have to send out the *velites*** to follow up the cavalry and drive off Mago's supports before we had the situation in hand. But enough of Mago, it's Hasdrubal and his mind that is my first concern," I said.

"Your concern may be his mind, but it was the array of his army that impressed me this afternoon. Your army, fully deployed, has a frontage of six thousand yards, yet Hasdrubal's overlaps it on each flank by another thousand yards, and the phalanx of his veteran African infantry may have greater depth than our legions which oppose it," Gaius said.

I picked up the sketch that I had made that afternoon and unrolled it so that we could both examine it.

"Let's commit these deployments of ours and the enemy's to memory so that we can talk of them tomorrow, and later if necessary, without referring to the sketch again," I said.

"It's simple enough. Here our two camps on their ridge crests about three miles from each other. Down here is the

---

*The Numidian horsemen, though without peer in their world, rode with neither saddle nor bridle, controlling their horses with their legs and body movements; thus they could be unseated when taken by surprise.
**The lightly-armed, mobile infantry of the legions who fought usually as skirmishers, opening the battle before the commitment of the heavy infantry.

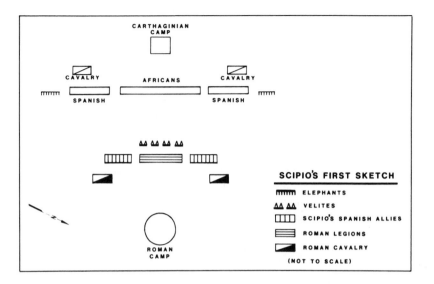

plain where we both deployed today, both armies in standard array, lined up almost a mile apart; it all looks as straightforward as it could be," Gaius said.

"Doesn't it though. Our legions—my only dependable troops—are opposed directly to Hasdrubal's Libyan infantry, his only tried veterans. And on the wings of each array the Spanish allied infantry, extending as you say in Hasdrubal's case, beyond our flanks, with his elephants extending protection to his allies and threatening ours. A rather formidable show on Hasdrubal's part, wouldn't you say?"

Gaius looked up from the sketch, his dark eyes clearly showing his concern.

"More alarming than I'd ever say outside this tent—in spite of the trust we both have in the legions' fighting abilities. Yet you've got to use all that fighting power to stop Hasdrubal's Libyan infantry, not to mention the elephants," he said.

"Gaius, you are repeating here just what your eyes told you this afternoon. Now you must see beyond that Carthaginian array there on the plain."

"How beyond it? There are times when you taunt me with mysteries. How can I see 'beyond' something that is no longer there?"

I rolled up the sketch and tossed it onto the red coals in the brazier standing between us and the tent wall. When the papyrus had turned brown, then black as it burst into flame I looked back at Gaius. He was still staring at me with puzzled eyes.

"I don't taunt you—never have," I said. "Now if I know you at all, and if I were to ask you to describe every element on that sketch you would recount it all without hesitation or doubt. Why? Because you see beyond those mere markings. You could do the same with the eye of your mind in thinking of the line-up of the armies this afternoon; and do it by conceiving changes, perhaps radical changes, in the future."

"What do you see that can be changed?" Gaius asked.

"I see such things as finding ways to better employ the legions, but I cannot tell clearly yet how to do it. And we've long ago learned how to handle elephants with our light infantry, given the right conditions."

"The gods will give you that inner sight, as every soldier out there knows."

"They can believe that piffle, and well that they do. You've known for years that I wouldn't expect it of you, so enough of that. But I do see one great thing the gods have given us, if we'll just use it," I said.

"Yes, what?"

"They gave me the foresight and the means to defeat Mago's attack. But there was far more to that defeat than just breaking up Mago's formations and driving them off with heavy loss to them and little to ourselves. Did you notice this afternoon that while our main force and Hasdrubal's stood in rank confronting each other across the plain the cavalry and light infantry skirmishes ended with a definite character in our favor?"

"If you mean the reluctance of Hasdrubal's African and Spanish cavalry to become engaged, yes I did," Gaius said.

"Well, that was clearly the result of our victory over Mago, brief though that fight was. The enemy's cavalry not only avoided decisive action, they were always the first to withdraw to safety behind their infantry formations. Which means they've got a bit of the wind up and Hasdrubal must see that as plainly as we do," I said.

"Then why did Hasdrubal march out of his camp and deploy on the plain before we did? And why was he first to withdraw to his camp this evening at sundown?"

"I don't know—yet. Perhaps there's some bravado behind it, perhaps to convince his army that he will not avoid battle, that he stands ready to fight. If so, he withdraws first to show his men that they've challenged Romans all day and they have not responded, so that makes him look the better for it."

"Do you intend to let him look better tomorrow if we deploy again?" Gaius asked.

"If he wants to consume time with these shows, we will make that time work in our favor. Let's see when and how he acts tomorrow. For now, let's take advantage of the time and get a good night's rest."

There are two reasons why I have made my escort ride back to our lines at a walk. First, when I had finished my reconnaissance we had to turn our backs on Hasdrubal's battle array, for it would be an unseemly action to ride away from the enemy in haste. Further, I will not have dust stirred up by our horses, dust that would blow in the faces of my legionaries. They have stood here in ranks, facing the Carthaginians across the plain, for a good six hours, and there's no need to add to their discomfort. Besides, my men have had to face to the southwest in order to oppose the enemy. Now, at an hour before sundown, the sun is in Roman eyes which tells me that I will not bring these men into battle in an afternoon. In fact the earlier in the morning the better.

This ride should end my last reconnaissance, for we are ending our third day of confrontation on this plain. I am ready to make my battle plan and I will start after the evening meal. These shows of force and challenges to battle for three days running have been wearing on all, but they have been rewarding to me. Hasdrubal and I have become unwitting—at least I believe unwitting on his part—partners in setting up a fixed pattern. For three mornings, always at a late hour, he has marched his army out of its camp and deployed it on the plain, always in the same order that I showed Gaius in my sketch—his veteran Libyan infantry in the center flanked on each wing by his Spanish infantry, with half his elephants extended on each flank. Each morning I have let him sally out first, then followed and arrayed my army in the same fixed deployment—my legions in the center, facing Hasdrubal's best troops, then my Spanish allies on the wings flanked by my cavalry. At the end of each day, near sundown, Hasdrubal has withdrawn his force back into his camp, and I have followed suit with mine, closing back into my camp at sunset.

Now the pattern has become such a matter of routine in both camps that it is no longer a subject of camp gossip. But of far greater importance, the whole procedure has become fixed in Hasdrubal's mind. And the seeds of that impression will give root to the groundwork of my plan. But first there is the matter of getting the army back to the camp, dispatching my aides with orders to the *legati** and the other commanders to march back in the usual formation.

I looked around the command group assembled that evening in my tent. I had restricted the group to the four *legati* as well as Gaius Laelius, Lucius Marcius, and Marcus Iunis Silanus. These key officers were the only ones to whom I would confide my battle plans, trusting them with its security until they would give their own orders to their troops tomorrow morning. I began by reminding them that the only troops on either side that had seen action so far had been the cavalry and a few light infantry.

"As you know," I said, "these petty skirmishes have shown no result except to exercise some cavalry and *velites*. Tomorrow's action will be another story. Know now that the whole army moves to attack Hasdrubal tomorrow at first light—no more shows of force or skirmishing. This will be the battle that we have been waiting for."

I caught Gaius's knowing eye and saw that he had managed to assume the same intent look that marked the faces of the others.

"I begin," I went on, "with the conclusions I have reached about our enemy and how we must act to destroy him. I have determined that, by now, Hasdrubal and his officers have fixed in their minds the habitual deployments of both armies. You must understand that that is the key to the four things we must accomplish tomorrow in order to gain the victory.

"First, we will defeat Hasdrubal by surprising him. I will come back in a moment to the means we will use.

"Next, we must use the legions to deliver the decisive stroke and that must be against Hasdrubal's weakest elements, his Spanish allies on the wings of his army.

"Third, we must 'fix'—pin down—the best of Hasdrubal's infantry, the Libyan phalanx that forms his center.

*Legion commanders.

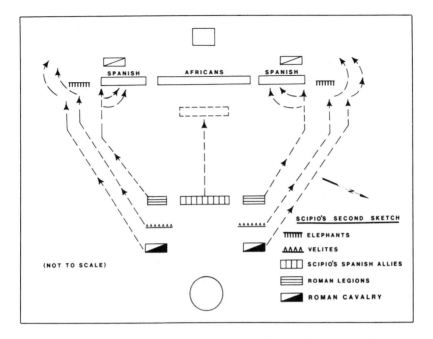

SPANISH   AFRICANS   SPANISH

SCIPIO'S SECOND SKETCH

ꕮꕮꕮ ELEPHANTS

ᴧᴧᴧᴧ VELITES

[[[[SCIPIO'S SPANISH ALLIES

▤▤ ROMAN LEGIONS

◣ ROMAN CAVALRY

(NOT TO SCALE)

"Lastly, we must destroy the Spanish on the enemy's wings before we can attack and defeat his center."

I could see that Marcius and Silanus were bursting with questions while struggling to make an outward show of stoic composure. The rest of the group were equally intense though various degrees of control were evident. Clearly there was no need to excite their interest further, so I launched into the matter of tactical surprise.

"We start by surprising Hasdrubal and his army in their camp in the morning. This means that our cavalry and the *velites* must move out to the attack at first light, and so they must be fed, armed, and the horses saddled before dawn."

Silanus could no longer control his old soldier's impatience with the idea of cavalry and light infantry attacking a fortified camp.

"I fail to see what is accomplished by this attack if it is unsupported," he said.

"It won't be—but must seem so to the enemy," I said. "While the light troops are throwing everything they can at the enemy's camp the rest of our units—under cover of that attack—will be falling in to move out as soon as the troops have been fed. But before we go into the advance of our army across the plain, let us see what we can accomplish by the light troops' attack.

"In the first place the alarms sounded in the Carthaginian camp will cause Hasdrubal to arouse his army in all haste and rush to deploy it on the plain, especially when it is light enough for them to see the rest of our army advancing to the attack. Now here comes the most important point. Hasdrubal has always moved his army out in late morning and has taken his own good time in deploying. But now what will happen to the Carthaginian army when it will have to be assembled so hastily?"

My question caught all but Gaius with their tunics showing. But of course he had the advantage over the rest of having some prior knowledge.

"It's quite clear," Gaius said, "that the enemy will have no choice but to form in the same order they've been using for the last three days."

The abrupt silence that followed Gaius's answer showed that its meaning was lost on the group. It was time for me to produce my new sketch and explain what it meant.

"Here is where Hasdrubal will get his second—and by far his greatest—surprise. Assuming that Gaius's answer is a sound one, and I believe it is, Hasdrubal will have his troops formed in his standard array expecting to find us opposing him with the same deployment we have confronted him with for the past three days. Instead, here is what he will see."

I unrolled the sketch and held it out for them to see.

"As you see," I went on, "our deployment will be reversed, with the Spanish in the center facing Hasdrubal's Libyans, and the legions will be on the wings. You will recall that I said that the decisive stroke must be made by the legions, and it must be against Hasdrubal's Spanish infantry on the wings. Here is how it will be done."

I paused to point out the movements of the legions.

"Each wing moves out obliquely at its fastest pace to move where it can outflank and strike the enemy wing. In the meanwhile our Spanish move at a slow pace to advance directly on the enemy center. Thus, so far, we will be accomplishing three of the four things I told you were essential— we surprise Hasdrubal as I've described, then deliver the decisive attack with the legions against the enemy's wings, and we will 'fix' Hasdrubal's center with our Spanish center. There remains the fourth and final stage—the destruction of Hasdrubal's Spanish on the wings followed by attacks against the flanks of his center."

The silence that followed must have been as profound as the thoughts in the depths of their minds. Never in the history of Roman wars had there been such a radical departure from the tactical norms built up through centuries of warfare. Indeed, what I proposed to do must have seemed more cataclysmic than radical to all but Gaius. When he put his question I could sense the conflict between loyalty and doubt going on within him.

"I see what you intend and how it should be done, but I must say that I fear for the dependence upon our Spanish allies against Hasdrubal's veteran Africans. What will happen if Hasdrubal's center charges into our Spanish and shatters their formations?" Gaius asked.

"Your fear is well founded. There is a risk in opposing Hasdrubal's center with our Spanish, but the risk is lessened by depending upon two things," I said.

"And they are?"

"Our center must be refused from time to time, avoiding close engagement."

"And if the Libyans continue to advance?"

"That brings us to my second point. Hasdrubal's center cannot advance too far without exposing its flanks to attack by units of our legions. Furthermore, he will not allow his center to break contact with his wings, thus leaving his allies on his wings without the support of his veterans in the center. If that were to happen, the same kind of attack by our legions would be an unacceptable threat to his exposed flanks."

"The risk is still there, but I see no way of lessening it, save as you say," Gaius said.

"I acknowledge the risk and accept it. In the morning we will seek the omens from the augurs after the sacrifice before battle, but I have no doubt of the outcome."

"Nor do I if you so believe. Also I see two other matters affecting Hasdrubal when he is surprised by an early morning attack," Gaius said.

This was the sort of contribution that I had always encouraged from commanders and staff officers.

"Let us hear them," I said.

"Since we will advance directly toward his camp his army

will deploy with its front facing us and that will cause his soldiers to be looking into the sun all morning," Gaius said.

I gave him and myself mental slaps on the back.

"Excellent. And the other?"

"Because of the alarms and the hasty exit from their camp Hasdrubal's men will miss breakfast, and they will have to stand and face us feeling their hunger growing, and with no chance of their being fed."

"Yes, and we will find ways to take advantage of that sometime during the morning. Now, are there other questions or ideas?" I said.

"I have a question," Silanus said, "I understand the part about the legions moving out in column from their wing positions so as to advance obliquely to attack Hasdrubal's flanks, but how do you propose to maneuver the legions at that point?"

"Maneuver? *I* maneuver? What do you mean?" I said.

"If the heavy infantry and the light troops have to wheel from column in opposite directions, won't the battle order of some units be reversed?" Silanus asked.

I'd no doubt that Silanus would soon realize that he had spoken without thinking first, and, what was worse, making me look as though I had not anticipated critical events. I dismissed this as it deserved—a matter of detail properly left to the *legati* and their tribunes and centurions.

"I don't propose to allow the mechanics of battle drill to obscure *real* tactical problems. Now if certain stages of the operation tomorrow call for changes in the execution of my plan I will, as always, handle them on the spot. Are there other questions?" I said.

This time the silence showed the relief of tension. It was a settling back after problems had been cleared away and issues settled.

"Very well then," I said, "there remain two matters we can deal with, and quickly, before you leave. First, Silanus and Marcius will command on the left wing. I will command the right wing seconded by Gaius Laelius. Until the legions of both wings march away from the center, my battle station will be in the interval between the center and the right wing. Finally, a detail that you should see observed by your officers, and the word passed among the troops when they fall in at first light. When your tribunes report here in the morning they will see displayed outside my tent one of my scarlet cloaks tied to a spear* I have kept you long enough, I know you are anxious to get back to your commands. Know all of you that Jupiter and Hercules ride with us on the morrow.** Gaius, on your way out please pass the word that I wish to see the augurs within the half-hour."

The dawn mists were rising around us as we rode, making us draw our cloaks tighter against the chill plumes stirred up like surf by our horses' hooves. Gaius and I were followed by a double file of aides and behind them at a little distance rattled and clanked the column of my cavalry escort. The light troops had long ago disappeared into the mists of the plain toward which we were riding. The cavalry columns had moved past us at a walk to allow the files of loping *velites* to keep abreast of them. We could still hear from the camp the distant shouted commands of centurions that grew fainter as we rode down the gentle slopes to the plain. I gave the order to halt when we reached a spot where the rough path crossed a shallow ravine. The horses sniffed around like hounds at the smells rising from the damp earth. Gaius sniffed too and I laughed, thinking of how he sounded like my mare.

"You laugh," Gaius said, "it is a good sign, but I'm sure I don't know what it's about."

"You and the horses, are you related in this way?—how you test the air?" I said.

"No, but there is some of the beast in me—like anyone I suppose. Really though I was thinking of the boar hunts in the early morning on your estate at Liternum. I remember the horses sniffing like dogs when we'd assemble to follow the trackers."

"And so I remember too. But I didn't halt here to sample smells, I want to look, not to smell."

"By the gods, what is there to see here?"

"Don't you think it's time to appreciate a sunrise? Even if we have to look back toward our camp," I asked.

"The sun does appear to rise behind our camp and the crest of the hill is beginning to lighten. Is that an omen favorable to you?"

*The symbol-signal used by Roman army commanders to tell their soldiers that battle was imminent.
**Scipio was linked, in the minds of the people, with the gods, principally Jupiter and on occasion Hercules.

We had been talking in low voices, but when I answered I raised my voice so the escort could hear.

"Truly, as it was augured, Phoebus Apollo joins Jupiter and Hercules in crowning Roman arms with success this day."

As I spoke we began to hear the first sounds of battle from the direction of the Carthaginian camp.

"Come, let us ride," I ordered, "I must see the array of Hasdrubal's army as it begins to form."

At the second hour* the morning mists had been chased from the plain by the sun and we could see the whole front of the Carthaginian array as it stood fast in its ranks, just as it had in the past days. Our light troops had been driven back on the plain by the enemy's heavy infantry as it advanced to take up its battle positions, and now there were only infrequent clashes between opposing flurries of cavalry and light infantry. Fortunately for my reconnaissance there had been enough heavy dew left on the damp ground to prevent dust being raised by the horses and swarms of light infantry, so we had a clear look at the enemy army. Over Gaius's objections I led my escort within five hundred yards of the enemy's center before turning to ride toward his left wing.

"I'm in no danger here," I told Gaius, "we're hundreds of yards beyond the range of any archer and if any of their cavalry start to move this way in force we'll see them in plenty of time to get safely back to our lines."

He grumbled something I didn't bother to hear, but I did hear him charge the escort commander to be alert for the approach of groups of horse.

We rode at an easy canter, halting briefly now and again as I tried to get a closer look at Hasdrubal's men. After we had cleared the front of the enemy center I paused to get a glimpse of the Spanish auxiliaries who made up Hasdrubal's left wing. They too were formed in phalanx though not in as deep a formation as the center. They were easily distinguished from Hasdrubal's Libyan-Phoenician infantry even though both could be called heavy infantry. These *scutarii* were leaning on their long, flat, oval-ended shields with each man's pair of javelins, one light, one heavy, thrust into the ground at his right. They too wore a variety of headgear, though most

*The hours of the Roman day were counted from sunrise.

of them wore the sinew cap which protected the head and back of the neck but left the ears and face exposed. Most also wore belted white tunics edged in purple. Some had pieces of body armor such as flat breastplates, others had none. They were a tough looking lot but we Romans were well aware of their chief weakness as soldiery—they were fierce fighters as individuals but subject to sudden fits of mass panic making them unreliable in organized fighting formations.

When we were close enough to the left end of Hasdrubal's line I stopped long enough to count the elephants standing on the flank. There were sixteen, looming like distant miniature castles, the bulk of the huge beasts surmounted by their mahouts seated on their high-backed saddles. It was evident that Hasdrubal had, in his usual fashion, split his elephant force, placing half on each flank of his army.

"Fearsome beasts," Gaius said as though echoing my thought.

"Yes, until one's infantry learns their weaknesses, as ours has—sometimes the hard way. Though we may be past those trials," I said.

"I've been checking the training of the *velites* in that respect ever since we approached Ilipa. Just yesterday you'd have had to choke back a laugh as I did when I heard a *primus pilus** supervising *velites* in battle drill. After the centurions' usual summing up of the elephant's vulnerable spots** he would break in with his version of the decisive stroke—'What's the best way to stampede an elephant? You slip up behind his tail and jam your javelin up his ass!' On the crude side, but effective wouldn't you say?"

"Of course I've heard of that tactic, but never heard it put so delicately. Excellent though. Now, I've seen enough, it's time we started back to our battle station," I said.

"Right, it's now past the fourth hour. Do you want to order the cavalry and the *velites* back to join their legions?" Gaius asked.

"Not yet, at least not all at once. You remember the point you made last night about the enemy having to charge out of his camp without breakfast? Well, I want that hunger to

---

*The highest ranking centurion of the legion, the position aspired to by every professional officer of the legion.
**Those vulnerable areas included not only the trunk (which could be slashed by spear or sword) but also the soles of the feet and the tender skin of their rumps.

go on working on Hasdrubal's men as long as we can prolong it to our advantage. But you can order the light troops to disengage and withdraw by detachments so that they will finish passing through their legions before the seventh hour. When they have completed their withdrawal I want them formed in rear of their legions, the *velites'* formations in front of the cavalry.

"By the seventh hour?"

"Yes, that will be the noon hour. By that time we will have played out this waiting game for all it's worth. Then I will signal a general advance."

Hasdrubal's Libyan infantry was drawn up in phalanx and I could make out the *speirai** that formed it. I was close enough to see their armor and weaponry—the long pikes, the round Greek-style shields, and a mixture of helmet types, Corinthian, Chalcidian, and even Roman. Gaius had noticed the Roman helmets and was cursing the wearers for their wearing the captured Roman body armor as well. Taken in all it was impressive array especially when one could imagine the long pikes, now rested upright, levelled in the fearsome hedge that would precede the advance of the phalanx.

At noon I rode forward alone from my station between the center and the right wing. I halted my horse at a hundred paces and turned to face about. By turning my head from left to right I could survey the whole order of my army. It was a splendid sight—forty-five thousand men aligned in their formations on a front, extending from flank to flank, of almost three miles. Every legionary, every Spaniard was at his appointed station. The last centurions and *optiones* had given their final commands, and the plain had fallen silent. As far as the eye could see the sun was reflected from crested helmets, steel cuirasses, and spear points. For the briefest moment I was seeing thousands upon thousands of steel statues arrayed as if they had stepped out of an immense frieze on some unearthly temple, then my mind snapped back to reality. These statues were living, breathing men who were on the verge of leaning forward, waiting for the command to step out in the advance against their enemy.

---

*It is believed that the Carthaginian African heavy infantry fought in a Macedonian-type phalanx made up of *speirai*, each *speira* could have been (if it were truly Macedonian in nature) formed in close order with a depth of sixteen men and a width of the same, i.e., a total of 256 men per *speira*.

The sun was directly overhead when I raised my right arm to give the signal. I dropped my arm, my *tubicen* sounded his trumpet, my *signifer* dipped his standard, and the horns of the legions' *cornicens* blared out, blast after blast, and the long line began the advance.

I beckoned Gaius to my side and we rode forward together in the interval between the center and the right wing. The sun had long since dried the hard ground, and now dust from thousands of marching feet rose in thin brown clouds over the helmets of the legions and the Spanish cohorts. Yet from my vantage point on horseback I had a clear view of both armies. The Carthaginian line was standing fast, an immobile wall of armed men awaiting the onslaught. I set the pace for the advance, a battle-drill pace so even the Spaniards could maintain their alignment.

We crossed a half mile of plain moving directly toward the enemy until I estimated that we were nearing a point eight hundred yards from his line. I gave the orders, and aides went flying to Silanus and Marcius on the left and the senior prefect leading the Spanish allies in the center—the left wing to break off from the center and begin the maneuvers that would become mirror images of what my right-wing legions would execute; the prefects in the center would take up the slow march so that the Spanish would be moving forward at a slackened pace, less than half that at which the legions would be marching.

At the eight-hundred-yard point I signalled a general halt and nodded to Gaius. He gave the commands to face the legions to the right, then rode off to lead the legionary columns as they began their march taking them away from the center at an oblique angle of 45 degrees. Following Gaius's orders, the legions were marching at the quick step, moving in the four columns that would wheel into line of battle when the command was given. I rode across the rear of the columns to make sure that all was in order. From left to right the columns were composed of the *hastati* whose maniples would form the first line of battle. To their right were the *principes* of the second line, next to the right were the old veterans, the *triarii* who would form the third line of battle.* The rightmost column was made up of the bodies of *velites* and cavalry which

---

*Appendix E contains a summary of the legion's tactical formation and manipular tactics.

would wheel outwards—to their right—on my command in order to start the maneuver which would outflank Hasdrubal's elephants and his left wing.

Satisfied with the formations and their order of march I trotted up the right side of the column of *velites* and cavalry, checking as I rode on the condition of the men and their marching pace. It was a cheering sight. The dust-covered, sweating soldiers were swinging along, hard-muscled men in the top of condition and eager for action after days of standing uselessly—at least in their minds—in ranks facing an enemy with whom it seemed they could never come to blows. Now they were spoiling for a fight, anxious to get the day's dirty business behind them. Nothing would have suited me better, and I was going to see that they all got a full measure of fighting.

When I reached the head of the rightmost column Gaius trotted over from his station at the head of the infantry columns.

"I'm getting a sore neck from trying to look back at these legions' columns and keep an eye on the enemy's flank, all at the same time," he said.

He was grinning like a boy beating his opponents at trigon,* whether at his idea of a joke or at the prospects of getting the legions into action I couldn't tell.

"We'll both get a little more neck exercise in trying to follow what's happening to our Spanish in the center," I said.

We both turned in the saddle to look back over our left shoulders at the now distant center which we were leaving farther behind with every step.

"They're moving slow enough all right. I see a gap of at least a couple of hundred yards between them and Hasdrubal's center," Gaius said.

"So thus far all is well there, for you can see that the Libyans haven't moved a foot. That means that Hasdrubal will keep them on the defensive, at least for now, and we couldn't ask for more. Every minute that passes in this way gives me more assurance that Hasdrubal's center will continue to be fixed in place," I said.

We rode together, each judging the width of the narrowing gap between the heads of our columns and the flank

---

*A game with three players who try to make an opponent miss catching the ball.

of Hasdrubal's Spanish infantry. There was no time now for checking on the march of our center or even our columns following at our heels. When I saw that I was opposite the last enemy file and three hundred yards from it I turned to Gaius.

"This is the moment we've waited four years for. May the gods ride with you," I said.

His only reply was to raise his hand to his helmet, and he and his tribunes were gone. Our next moves were prearranged, leaving me no time to watch what was happening with the rest of the army. Gaius's duties lay with the redeployment of the legions' heavy infantry which now had to wheel to the left, going from column into their lines. My part was to oversee the wheeling outward—to the right—of the light troops so they could come up into line and advance to attack the elephants and the flanks of the enemy infantry. I sent an aide galloping with word to the tribune commanding the light troops to begin his maneuver.

That done I was free to take station with my staff on a low knoll which allowed an overview of the action. I watched the next moves of the legions, fascinated at the drill-ground precision with which they came into line to attack Hasdrubal's Spanish. Gaius had halted the four columns, faced them left into line, then each line—following in turn—wheeled through 45 degrees to come into line facing the Spanish. When the maneuver had been completed Gaius gave the order and the legions were launched into the attack. Even at my distance from the battle the din was deafening. The trumpets were blaring as the first maniples shouted their war cry and dashed forward to get within javelin range of their enemy. At the same time the second and third lines were clashing their javelins against their shields and shouting themselves hoarse as they cheered on the *hastati*. The front line halted long enough to volley their javelins—first the thin one, then the thicker—into the ranks of their enemy. As the two volleys crashed into the enemy the *hastati* had already drawn their swords and were charging full tilt into the shaken Spanish. The young Roman legionaries threw the full weight of their bodies against the flat shields of the Spanish, raising a clamor that could be heard all across the plain. They were trying to knock their enemies off balance while thrusting at them with their swords. In individual encounters where a Roman had not overthrown his enemy he would rest the bottom end of his shield on the ground, put all his weight behind his left shoulder and his shield, and continue his sword-thrusting attack.

In the meantime the deployed maniples of the second line, the *principes*, were followed by the third line of the *triarii* as they advanced within supporting distance of the now-committed first line. The second line, made up of the finest fighting men of the legion, were waiting their turn at the enemy in case the first line's attack failed to shatter the enemy formation. As I watched I could see that the Spanish were fighting back furiously in spite of the terrible losses in their front ranks. It was time for committing the second line, and I could hear the first trumpet blasts that were signalling the recall of the first line. This was carried out with precision despite the heavily engaged front ranks. The forward centuries disengaged, moving back under the protection of the other centuries, then withdrew through the gaps between the maniples of the second line. After the *hastati* had passed through, the rear centuries of the second line moved up to close the gaps, forming a solid phalanx. On the next trumpet blasts the *principes* volleyed their *pila* into the enemy, just as the *hastati* had done, and charged. The worn down and dismayed Spanish could not withstand the attack of this fresh, battle-tried infantry. As the first ranks of *principes* smashed into their enemy I witnessed the sight that never ceased to surprise me during these clashes of heavy infantry when a beaten formation begins to break up. The foremost ranks of Spanish infantry continued to resist, individual soldiers standing and fighting back, fearing to turn their bodies to enemies who were within sword's length. But it was the rearmost ranks who turned and fled, followed by their companions who had been ranked between them and the engaged front. It was that ever-strange phenomenon of a phalanx beginning to disintegrate from the rear instead of from its front, which could not disengage.

Despite my fascination with the infantry combat my attention had to be directed next to the attack of the light troops against the elephants and the rest of Hasdrubal's left flank. The *velites* and cavalry had wheeled into line at right angles to the enemy flank behind which a detachment of his cavalry had formed. The line of light troops was made up of alternated bodies of *velites* and cavalry. Following my orders the *velites* ran forward out of the line while the cavalry stood in place. There were good reasons for this—while the *velites* went for the elephants the cavalry waited to support them or, if necessary, take on the enemy's cavalry if it interfered. Our cavalry would have been more hindrance than support to the *velites* at this stage, for the horses feared the elephants, even their smell frightened them.

Each advancing body of *velites* broke into two groups as the running men charged around the line of elephants, one element going for the enemy's light infantry in the intervals, the other for the elephants. As they ran they raised enough racket to alarm men as well as animals, clashing swords or javelins against their shields, every man shouting at the top of his voice.

What followed was over in no time, an action as swift as it was involved. As swarms of *velites* poured through the intervals and battled hand-to-hand with the Carthaginian light infantry, their comrades attacked the sides and rear of the elephants, slashing at trunks, thrusting javelins into their rumps, and spearing the mahouts or leaping up to pull them from their saddles. The uproar that rose out of this milling mass of men and animals would easily have drowned the clamor that the *velites* had started. Clouds of choking dust rose from the melee obscuring the men and at times even the elephants. The shrill trumpeting of the maddened beasts made my hair rise as I tried to imagine what it was like to be caught up in that deadly game.

That part was over in seconds. The violent action was spread in all directions by the panicked elephants, like rushing waters thrown from the vortex of a whirlpool. All control of the great beasts had been lost at the height of the *velites'* attack, and now the elephants—trunks upraised and great ears spread wide in terror—broke and ran in all directions, trampling friend and foe alike, anyone who was unlucky enough to get in their path. Some even reached the withdrawing Spanish heavy infantry, while two other beasts tore through the closed ranks of the nearest legion leaving a welter of dead and maimed in their wake.

Then occurred an event that I can ascribe only to the intervention of Jupiter himself. A half-dozen of the panic-stricken elephants had whirled about and plunged through the ranks of the enemy cavalry which had been formed up to support Hasdrubal's left wing. The Spanish horsemen, their white tunics flying in the wind, broke and scattered, all organization lost in their flight. After the elephants had passed on to disappear in the distance I could see officers trying to rally knots of Spanish cavalrymen, and several had succeeded in forming a semblance of order among a half-dozen troops. It was what our cavalry had been waiting for—there had been no point in committing them into the violent melee that had just broken up—and the prefect commanding the cavalry had seen the opportunity as soon as I had. He launched all his squadrons with one trumpet blast and they swept across the field in a knee to knee charge that sent the rallied remnants of the Carthaginian cavalry flying, never to be reassembled.

While I was watching our cavalry complete the defeat of Hasdrubal's left wing, one of Silanus' aides galloped up with the best news I would receive that afternoon: Silanus and Marcius had smashed Hasdrubal's right wing in an attack that had gone almost like a duplicate of our victory over the left. But the battle as a whole could never be won until we could crush Hasdrubal's center. I sent an aide with an order to Silanus and Marcius to attack the right flank of the Libyan phalanx as soon as possible while I would take immediate steps to launch my legions against the left of the Libyans.

There was no time to lose in my sphere of command. I could see that my Spanish allies, while trying to withdraw from the grip of the Libyans, were getting seriously entangled in combat. Also *speirai* of the Spanish infantry that my legions had just broken were being rallied and regrouped in an obvious effort to protect the center's left flank. The Spanish enemy were being formed up to face toward my reorganized legions. I sent two aides galloping—one to Gaius directing him to advance directly against the enemy's Spanish infantry, destroy it and continue the attack to smash the left flank of the Libyans; the other courier carried orders to my cavalry to re-form on the right of the legions prepared to exploit the destruction of the enemy infantry.

When the legions signaled their readiness I had my trumpeter and *signifer* give the signal for a general advance. I started to ride forward when another messenger arrived, this one from Gaius. He also brought welcome news—while my attention had been riveted on the engagement of the light troops and the subsequent destruction of the enemy cavalry, I had missed seeing more widespread effects of the elephant stampede. A number had charged through the Libyan infantry spreading destruction and confusion and now was the time to strike and reap the harvest of my enemy's troubles.

Since Gaius's legions were already launching their renewed attack, all the necessary orders had been given, and I found a low rise behind the legions where I could observe the action. It was obvious that Gaius must finish off Hasdrubal's rallying Spanish infantry before the legions could get at the Libyans, and that began to happen under my eyes.

The *hastati* repeated their earlier attack against the Spanish who were only partially re-formed and scarcely the threat they had been in the beginning. Again the *hastati* threw their *pila* and dashed into the disorderly array of spears that were lowered against the attackers. The ragged spear hedge proved to be no obstacle to the leading rank of *hastati*. They either thrust aside or battered down the spears, and then were among the spearmen, thrusting and slashing. And again the rearmost ranks broke and fled leaving the foremost of their comrades to their fate. It was a fate that came as suddenly as the throwing of the javelins into the Spanish. There was no need for the legions to commit the *principes*. The job was done. The Spanish phalanx disintegrated into a horde of fugitives who were dashing to either flank and some even sought refuge among the Libyans who, of course, were facing to their front against my center. Libyan officers coolly faced their two outer files to the left to present a bristling line of pikes to the fleeing Spanish. However, the greater mass of fugitives was running toward what had been the Spanish left—the right of the legions—in the direction of their camp. Now if I could drive that mass into the rear of the Libyans that might create confusion on that quarter. I sent an aide to my cavalry commander who led off at once in a cavalry charge that thundered down into the broken Spanish and scattered them across the plain. There was no discernible damage to the rear of the Libyan phalanx, so I sent another message to the cavalry commander to reassemble in his last position to the right of the legions.

There was no need for an order to Gaius to continue the attack to strike the Libyan left flank. The *hastati* had again withdrawn through the gap left by the *principes*, and now the elite of the legions dashed forward against the Libyans. This threat had long been an obvious one to the Libyans' leaders, who faced more files to the left to counter the legions' attack. If the Libyan phalanx had had only to take on the attack of Gaius' legions, they might have succeeded in beating it off. But the plight of Hasdrubal's center—the only fighting force left in his army—was truly a prelude to disaster. Silanus and Marcius were attacking the Libyan right in concert with Gaius's attack, and the prefects commanding my Spanish allies seized their opportunity to switch from skirmishing tactics to an all-out frontal attack on the Libyans. In addition to all these troubles, I recalled that these veterans of Hasdrubal's had been fighting—or the majority just standing in ranks—since early morning, over eight hours without breakfast and with no hope of getting food or water. Now, since they were surrounded on three sides, with my cavalry threatening their rear, their leaders had no choice but to try to withdraw to the security of their camp a good half-mile to their rear. Their retreat began in an orderly manner, step by step, keeping their ranks as veterans should. However, by this time every Roman and allied soldier could see that victory was in sight if only every man would put forward his best, and they did.

Later I heard that Hasdrubal, after taking personal command of his center, had sought to encourage his men by shouting, "the hills in the rear will afford a safe refuge, if you will but retreat without hurry." I will never know if that desperate cry marked the beginning of the end, but in any event something happened within the Libyan phalanx as it tried to make a final stand at the foot of the ridge on which they had built their camp. Just when the Libyans had halted and renewed the fight, panic struck in their rear, and the rear ranks turned tail and bolted. The phalanx crumbled like a sand castle in the surf as more rearward ranks broke and joined in the flight. In minutes what had been a steadily moving fortress became a disorderly mob running for its life—and its camp. My light troops were nipping at the heels of the fleeing rabble while the legions and allies were closing ranks to assault the camp when it happened.

If the gods had chosen to aid our cause throughout the battle they must have decided at this point to call it a day and return to Mount Olympus. The hot skies were suddenly darkened with thick thunder clouds and before my legions could ascend the slope rain fell in sheets that turned the dust to mud. The slippery mud soon became ankle deep under thousands of churning feet. If it had been a passing shower, I would have ordered the attack renewed. But the downpour showed no signs of slackening, and with the greatest reluctance I had to order the withdrawal to our camp. I left behind enough light troops with legionary infantry reliefs to screen Hasdrubal's camp, and we marched back in the rain.

While we marched I sent orders to see that the men got fed and assured of a good night's rest because I knew they would need it at first light on the morrow. I knew also that my plans must be completed and the orders given before I could sleep, for this victory would be meaningless if I did not destroy the remainder of Hasdrubal's army.

The finish of Scipio's story is the story of the finish of Carthaginian aspirations in Spain. At daybreak the morning after Ilipa, Scipio's light troops reported that Hasdrubal's army had evacuated its camp and was trying to escape on the road to Gades. Scipio immediately launched a pursuit, one that turned into a strategic pursuit scarcely matched in history and never surpassed until Napoleon's destruction of Prussian armies after Jena twenty centuries later.

The Roman cavalry and light infantry caught up with Hasdrubal's rear guards—in spite of losing their way in attempting to cut the Carthaginian line of retreat—and kept up such a series of flank and rear attacks against Hasdrubal's columns that forced frequent halts, allowing the legion infantry to catch up. What followed, in Livy's words, "was not a fight, but a carnage of cattle." This relentless slaughter and the pressure on the fugitives were kept up until Hasdrubal, with only 6,000 out of his original 74,000, escaped into the hills and fortified a camp on the highest hill. That night Hasdrubal deserted his men, reached the coast, and took a ship to Gades, followed by Mago. It remained only for Scipio to leave Silanus with enough troops to take the surrender of the doomed camp while he marched back to Tarraco, now the undisputed master of Spain.

In regard to the conduct of the battle of Ilipa, it is only fair that the reader be aware of the controversy among some commentators concerning the complexity of Scipio's maneuver of the legion infantry and cavalry in their attack on the enemy's wings. There has been some "quibbling over the minutiae," over the wheeling inward (by legion infantry) and outward (by the cavalry and *velites*) resulting in some cases in reversed order from "normal" formations just as the troops moved to the attack. I have dealt with that problem exactly as I believe Scipio would by leaving the mechanics of the maneuver to subordinate commanders. I likewise believe that if the commentators paid less attention to Polybius's remarks on the complexity of Roman battle drills at Ilipa, and gave more heed to his comment on generalship (Book XI, 23) the controversy might yet die a natural death. Polybius, the innocent perpetrator of all the fuss, went on to vindicate himself (to anyone who would listen): "But the general [Scipio] regarding this [all the wheeling] as of small importance, devoted his attention to the really important object—outflanking the enemy—and he estimated rightly, for a general should, of course, know the actual course of events, but employ those movements which are suited to an emergency." Amen—to another case for learning about leadership from leaders.

Leaving those small potatoes to wither in their jackets, two salient points in Scipio's planning and conduct of Ilipa demand recognition. His study of his enemy and his exercise of imagination were the bases of an innovation which remains a tactical masterpiece, in its conception as well as in the simplicity of its execution. The other factor was Scipio's step-by-step course from perception to deduction to action, making Ilipa more than a victory; it was a triumph of practical reasoning.

Once Scipio had proceeded from deduction to action, it is the nature of his action that sets his genius apart. Before he resorted to physical action—battle itself—his operations were being carried out on an intellectual plane: he was working on the mind of his opponent before any major forces came in contact. In today's terms, Scipio "conned" Hasdrubal into a comfortable mode of thought. The fixed pattern set up in Hasdrubal's mind was designed to lure him into two nasty surprises. He got the first one in the early morning because he had fallen into the rut of a daily sequence he himself had established—moving his army out of camp first, then, after offering battle all day, withdrawing first to his camp at sundown. Hence Scipio's attack at first light tumbled Hasdrubal and his men out onto the plain sans breakfast and sans choice of deployment since they were given no time for "falling in" in any order other than their standard one.

And the second surprise: "indeed it followed hard upon" the first. This was caused by Scipio's reversal of his order of battle which resulted in his best troops attacking his enemy's worst, while Hasdrubal's best troops, in his center, were pinned down during the critical phases that followed.

Flexibility

THERE REMAINS IMBEDDED in our American mores the obligation to quote Mark Twain at least once in a lifetime. It is my turn to sin. In *Life on the Mississippi* there is a passage that puts to shame any other writer's attempts to dramatize flexibility.

> This . . . brought back to me the St. Louis riots of about thirty years ago. I spent a week there, at that time, in a boarding house, and had this young fellow for a neighbor across the hall. We saw some of the fightings and killings; and by and by we went one night to an armory where two hundred young men had met, upon call, to be armed up and go forth against the rioters, under command of a military man. We drilled till about ten o'clock at night; then news came that the mob were in great force in the lower end of the town, and were sweeping everything before them. Our column moved at once. It was a very hot night, and my musket was very heavy. We marched and marched, and the nearer we approached the seat of war, the hotter I grew and the thirstier I got. I was behind my friend; so finally, I asked him to hold my musket while I dropped out and got a drink. Then I branched off and went home. I was not feeling any solicitude about *him* of course, because I knew he was so well armed now that he could take care of himself without any trouble. If I had had any doubts about that, I would have borrowed another musket for him. . . .

I am not, of course, foolhardy enough to imply that Mark Twain's "branching off" was an exemplary act. I view his conduct with fascination when it comes to flexibility, but after that one has to draw a line.

On the other side of that line there is a manifest responsibility—within the bounds of this book—of defining flexibility as a quality contributing to intellect. Such a definition should take into account the certainty that the leader will have to exercise his flexibility in the face of such battlefield dynamics as danger, uncertainty, and frustration. With that in mind flexibility can be seen as *the ability to shift mental gears under pressure without confusion of purpose*. The key conditions are clear: there will be pressure and the leader's decisions must be taken without losing sight of the overriding consideration—his mission.

In the next example we will see a leader under a host of pressures that threaten not only his mission but the very survival of his command. First, however, we should recognize the two elements that must be appreciated in following the action: the man and the conditions he had to master before he could hope to win his battles.

Henry Bouquet has been called a soldier of fortune serving in the Army of King George III. Lest he be tarred with the same brush as the mercenaries of our times, Bouquet should be seen for what he was—a professional soldier, born of a good Swiss family, who was following the custom of his day by seeking combat experience as a commissioned officer in European armies. Born in Canton Vaud in 1719, he entered the service of the States General of Holland at age seventeen as a cadet, and two years later was commissioned a lieutenant. In the War of the Austrian Succession (1740–1748) he served in the Sardinian Army, where he showed such coolness and tactical skill in action that the Prince of Orange engaged him, promoted him to lieutenant-colonel, and made him captain-commandant in his regiment of Swiss Guards. After the war he traveled through Europe with Lord Middleton, from whom he began to learn the English which he eventually mastered to a high degree of fluency in speech and "grace and precision" in writing. This association also laid the foundation for a lifelong and amicable relationship with the British military. Their recognition of his abilities led to an offer of the lieutenant-colonelcy of the yet-to-be-formed 1st Battalion of the 60th Royal American Regiment (later, after the Revolutionary War, to be re-titled the King's Royal Rifle Corps) which he would have to assist in organizing and recruiting. He accepted, and in 1756, the third year of the French and Indian War, found himself recruiting among the Germans of Pennsylvania. He liked the Americans and they liked him, a great deal due, no doubt, to his patience, intelligence, and friendly manner. He is said to have been both handsome and ordinary in appearance (if that was an inconsistency it has not been explained), with a tendency to portliness. However that may have been, it is the composition of Bouquet's

Colonel Henry Bouquet

upstairs that should concern us more than the configuration of his downstairs, for he was an exact opposite of the British officer Churchill described a century and half later as being so stupid that even his brother officers had begun to notice it.

Bouquet had a love for mathematics and scientific inquiry that formed a natural base for the working of his inquisitive and analytical mind. He had none of the make-up of the British professional soldier who despised the colonials and who showed a closed mind to their problems and the conditions under which they had to fight the French-supported Indians on their frontiers. The Swiss colonel was not too proud to seek the best advice and instruction available in order to learn the ways of frontier rangers and their Indian enemies. His inquiries led him to concentrate on developing tactics for employing regular troops against Indians. To his inquiring mind this meant finding ways of adapting the advantages and disadvantages of European-type discipline to the conditions of wilderness warfare. When his ideas had crystallized, he began to train his Royal Americans as mobile light infantry in methods that would make them effective in the fluid kind of fighting that characterized Indian warfare. By the time he could put his ideas into practice Bouquet had come to know something that no other British commander knew—his enemy.

Bouquet knew too that provincial soldiers—like his Pennsylvania Germans—could be molded into elite units if properly led, disciplined, trained and equipped. He made his Royal Americans a model light infantry, armed with light fusil instead of the heavy musket, with hunting knives and tomahawks instead of clumsy swords, and with a light pack designed for forest warfare. And instead of close-order drills and firing by volleys, his men were trained to fight as skirmishers in open order so that they could fire and maneuver more effectively than large bodies of Indians. One observer of this training wrote in 1758 (the year Bouquet was promoted to full colonel): "Every afternoon Colonel Bouquet exercises his men in the woods and bushes in a particular manner of his own invention which will be of great service in an engagement with the Indians." In the years that followed this proved to be of great service indeed in the minor actions that the battalion fought against the Indians on frontier outposts. When the war ended in 1763 it would have seemed that the need for Bouquet's men and his tactical skill had finally ended. This turned out not to be the case, in fact the greatest challenge Bouquet and his light infantry would ever face was in the making.

The victorious British commander in North America, Lord Jeffrey Amherst, may have been a fine administrator but he was contemptuous of the Indians and the means the French had used to secure their alliances. The Indians, in turn, resented their new masters and saw them not as new allies but as a mounting threat to their lands and peoples. Their resentment was abetted by the French who wanted the Indians to rebel and so spread rumors that the French would renew the war by sending an expedition to recapture Montreal and Quebec. A remarkable Indian leader arose in the midst of this situation: Pontiac, an Ottawa chief with amazing political and military abilities. In April, 1763, Pontiac exhorted a council of chiefs to unite in a great confederacy that would join all the tribes from the Great Lakes to the Gulf to fall upon the British settlers and drive them from Indian lands. Pontiac's grandest schemes never worked out, but what did follow—known variously as Pontiac's War, Rebellion, or Conspiracy—was a series of bloody, concerted Indian attacks of an intensity that the colonists had never experienced, even when the Indians had been led by the French. The onslaught was cleverly planned and carried out under cover of the In-

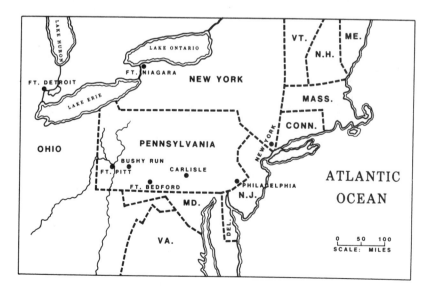

dian gatherings during the trading season, quiet assemblages that had become customary over the years. At a given signal war-painted warriors sprang from hiding, burst into stockades and slaughtered the British settlers. Panic-stricken settlers who escaped fled to frontier outpost forts. By the end of June the terror had flamed across the whole frontier, and in the end only two westernmost posts still held out: Fort Detroit and Fort Pitt.

Finally Amherst became convinced that the Indian attacks were not mere sporadic outbreaks and that full-scale Indian warfare threatened the provinces that would become the states of New York, Ohio, Michigan, and Pennsylvania. Correspondence between Amherst and Bouquet resulted in the latter hurrying to Carlisle in Pennsylvania to assemble a relief column which he would lead westward to save Fort Pitt.

Bouquet's "army" when assembled totaled 460 regulars—his battalion of the Royal Americans, 214 men of the 42nd Highlanders (later the "Black Watch"), 133 of the 77th (Montgomery Highlanders), and a small detachment of rangers. Welcome as the reinforcements were to Bouquet, there were, as he saw it, two serious shortcomings in the build-up of his force. Now his Royal Americans, the trained forest fighters, would be in the minority, and the Highlanders were worn down from their recent service in the West Indies. There were, however, some comforting thoughts: the Scots were well-disciplined, with good morale, and all born fighters. Bouquet consoled himself by determining to make Indian fighters out of the whole force if it meant on-the-job training.

He was ready to march by the end of June, but was held up until July 18 because of the difficulty in getting volunteers from the terrified settlers to serve as wagoners for the wagon train—a logistical liability even Bouquet could not dispense with. A week after his departure Bouquet reached Fort Bedford, where he was delayed for another three days. On August 2 he had gotten to Fort Ligonier when he learned from Lieutenant Archibald Blane that Fort Ligonier had had no word from Captain Ecuyer at Fort Pitt since May 30—no communication for sixty-four days! This lack of intelligence could only mean that Fort Pitt was under siege, if it had not already fallen.

Bouquet acted with his usual alacrity. He stripped his command down to the bare essentials, his only unavoidable burden being the supplies for Fort Pitt. He had the flour barrels emptied into sacks, and rid himself of the wagons by transferring the flour and ammunition to 350 pack horses. He led the vanguard of his force out of Fort Ligonier in the early morning of August 4. He still had learned nothing of the situation at Fort Pitt, and was of course unaware that Captain Ecuyer, staring out of a blockhouse loophole while nursing an arrow wound in his leg, had come to realize that the Indians had lifted the siege and had disappeared into the woods, heading eastward. Simeon Ecuyer, a Swiss professional like Bouquet, knew that they were going to ambush a relief column. Would its commander and his men meet the same fate as had Braddock's force in the same wilderness eight years before?

Bushy Run: Indians, Highlanders, and Light Infantry Mix it Up

Bouquet rested his right foot on a stump, plunked his gold-laced hat down on his knee, and wiped back his sweat-streaked hair with his linen handkerchief. He could see all kinds of low stumps that offered inviting seats, but he was not going to rest while his men were still marching. As far as he could see to his front, the double files of his Royal Americans shared Forbes Road with companies of the 42nd Highlanders from the main body of the column. It was a road in name only, really a track hacked out by General Forbes' axmen five years before and now walled in by dense stands of timber and matted thickets. Some of the tall oaks had since grown canopies whose tops almost joined over the wilderness trail. The forest with its towering trees and thick underbrush held in the August heat, and although it shaded the plodding files from the noon-high sun, the scarlet jackets of Highlanders and provincials showed dark sweat patches under the arms and down the open fronts. Most of the light infantry and the Scots marched bare-headed, their caps or bonnets tucked under the tops of their packs, but Bouquet could see an occasional bear-skin-tufted, blue bonnet topping a stubborn Scottish head.

This is the eighteenth day, he thought, *since we marched out of Carlisle. We've crossed the Alleghenies—easier done than I'd have believed—then the high Laurel Hills, and now Chestnut Ridge is behind us. We've made something like seventeen miles today and we should be approaching the site of the abandoned blockhouse near Bushy*

Run. If I'm not mistaken I see that Byerly has dropped back from the advance party to report something.

Andrew Byerly's battered cocked hat and stained brown homespun marked him clearly for the wilderness farmer he was. Bouquet had been delighted to recruit Byerly's services as a guide for this stage of the march since he had only recently been driven from his farm near Bushy Run Creek and knew the local terrain better than any scout. And Bouquet had heeded his suggestion that the column make an afternoon halt at the old blockhouse. After that Bouquet planned to make a night crossing of Turtle Creek, thus avoiding a daytime march through the steep defiles along that creek, an ideal spot for an ambush.

Byerly raised a knuckle to his hat, a gesture that amused Bouquet, as he acknowledged the "salute." The blond young farmer used the back of his saluting hand to wipe the sweat from his forehead.

"Colonel, your advance men are coming up on Edge Hill just off the right of the road. That puts them about a half-mile from Bushy Run," Byerly said.

"Good, but you needn't have brought the word yourself. Now you're going to have to run to catch up with the advance party," Bouquet said.

"I know a path that cuts across the long bend in the road, so I'll be back with them in no time."

"Very well, but is that all? Have the rangers seen any signs at all?"

"Not a thing that we know of. It has been a quiet morning's march, not a sound from the woods on either side."

"Just too quiet, I'd think. Well, be off with you, and next time let one of the soldiers carry back any message."

Byerly knuckled his crude salute and trotted off, slipping through the left file of light infantry and vanishing into a gap between two thickets. He was scarcely out of Bouquet's sight and mind when the first firing began. Up ahead and far out of sight there was a scattered banging of muskets followed by the sharper crack of rifles. In seconds the musketry grew in volume until it sounded to Bouquet like a series of ragged volleys. But he knew it for what it was—not volley fire but the uncontrolled firing of scores of Indian muskets, perhaps hundreds. He put on his hat and looked around into the wide-eyed stare of the young lieutenant at his side. No better time to teach this youngster how an officer should behave at the prospect of action; he fetched out his watch, looked down at it, and carefully put it back in a pocket of his waistcoat.

"Hardly on one o'clock. It seems that lunch will be delayed somewhat this afternoon. Would you mind going forward and telling Major Campbell with the advance guard to be prepared to send his companies to the support of the advance party? Messengers will find me at the head of the main body," Bouquet said.

The lieutenant's stare was still awe-filled, but he had the presence of mind to salute before he took off at a run up the column.

In a matter of minutes Major Campbell's return message convinced Bouquet that his first fears had been well founded.

If my ears and Campbell's messenger tell me the same thing this is no mere harassment of my column. No, they're in numbers strong enough to make an ambush. But why have they attacked only the advance party? I've gotten no reports from the rangers covering each flank. Perhaps the Indian chiefs haven't coordinated their movements yet; that has happened more than once in their attacks. And if that's the case a quickly mounted counterattack, in force, could wreck their schemes for an ambush.

Bouquet's orders to the assembled company commanders and the officers with the convoy were, as always in an action, brief and to the point.

"We will deploy the forward companies on line in advance of the convoy for a frontal attack to pass through the advance guard. We'll rely on the bayonet after the men have fired their first shot. When the advance guard has been passed through, it will re-form as the reserve.

"I want the pack horses assembled off the left side of the road on that hill slope back there.

"The rear guard will close up and form to protect the assembly of the convoy. That is all; we move out at once."

Bouquet went forward to take post in an interval between his Royal Americans, deploying on the left of the road, and the companies of the 42nd, coming into line on the right. He took advantage of a felled oak log to stand and observe the deployment. Bouquet's provincials, accustomed to moving in open order, came into line long before the Scots. Seeing that they were under the eye of their commander, the Royal Americans, their scarlet jackets and blue facings flashing through the trees and thickets, darted into line and waited derisively for the Highlanders to come up even with them.

Bouquet watched the colorful 42nd line forming deliberately, marching with shouldered arms, bright red jackets contrasting with the *feilidh beag,* the small kilt with the dark green background of the Campbell tartan. For a moment Bouquet felt himself the victim of an illusion, for the Highlanders' lower legs were hidden in the undergrowth while the dark green tartan of their kilts had blended so naturally with the shaded green of the forest that their scarlet jackets seemed to float by themselves through the underbrush.

He had no time to muse about illusions. The company commanders were signalling their readiness to advance, the Scots with an upward flash of their claymores,* the Royal American officers with their hats raised overhead. Bouquet dropped his arm to the front and the double-ranked line went forward as shouldered muskets came down to Charge Bayonet to present a gleaming hedge of steel to the enemy. Drums were beating the long roll and high above the steady drumbeat came the high-pitched skirl of the 42nd's bagpipes. This was no shoulder-to-shoulder drill-ground maneuver since the companies had to move in open order to make their way around thickets and through the trees. Yet Bouquet was noting with approval that the overall formation remained intact so that a line was maintained in spite of the rugged terrain.

As the attack swept forward, the skirl of pipes and the roll of the drums began to fade under the crashes of musketry in the woods ahead. When Bouquet's line came up to the rear of the advance guard's line, he saw that Major Campbell had deployed his companies in extended order with the men taking cover behind trees and logs, firing back individually at their enemy. Bouquet's spirits lifted at the sight.

Mon dieu, it may be that these Scots can learn after all. So my instructions to their officers and sergeants at Carlisle and on the march haven't been wasted. I must find Campbell before I can follow the attack.

Bouquet found that Campbell was waiting for him. The red-faced, perspiring major had discarded his scarlet, gold-laced coat and hung it on a stump along with his sword belt and scabbard. His white waistcoat showed grey patches of sweatstains, but it was clear that it was not simply the steaming heat of the forest that was sending rivers of sweat down his chest and back. He was the picture of the clansman rel-

---

*The Scottish basket-hilted broadsword.

ishing the heat and smell of battle as he paced back and forth, bared claymore in hand, meeting messengers and dispatching them back to their companies with new orders. When he caught sight of Bouquet he saluted and made his report.

"Twelve of the eighteen rangers with the advance party fell in the surprise attack on them. I carried through with a bayonet attack but the Indians just kept melting away before us. They'd stand and fire until the bayonets bore down on them, then they'd simply disappear in the woods. So after I got the word of your general advance I formed up here, as you see. I've no count of killed and wounded yet, but that will be in soon. I'm ready to reassemble my companies as soon as your line has passed through."

"You've done well and that won't be forgotten," Bouquet said. "When you speak of the count of killed or wounded, remember that the tactics you've used here will cut that accounting to a fraction of what it would have been if your men had tried to stand and fire in close order. Now I've got to catch up with the advance. One thing you must do when your companies have re-formed—be prepared to deploy a company to each flank to act as flank guards in case I must withdraw this attacking force back to the convoy." Bouquet was gone without waiting for Campbell's acknowledgement.

There was a lull in the Indians' firing as they became aware of the advance of the British main body. The lull died to silence before the steady advance of the long line of bayonets, and the braves faded away into the dense forest just as they had when Campbell's men had made their bayonet attack. The elation Bouquet had felt on seeing Campbell's firing line faded away too as he realized what was coming. In another hundred yards the silence was shattered by a fusilade from the forest to front and flanks. The only signs of the new ambuscade were the muzzle flashes of the Indian muskets and the puffs of white smoke that followed; nothing else was revealed, not a feather or scalp-lock, so cleverly concealed were the Indian warriors among the trees and underbrush.

Following Bouquet's orders, the British infantry had withheld their fire until this moment. The line halted long enough to deliver a crashing volley and dashed forward with lowered bayonets. A new sound arose to replace the banging of musketry. All through the woods resounded the war whoops and shrill yells of the Indians as they darted back to new cover.

As he had feared, Bouquet's attack was having the effect

of a sword thrust piercing thin air, and that was only the prelude to a new predicament. Hardly had the bayonet assault been launched when a buckskin-clad rifleman arrived with a message from Lieutenant Randall, commanding the rangers. The Indians had started to mass on the flanks of the British advance in such swarms that the ranger flank-guards had had to fall back in haste to avoid being overrun. There was nothing to do but order a withdrawal, and Bouquet wasted no time in sending aides scurrying to the companies with the order. His last message went to Major Campbell.

"Tell the major to deploy a company to each flank as I had directed him. He must see my flanks secured so that my main body can make an orderly withdrawal," Bouquet ordered, as he turned his attention back to his companies.

To his great relief the troops were retiring in good order, in steady lines with no confusion showing anywhere. Off to either flank the growing rattle of musketry told all too well of the new threat of the extending Indian attack.

Moving just as they did on Braddock, Bouquet thought, *to encircle the whole force. But these are not Braddock's troops, and I'm not Braddock. We're going to do this right and we're going to join up with the rear guard to form a perimeter around the convoy. That hill where I had the pack horses drawn up will make a good defensive position, and my next concern is to get the position organized—as soon as I can get the companies directed to their positions.*

Now the war crys and firing of the Indians were concentrating on the flanks, though the retreating British main line was still getting a harassing fire from muskets and arrows. But Campbell's Highlanders were keeping the flanks secure, and Bouquet used the brief breathing spell to get new orders to his company commanders.

When the last company had reached the lower slopes of the hill and contact had been established all around, Bouquet sent new orders to assemble his commanders on the hilltop. He had hoped for a respite in order to get in reports and make the inspections to assure that the dozens of details for the defense were attended to: carrying in the wounded to a central point, directing ammunition parties to the supply point, and a host of others. But his enemies were not going to slow down their assaults, and a fresh disaster was looming that could destroy the convoy.

As war whoops rose around the perimeter, new assaults were launched time and again against each part of the circle.

Each party of painted, screaming braves was repulsed with aimed fire and then the bayonet when the Indians charged up to a section of the defensive ring. The Indian chiefs were quick to seize on a new opportunity that would threaten the British from an unexpected quarter. They pressed new attacks with arrows and muskets against the circle of pack horses. Whinnying horses—mad with fright—broke loose, plunging and rearing, to break out of the cordon and into the woods. There was no use in trying to restrain or capture the horses, for their civilian drivers and teamsters had sought cover in the thickets at the first sign of attack.

After a counterattack by a company of Royal Americans had driven off the threat against the convoy, Bouquet was able to take stock of the situation. He called his commanders to a hurried conference on the hilltop. The grave faces of his officers reminded him that it was going to take leadership of the highest order to keep the morale of the men at a fighting pitch, and it was only from him that the officers could catch that spirit. He began by looking at Major Campbell who returned his look with a fighter's grin.

"Well," Bouquet began, "they have got us surrounded— the poor devils!"

A quick glance around the half-circle of faces revealed eyes bright with surprise and a sense of relieved tension. This was the Bouquet whose name was known to every soldier and ranger across the frontiers, the strange foreigner who knew more about Indian fighting than the Indians themselves. If he stood confident in this situation, then things couldn't be hopeless. Bouquet went on quickly to seize the advantage of his pause.

"The rangers report at least five tribes' warriors out there—Shawnees, Mingoes, Delawares, Hurons, and Ottawas—and there may be others. They may outnumber us, but we don't know that to be a fact. What we do know is this: it's got to be our fight all the way because there'll be no column coming to relieve us. But remember this, we've got plenty of food and ammunition, and we have the best men with us because all the sickly and weak were dropped off to garrison Forts Bedford and Ligonier. Every man is a fighter, and all they need is you to keep their spirits up. But above all remember this—those whooping devils out there are, sooner or later, going to make a mistake. They always have because they have no organization and no discipline to act as a controlled force, and their chiefs have no overall control of this hodgepodge of tribesmen. Finally, if there are any signs of faint hearts—though I don't anticipate any signs of such—a gentle reminder will suffice to restore the fight in a man; if we were to give up and surrender, the same fate would await every man. There won't be any lucky ones to die by the tomahawk; to be roasted alive is the least to expect. Now, to the business of organizing our defenses."

Bouquet went on with the details: closing gaps between companies, the exercise of fire discipline, ammunition resupply, followed by a quick dismissal of the officers to their units.

The lull that followed Bouquet's counterattack was short-lived. No sooner had he overseen order restored in the convoy area than the Indians' attacks were renewed all around the beleaguered perimeter. But Bouquet was quick to sense the lack of concerted control by the tribal chiefs. Although the succession of stinging attacks was battering the defenders unmercifully, the assaults were repulsed with bullet and bayonet because each effort, no matter how fiercely mounted, was a local effort. Bouquet had the satisfaction of knowing that his officers were realizing the truth of the counsel he had just given them. Still, Bouquet knew, the enemy's leaders were well aware of the great advantage that now lay with their cause. The British were surrounded, cut off from any conceivable relief, and without access to water. Thus time was on their side and their local attacks, even if they subsided to occasional sniping, would make the battle one of attrition.

Yet, as the afternoon wore on, the Indians continued their ferocious attacks at different sections of Bouquet's defenses, seemingly careless of casualties. A group would deliver a heavy fire from concealed positions then spring to the attack with yells and war whoops intended to terrify the defenders as the painted braves drove to break through the cordon. Each time the assault was met with a controlled volley followed by platoon-strength bayonet charges. And each time the Indians, leaping from cover to cover, vanished like smoke in the forest.

Bouquet, observing the pattern of these local attacks and counterattacks, carried his admonishing word in person and by messenger to his commanders:

"Stop making counterattacks with the bayonet. They do no good and the Indians know they're wearing us down when they run to cover. Instead, make the men lie flat, even though it's hard to load a musket in that position. Then pair off your men for loading and firing, so that one man's musket is always loaded and can cover his partner while he is reloading."

Nom de nom, am I the only one who seems to remember what happened at Braddock's ambush? Bouquet asked himself. *How he raged at the Virginia militia when they took cover on the ground, and how he ordered them to stand up and re-form in ranks—so that instead of killing Indians with aimed fire they could stand in formation and be slaughtered like his British regulars! Well, with God's help I've stopped that nonsense. Now there is the matter of getting the wounded under cover and tended to.*

By three o'clock Bouquet's wounded totaled thirty-five, all of whom had to be carried up to the open hilltop and laid out in an area where they could be cared for. Even in that location they were not safe from enemy fire, since every point within the circular defense could be reached by an Indian bullet. Bouquet listened to the suggestions made by his convoy commander and ordered a work party formed from teamsters and drivers to haul flour bags up the hill. At the top Bouquet's adjutant directed the construction of a circular wall of bags to protect the wounded.

That matter attended to, Bouquet resumed the point-to-point round of his units over the protests of the company commanders, who appeared to be far more concerned for his safety than he was. He did yield to Capt. Tom Basset's persuasion that he shed his scarlet uniform coat and hand it to a sergeant, who hung it over a tree limb. The wisdom of the captain's suggestion was shown to Bouquet on a later visit to the position when Basset pointed out fourteen bullets imbedded in the tree where the coat had hung.

Moving on in white breeches and waistcoat Bouquet used his calm presence and resolute bearing to steady his men and maintain their confidence in him and in themselves. With his sure insight he could feel that confidence had bred confidence, and his eyes told him that his system of fire control was showing its worth all around the perimeter. His tactical methods continued to pay off as the Indians found that their rushes to break through the cordon were proving too costly in casualties and were no longer effective in drawing the British from their covered positions to waste their strength in futile bayonet charges.

Yet, in spite of Bouquet's show of optimism and his soldiers' trust in him, time was on the side of his enemy. The chiefs knew as well as Bouquet that any attempt on his part to advance or retire with his whole force would expose his command to disaster. They knew too that the encircled British were running out of water with no hope of getting any even by digging. What they did not know was that their enemy had long since emptied every water bottle and there was none left even for the wounded whose sufferings were being redoubled by thirst.

By late afternoon the Indians had resorted to sniping and shooting arrows while constantly moving from one hidden cover to another. But they showed no intention of letting up on the harassment of the British, and their change in tactics was causing casualties and tying down the defenders as much as had their earlier rushes.

This kind of action continued to wear down the British until nightfall. The exhausted men had been fighting for seven hours, from the initial ambuscade at one o'clock until eight when the blessed darkness closed in. And that seven hours of fighting had followed seventeen miles of marching over rugged terrain in the worst of the summer's heat. One consolation alone could comfort Bouquet's men: the Indians feared to attack an unbeaten enemy at night. Yet that knowledge was to be offset by sporadic sniping and shouted taunts coming out of the darkness. Even so, rest could be taken in relays so that each would get his turn. Each except the commander.

Major Campbell had to take off his hat and stoop to enter the candlelit shelter where Bouquet sat writing his after-action report. The tiny cubicle, walled with flour bags and roofed with a stretched tent, was so cramped that the only other seat was Bouquet's cot. The Colonel motioned for Campbell take his seat on it, laid aside his pen, and stared for a moment into the Major's blue eyes.

"That cot was not intended for a chair, so feel free to stretch your legs out there," Bouquet said.

Campbell, glad to take a rest, did as his commander suggested and stretched his booted legs toward the entrance.

"You're here to report on security measures, I know, so get on with it," Bouquet said.

"Yes, but first, Sir, the confirmed dead and wounded, if you don't mind," Campbell said.

"Of course, Allan, I didn't know you'd made another count."

"Late returns, Sir. There are twenty-five dead out there and—"

"You don't have to say it," Bouquet broke in, "we have no way to recover them after the withdrawal to this hill, and those bodies will, by now, have been under the scalping knife. Go on."

"Thank you for saving me that. The wounded total thirty-five, some uncertain of recovery, and there's no water for them."

"Or for anyone, I know. Have you finished your check with company commanders on security measures for the perimeter?" Bouquet asked.

"I have, Colonel. No fires anywhere and no pipes to be lit by officer or soldier—"

"Standards good for any forest bivouac, but I think the business about tobacco a bit *de trop*. Is there a man out there whose throat is not drier than his tobacco pouch?"

The tough Campbell face cracked enough to allow a dour smile. He had long since given up trying to anticipate what this incredible colonel would say next.

"Every company has double sentries at least fifty yards advanced from the perimeter and these are backed up by outposts. Reliefs have been assigned at short intervals so that there's no danger of men tired as these falling asleep on post," Campbell said.

"Excellent, now one more thing. Have arrangements been made for the men not on guard to lie down in their formations?"

"The men are sleeping—if you can call it that—under arms, each where he can take up the firing position he'd been in at nightfall."

"Thank you, Allan. Now why don't you see if you can get some sort of rest. I don't have to tell you that those painted fiends will be after us again at first light."

Left with his thoughts Bouquet picked up his pen, then laid it down.

Mon Dieu, what did I do to deserve such rotten luck? My frontal attack took us within a half-mile of the creek, but of course I had to withdraw to save the convoy and to set up the defense back here. So now every man has to suffer from thirst and with no promise of relief. And to think of young Byerly volunteering to make his way through the Indian lines to fetch water for the wounded! If he could have carried a hundred water bottles like I'd carry my hat, he wouldn't have gotten two hundred yards before those devils got him—then what would have happened to him? No, I was right in keeping him here.

I've read that Cortés and his army had their noche triste *when they were driven out of Tenochtitlan, but at least he could share that with his men. Henry Bouquet has to spend his "sad night" alone, at least where it comes to sharing the anguish of the mind. But no one made me take this command, and this must be a part of it.*

There is no use in my wasting time tonight in making plans that will never come to fruition. I must wait until those Indians present me with even the slightest opportunity, one mistake of theirs, one chance that I can seize on. Something to make them stand and fight, something that will allow my troops to get at them with the bayonet as well as the bullet. But there I go, enough of wishful thinking, it is simply that I must be ready to seize my opening.

If there is no victory for me tomorrow, then there is no hope— no hope for this command, for Fort Pitt, and for all the Northwest Territory. With my force gone the last settler will be driven from his land or he and his family massacred.

I must get on with this letter to Amherst. If we fail tomorrow there may be a chance for a mounted and escorted courier to escape with this. But I am not going to fail tomorrow.

He picked up his pen again and went on with his next paragraph:

"Whatever our fate may be, I thought it necessary to give your excellency this information, so that you may, at all events, take such measures as you will think proper with the provinces for their own safety and the effectual relief of Fort Pitt. In case of another engagement I fear insurmountable difficulties in protecting and transporting our provisions, being already so weakened by the losses of this day, in men and horses; and there is the additional necessity of carrying the wounded, whose situation is truly deplorable."

The sentry outside the commander's tent paused in his pacing to listen to a renewed burst of Indian war-whooping and a ragged salvo of musket shots. As he turned back to his duty he could see his colonel's shadow silhouetted like an outline of a bust in the candlelight. His head was bent to his writing and he didn't look up.

The restless night wore on into early morning with the men catching a few winks in relays in spite of the sniping and howling from the dark forest. Most were exhausted enough to at least rest their bodies even if sleep would not come.

Promptly at first light the Indians launched a new series

of attacks much as Bouquet had anticipated. Although the British were as prepared as men could be under the conditions, casualties continued to mount. The greater part of the encircled cordon was suffering under a hail of bullets and arrows fired by an unseen foe who was taking every advantage of the plentiful natural cover. As the August sun rose higher and grew hotter, renewed torments of thirst began to plague the men until—as Bouquet would say in his next report—they were "distressed to the last Degree by a total want of Water, much more intolerable than the Enemy's Fire."

The weakening condition of the troops was not lost on the Indian chiefs who led their braves to come in even closer, becoming more brazen with every effort. There were taunts in broken English, and Bouquet caught a glimpse of a Delaware chief whom he recognized as Keelyushung, a bold leader whose English was better than most.

"You have thirst now, Englishmen, but wait until we roast you as soon as the sun is high," he shouted from behind a thick tree.

Bouquet resumed his rounds of the companies, continually encouraging the men to reserve their fire for clearly exposed targets and not to waste breath in shouting replies to the insults thrown at them from the woods.

"Better one good shot for revenge than all the hollering in the world," he told a section of Highlanders on the north side of the circle.

At the end of the fifth hour—the renewed Indian attack had begun at five o'clock—Bouquet's spirits had reached their nadir, though he could still conceal that from the officers and men. He had to shake his head to clear away the numbness brought on by physical and mental exhaustion.

These men have performed wonders for the past twenty hours, but they can't endure much longer. And if we all weaken to the point of collapse, all about the same time, the Indians will discover it and overrun us, especially if they can manage some kind of final concerted effort.

He leaned against the trunk of a great oak on the eastern slope of the hill and tried to look out over the companies farther down the slope. He strained his reddened eyes trying to detect the movement of any enemy in the distant trees, but he could make out nothing. It certainly was quiet in those woods in front of this sector. There the realization struck him like the blow of a fist.

Those companies down there are as alert as could be expected, but they're not firing a shot! And there's no fire coming from the woods in front of them! Can it be? Can it be what I am thinking?

He ran as fast as his stiff legs could carry him back to his tiny command post.

"Lieutenant Dow," he shouted, "send for Major Campbell, Captain Basset, and their company officers. Run, man, and tell them to get up here at a run!"

In minutes he was issuing orders to the assembled officers in a flow that threatened to inundate their weary minds, yet all were following him intently.

"Listen now and carefully, for I've got no time for questions and answers. By God, they have done it! The Indians have finally given us the chance to strike them where we can beat them on our terms.

"Their circle around us is no longer complete. They have thinned out to nothing for at least two hundred yards on each

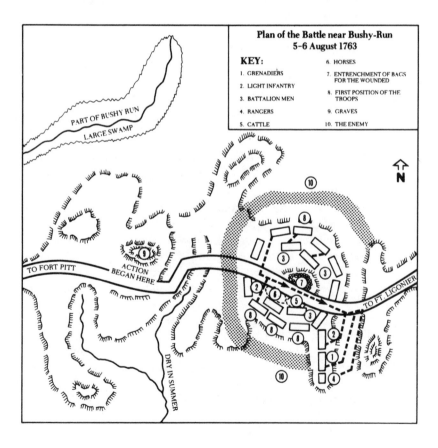

Plan of the Battle near Bushy-Run
5–6 August 1763

KEY:

1. GRENADIERS
2. LIGHT INFANTRY
3. BATTALION MEN
4. RANGERS
5. CATTLE
6. HORSES
7. ENTRENCHMENT OF BAGS FOR THE WOUNDED
8. FIRST POSITION OF THE TROOPS
9. GRAVES
10. THE ENEMY

PART OF BUSHY RUN

LARGE SWAMP

TO FORT PITT

ACTION BEGAN HERE

DRY IN SUMMER

TO FT. LIGONIER

N

side of the road back toward Fort Ligonier, on the eastern face of our perimeter. They have left two flanks open, and they don't yet realize it. Now see that spur that extends southward from the lower slope of this hill. Note that the spur begins just about where the Ligonier road starts to ascend our hill.

"We are going to use that spur to hide our counterattacking force. Major Campbell, you will lead the attack and you will have two companies, the 3rd Light Infantry Company and the Grenadiers of your 42nd. Your left flank will be covered by a detachment of rangers. You will form your line under cover on the east side of the spur, prepared to attack, on my signal, to the west against the Indians' south flank. Major Campbell's force will be supported by two companies of the 60th under Captain Basset. All four companies—Major Campbell's plus Captain Basset's—will be withdrawn from the west side of the perimeter."

Bouquet's orders continued to pour out in a torrent as the details of his battle plan fell into place, and every officer involved in its maneuvers knew his role in executing the plan. When Bouquet had finished, he dismissed his officers with this charge:

"Every man in this command has been aching to thrust a bayonet into one of those red devils, and here is his opportunity. I want to see every Indian we get in the open slaughtered or driven, like the mad beasts they are, from this ground. Now, to your stations."

He took post on the western slope of the hill just below the flour bag fort. From there he could watch the withdrawal of Campbell's and Basset's four companies. As the men of those companies rose from cover and assembled into ranks, he could see other companies on either flank extending their fronts to cover the gap that would be left by the four withdrawing companies. The men who were closing the gap passed just below him as their officers directed them to new positions, tightening the circle into a greatly shrunken perimeter. While the extending files were taking cover on the hillside, Bouquet saw the red jackets and green kilts of Campbell's Highlanders moving to form column on the road below him. Their commander was losing no time in moving his companies out. As the last files came out of the trees and onto the road, Campbell was ordering them into a double-time march that moved his two companies as fast as the stumps and ruts of the road would allow. While the Highlanders and the light infantry company were double-timing to the east, Basset's two companies had completed their withdrawal and were following on the heels of Campbell's men.

When he was satisfied that the gap had been closed and the new west side of the perimeter tightened in, Bouquet moved to the east end of the flour-bagged enclosure where he could get a panoramic view of the south half of the perimeter and the ground sloping outward from it. Peering through the trees he watched the scarlet flow of Campbell's column come to a halt and face into line. At Campbell's next command the companies wheeled to their right to disappear into the forest on the east side of the spur. He waved an acknowledgment to the courier Campbell had posted on the roadside to await Bouquet's signal to launch the attack.

He turned his attention to Basset's companies who had halted on the road just short of Campbell's courier. The late morning sun was reflected in flashes from the bayonets of the light infantry as they filed southward to positions at the bottom of the hill below the cattle corral. Then they too disappeared as they sought cover for their new firing line.

A renewed roar of musketry and wild whooping told Bouquet that the Indians were closing in on the west side of the perimeter.

This will be the boldest attack the chiefs can launch, he thought. *They think we've been beaten into a retreat and they will be going all out to overrun us from the west and take this hill and all the "victims" on it. Now if they will only mass on the west and south to make that final attack, we will have them where we want them.*

Bouquet's thoughts became reality as the whooping and firing reached a new crescendo. Painted warriors burst into the open, dashing forward against the British circle from the west and south. The braves were recklessly exposing themselves as they came running out of the thickets. He watched, fascinated by the naked bodies flashing through the trees, shaven heads and scalplocks shining and bobbing, as the Indians came on at a dead run. Most of them had discarded their muskets and ran with tomahawk in hand, ready to close in for the kill.

He saw that the officers were carrying out his orders to withhold the fire of the companies until every shot would tell. When the foremost warriors were within fifty paces the volley crashed out from the defenders. The volley smoke had not cleared as the infantrymen stood up and rapidly reloaded their muskets. A second volley rang out as Bouquet saw a scattering of Indians burst through the smoke to be met by the bayonets of the soldiers. As the smoke cleared he saw the ground littered with Indian dead and wounded, but beyond them new waves of warriors were massing among the trees two hundred yards beyond the littered ground.

This was the moment. To wait any longer would risk the rupture of the British cordon and certain destruction of the command. Bouquet picked up his fusil and held it overhead at arm's length, then dropped his arms bringing the light musket to the level of his knees. He saw Campbell's courier repeat his signal before he darted into the forest toward his commander. In seconds Bouquet witnessed the most pleasant sight of his career.

The long line of Campbell's Highlanders and light infantry emerged from the forest at the foot of the western slope of the spur. The scarlet line, topped by a crest of gleaming bayonets, swept forward toward the exposed flank of the Indians who were renewing their attack on the south perimeter. Bouquet heard the distant ring of Campbell's command, and the British line snapped to a halt. A hundred muskets came down as one at the next command, all levelled at the mob of yelling savages. He saw Campbell's claymore flash downward and heard his shouted—"Fire!"

The volley crashed into the crowd of warriors at a distance of thirty yards, leaving scores of dead and wounded heaped in front of the advancing British line. Campbell had not allowed time for his companies to reload. The Scots and the Royal Americans charged into the mass of Indians with lowered bayonets. A number of intrepid braves stood and fired back, but the greatest number stood for a second or two, stunned by the surprise volley and the sight most dreaded by Indian warriors—the line of cold steel charging at their naked bodies. The mass then turned and fled westward, but their troubles had only begun. Their headlong retreat led them straight across the front of Basset's waiting companies. A beautifully-directed volley laid low another swath of braves before Basset's light infantry broke from cover. They fell into line on the right flank of their Highland comrades and joined in the bayonet assault. There arose a combined chorus of ferocious Highland yells and American cheers as the pent-up fury of the long-suffering infantry was unleashed on their

The Black Watch at Bushy Run by C. W. Jeffries

hated enemy. Now the bayonet came into its own as the charging British infantry thrust away at the backs of the fleeing Indians. The Scots and the Royal Americans left a mounting trail of Indian bodies in their wake. The four united companies continued their attack to the west, then on command wheeled and fell on the now-exposed flank and rear of the mass of warriors who had been attacking the perimeter from the west.

This body of Indians, seeing destruction bearing down on them, became a pack of fugitives which Campbell's and Basset's companies pursued, leaving a new trail of Indian corpses behind them. Bouquet watched the Scots and Royal Americans vanish into the woods still in chase of bloody retribution. Bouquet was to learn later from Campbell that the pursuit had been a complete success; the Indians had dispersed in hopeless confusion, never to reunite.

For a matter of minutes, while Campbell's and Basset's men were driving off Indians from the south and west of the circle, the rest of the Indians broke off their attacks. Then, seeing the fate of their comrades, they turned and joined in their flight.

Quiet had settled over the bloody hill and the corpse-littered forest to its south and west before Bouquet had time to sag down to a seat on the flour-bag wall to collect his thoughts. The stillness, after twenty-two hours of battle, had so stunned his senses that he sat motionless for a space of time. Finally, he could turn to his officers and give his orders for reassembling his command and marching it on toward Bushy Run and life-restoring water.

Bouquet's victory did not come without cost. His little force, fewer than 500 strong before battle, lost 50 killed, 60 wounded, and 5 missing, a total of 115, almost a fourth of the command. Yet damaging as the losses were to Bouquet, the effects of Bushy Run were indeed as far-reaching as they were rewarding to the British settlements in America. The most immediate effect was the relief of Fort Pitt, but that was only the beginning. Bushy Run had a powerfully negative effect on the Indian tribes. Not only had they been soundly whipped, they had been beaten at their own game of ambush. Additionally, Bushy Run was a decisive action, in spite of the small numbers engaged, because it proved to be a turning point in Pontiac's War. From there on, the Indians were no longer on the offensive, and eventually Pontiac's grand vision of driving the English into the sea led only to surrender. In 1764, a year after Bushy Run, Bouquet led an expedition of 1,500 men into the depths of Shawnee and Delaware country. In a display of force—not a shot was fired—he recovered over 300 white captives from the Indian tribes and made peace while laying the groundwork for the treaties that followed. In all, Bouquet proved himself an able statesman as well as a soldier honored by the frontier peoples, white and Indian.

In regard to the battle itself and the decisive moments in it, one aspect deserves examination. It seems to be fashionable to refer to Bouquet's decisive maneuver as an act of "desperation." The precedent may have been set by Sir John Fortescue (*History of the British Army*, 1911, III, 17) when he referred to Bouquet's action as "a last desperate resource." The adjectives are at best misleading. While there can be little doubt that Bouquet conceived and executed a plan in a dangerous situation, one should evaluate the man and his methods before accepting an implication that he acted in desperation at Bushy Run.

Although I have sketched Bouquet's background and represented dramatically his actions in the battle, a closer look

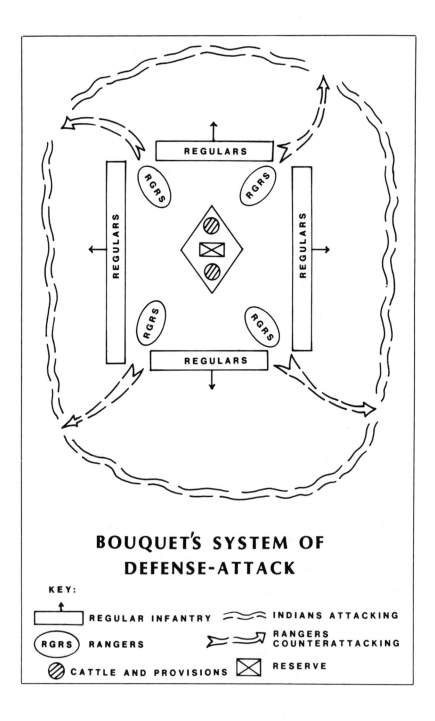

BOUQUET'S SYSTEM OF DEFENSE-ATTACK

KEY:

REGULAR INFANTRY   INDIANS ATTACKING

RGRS RANGERS   RANGERS COUNTERATTACKING

CATTLE AND PROVISIONS   RESERVE

at his tactical analyses and concepts will shed more light on the reasons and reasoning for his perception and decisions at Bushy Run. These brief extracts from Bouquet's writings will illustrate the man's insight and methods. He summed up Indian tactics this way:

> "The first, that their general maxim is to surround their enemy.
> "The second, that they fight scattered, and never in a compact body.
> "The third, that they never stand their ground when attacked, but immediately give way to return to the charge."

Bouquet went on to develop, in detail, conceptual models as guides for dealing tactically with Indian methods of forest fighting. The sketch is a simplified diagram of his system of shifting from the defensive to the offensive against an Indian force which has encircled a British force composed of regular troops and rangers. The essence of this tactical method lies in the counterattack (charges covered by fire from the defensive circle) that breaks the Indian encirclement into segments, thus creating artificial flanks which can be attacked in turn. In the final steps the regulars and rangers unite in rolling up the exposed flanks, demoralizing the Indians with cold steel charges (bayonet and tomahawk) followed by a relentless pursuit until the enemy is destroyed or dispersed.

These illustrative examples, taken from his extensive studies and correspondence, are positive indicators that Bouquet's experience and study led to the formulation of principles that were firmly set in his mind. What he exercised at Bushy Run was no more than an imaginative adaptation of his own ideas. He didn't need to be pushed to desperation in order to react effectively. All he needed was an opportunity to use his limited resources in a manner that would ensure success. His cool courage enabled him to wait until his keen perception could sense that opportunity, then his flexible mind came up with a practicable solution.

Judgment

> In the next place I experienced in myself a certain capacity for
> judging which I have doubtless received from God, like all the
> other things I possess; and as He could not desire to deceive
> me, it is clear that He has not given me a faculty that will lead
> me to err if I use it aright.
>
> —Descartes, *Meditations* (IV)

If we can accept Descartes' statement as he intended—that
is, not applying solely to him as an individual but to all rational men—we have a base for observing judgment in a
practical way. If we can further accept that base as being a
sound one (what other kind would we want?), it should be
enlarged by one assumption: that all rational men possess the
faculty of judgment, *but in varying degree*. Looking again at
Descartes' declaration, the last five words, "if I use it aright,"
point toward that difference in the quality of judgment as we
observe it in different men. There is no need to pursue this
thought with the idea of proving, through abstract reasoning,
that judgment varies from person to person. All that anyone
need do is search his memory to find examples of good and
bad judgment in private life or in public. Remember the time
your neighbor got fleeced by the con artists who were going
to resurface his driveway? Or the time your congressman finally did something right and voted against that tax bill—as
you had urged?

If we are going to observe the practical application of judgment, we should not overlook that twin quality that led Voltaire to point out: "common sense is not so common." We all use the term in daily life, but just what is common sense? The Oxford English Dictionary tells us that it is: "The endowment of natural intelligence possessed by rational beings; ordinary, normal or average understanding; the plain wisdom which is every man's inheritance . . . More emphatically: Good sound practical sense . . . general sagacity."

Then if we agree (as Voltaire would not) that we are generally sagacious, our next step would be to define judgment as it should be exercised by a leader in warfare. I would propose: *The ability to make a sound assessment of what he knows of the enemy and his own command, decide upon a practicable course of action, and act upon it.*

In the next case we will watch the actions of a leader that have caused his judgment to be questioned by some and defended by others.

The Battle of the Little Bighorn

Thus we see how all the judgements that are founded upon external appearances, are marvelously uncertain and doubtful; and that there is no so certain testimony as every one is to himself.

Montaigne, *The Essays* (II, 16)

Many Americans, old or young, might think of the Battle of the Little Bighorn as a contest between dance-band trumpeters, but if one calls it "Custer's Last Stand" everyone recognizes this minor military disaster that has been turned into a legend of almost epic proportions. Why such recognition?

In the most matter-of-fact terms it is the most written-about battle in American history, but that simple answer poses another "why." In over a hundred years no other event in our frontier history has so stirred the imagination of Americans. It was—is—a tragedy wrapped in a mystery with a bright side lit by heroic action and a dark side shadowed by the unknown. Its leader gained for himself glory in death and defeat that has far exceeded his grasp for it during his adventurous life. That glory and the legend that grew up around it have kindled a controversy that continues to be fanned by a succession of such a curious assortment of stokers as historians, dime novelists, responsible and irresponsible journalists, poets, military "experts," and movie scriptwriters. Out of all this has evolved an accumulated store of "Custeriana" which is continually being probed by Custerphiles and Custerphobes. The former maintain that the only orders known to exist gave full rein to Custer's aggressiveness, and had his subordinates Reno and Benteen given their full measure of duty things would have been different. The Custerphobes say that Custer disobeyed orders, began his battle prematurely, and risked the lives of his whole command in a reckless attack designed to restore the prestige which the "American Murat" had lost in the public eye.

Things have gotten so hot in a critical sense over the years that a friend of mine who had become interested in the battle essayed to enter the lists but quickly withdrew when his opening statement was challenged. When I asked him why on earth did he back out if only his first assertion had been disputed, he replied, yes, it was his only statement, but it had been that the twenty-fifth of June, 1876, was a Sunday.

There are things, however, that we do know. Foremost is the knowledge that when Lieutenant-Colonel Custer, formerly Major-General of Volunteers, led five companies of his 7th Cavalry down into Medicine Tail Coulee that Sunday afternoon, not a man was ever seen alive again by white men. There are other ascertainable facts that will be outlined in a moment in bare-bones form, but first the reader should be alert to a change in the way of presenting the leader in this battle.

In each of the seven cases we have examined, from Cowpens to Bushy Run, it has been possible to reconstruct the leader's thoughts and personal actions in a way that is both graphic and historically accurate. This has been possible because enough records were accessible for research and analysis to assure validity. However, when one approaches the quality of a leader's *judgment* one is stepping from firm ground onto quicksand. There are too many intangibles, even with the best of records, to portray the man's judgmental processes in a fair manner. Consequently, *just this once*, I will show in a narrated history what happened, in this case to Custer and his 7th Cavalry.

But, you may ask, why Custer and the Little Bighorn? I would reply that this case never fails to create an irresistible incitement to investigate the question of military judgment. Note that I am not saying that Custer's judgment was questionable. I *am* saying that the question will have to be resolved by each of us in his own way.

On a related point that cannot be questioned: to enter into this enigma can be a hazardous adventure in itself. So, if you are game, you will be ready to Stand to Horse and Prepare to Mount, for though we ride in company each man listens for his own bugle call.

The most important parts of the background are the figures of the chief players. First, without question, is George Armstrong Custer. Marshall has referred to him in *Crimsoned Prairie*, somewhat obliquely, as being cast in a stellar role as "the indispensable man," at the opening of his last campaign. With a greater show of sympathy the staid *Dictionary of American Biography* likens Custer's last days to those of "the central figure in a Greek tragedy, hemmed in by a closing net of adverse circumstances, while his every movement to extricate himself served only to hasten the inevitable end." Hardly an analogy likely to win the hearts of latter-day professionals, but there you have him—Custer the enduring enigma.

He comes on strong in this final act, still the dashing figure of the Indian fighter despite a put-down by President Grant that cost Custer the command of the expedition (which then went to General Terry) and almost the command of his regiment at the start of the campaign. Rescued by Terry and General Sherman, who were the chief instruments in getting Grant's grudging reprieve ("if you want General Custer along he withdraws his objections"), we see the star of the show, booted and spurred, wearing his buckskin battle jacket, ready to mount up and lead out his regiment—with the regimental band at parade ground's edge playing "Garry Owen."

How did he get to this stage entrance? Purely and simply by being the flesh and blood incarnation of the image he had fought to project throughout his military life. Never curbed by discipline (ninety-seven demerits his last half-year at West Point, three short of dismissal) he needed only battlefields and cavalry charges to blaze his name with *la gloire*. A second lieutenant at the first Bull Run, two years later he was the youngest brigadier-general ever appointed in the United States Army. The "boy general" went on to become Phil Sheridan's most trusted cavalry commander. Brevetted a major-general of volunteers in 1864, in the following year he wound up a meteroric career by throwing his cavalry division across the front of Lee's Army of Northern Virginia (in all fairness, by then the dying shadow of a once-great fighting machine) to block its final movement and cause its commander to meet Grant at Appomattox Court House.

In the cutbacks of the postwar years he was reduced to his permanent grade of lieutenant-colonel and began to have his ups and downs on frontier service. One of his downs was being found guilty by a court-martial in 1867 and sentenced to a year's suspension from the army. He may have been the scapegoat for the failure of General Hancock's campaign of that year—the major charge was deliberate absence from duty—but by the fall of 1868 he was recalled to command of his regiment by none other than General Sheridan, who had succeeded Hancock. That winter, on November 27, Custer redeemed his name by leading his 7th Cavalry in a surprise attack against Black Kettle's Cheyennes at the Washita River, where he gained a brilliant victory.

What is he like, now as we see him boarding Terry's steamboat, the *Far West,* for the final command conference? At thirty-six he is still as slender as he was at Appomattox, tall, with the rangy muscularity of the superb horseman. He looks through us with steady blue eyes, and we see that one of his most distinguishing features, his flowing golden locks, has been trimmed short for this campaign. He still wears his full mustache, which shows tawny gold against his sunburned face. He is in splendid physical condition, and his voice can be just as strong on the occasions he wishes it so, sharp and brusque; on others, earnest and appealing. He uses neither tobacco nor alcohol and in these later years has become a dedicated student of military science as well as a working and published writer. His courage is unquestioned and he has a high sense of integrity. He has a following of devoted relatives and friends (going with him on campaign are his younger brother, Capt. Tom Custer, his brother-in-law, Lt. James Calhoun, his nephew, "Autie" Reed, and his youngest brother, Boston Custer), but he has also accumulated a string of vindictive enemies. He can be positive to the point of brusqueness, but is also noted for the Custer charm. To his superiors—an acknowledged few—he seems obsessed with ambition and lust for glory; he can be erratic and impulsive, yet a hard driver and a ruthless fighter—a Peck's-Bad-Boy and the spirited earner of that other title, "the American Murat."

There is, of course, a succession of other dramatis personae, but we need concern ourselves with a look at only three. Alfred Howe Terry was a Yale man, a lawyer turned professional soldier after finishing his Civil War service as a corps commander. He is now the commanding general of the Department of Dakota and commands the column which includes Custer's 7th Cavalry. A kind and generous man, twelve years older than Custer, he has the full respect of both superiors and subordinates. His kindness was showing, as the story goes, when Custer implored him, on his knees and with tears in his eyes, to intercede on his behalf and get President Grant to relent and restore Custer to command of his regiment. That he did so intercede is proof of Terry's good heart and intentions, though some have not been so praiseful of his judgment in the matter.

Waiting in the wings are the two other officers with whom we cannot help becoming involved. Maj. Marcus A. Reno is the senior, ranking next under Custer in the 7th Cavalry. A West Pointer who graduated four years before Custer entered the academy, he attained the rank of brigadier-general of volunteers in the Civil War and earned two citations for gallantry. Older than Custer and used to his own command, he is anything but an admirer of his regimental commander. He is a darkly handsome man, stocky, looking back from his photographs with bland countenance and dark eyes. He will become the senior survivor of the battle and the one who will suffer most from that survival. He will be acquitted, in 1877, of misconduct in the battle by a court of inquiry, but will go on downhill until he will be dismissed from the army for drunkness and being a main contender in a tavern brawl. He is physically courageous and perhaps never should have arrived at the storm center of the recriminations and muckslinging that followed the American people's fascination with the "massacre."

Then there is Frederick W. Benteen, the senior captain of the regiment and from an altogether different kettle of fish than Custer or Reno. Born to an aristocratic Virginia family he chose to serve in the Union army despite the fact that his brothers served the Confederacy and his father had dismissed him as a disloyal son. He rose to the rank of colonel and after the war remained in the army, one of those few who were of independent means and who stayed in the ser-

Custer in dress uniform

vice simply because of love of the life. He is a year older than Reno and six years older than Custer. He is an uneasy ally of Reno's in the anti-Custer faction of the regiment—their only common ground being the dislike of Custer—and he is

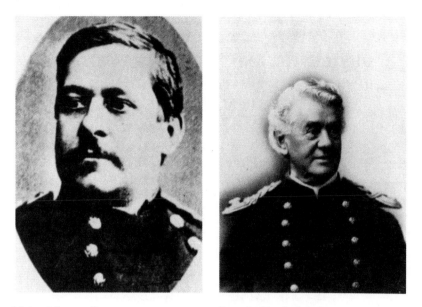

Major Marcus Reno   Captain Frederick Benteen

no doubt the stronger personality. His dislike of Custer had swelled to hatred after the Battle of the Washita. Benteen could never forgive Custer for what he considered the abandonment of Major Elliott and sixteen troopers. He had an unsigned letter published in the *St. Louis Democrat* wherein he took Custer to task for the alleged abandonment. When Custer read it he was enraged, summoned his officers to his tent, and, slapping his boot with his whip, said he was going to horsewhip the letter's writer. One of the officers present stated that Benteen calmly spoke up: "All right, General, start your horsewhipping now. I wrote it." Custer stared at him in astonishment, and turned and left the tent. Benteen hates Custer, but it is well to remember that Benteen dislikes almost everybody.

Our method of viewing the coming events may be compared to a photographer's coverage. First, things are seen in broad panoramic view as through a wide-angle lens. Next, we switch to a zoom lens to come closer to the action. Finally, we see things happening in a series of close-ups.

First then, are the column headings from the *Bismarck* [Dakota Territory] *Tribune's* extra of July 6, 1876:

MASSACRED

GEN. CUSTER AND 261 MEN THE VICTIMS

NO OFFICER OR MAN OF 5 COMPANIES
LEFT TO TELL THE TALE

3 DAYS DESPERATE FIGHTING
BY MAJ. RENO AND THE
REMAINDER OF THE
SEVENTH

FULL DETAILS OF THE BATTLE

LIST OF KILLED AND WOUNDED

THE BISMARCK TRIBUNE'S SPECIAL
CORRESPONDENT SLAIN

SQUAWS MUTILATE AND ROB THE DEAD

VICTIMS CAPTURED ALIVE TORTURED IN A
MOST FIENDISH MANNER

WHAT WILL CONGRESS DO ABOUT IT?

SHALL THIS BE THE BEGINNING OF THE
END?

In less lurid terms these are the bare-bones facts of the campaign and battle.

The Sioux nation and its allies took to the warpath in 1875 when a railroad and a gold rush threatened their territory. When the Sioux and allied tribes gathered in the Powder River country of southern Montana for the Teton

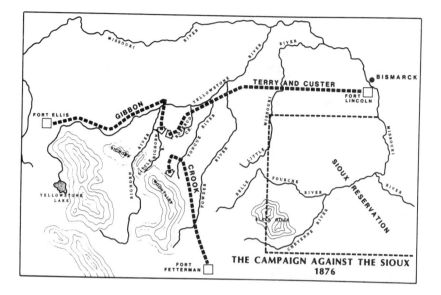

THE CAMPAIGN AGAINST THE SIOUX
1876

Council, the United States Army planned a three-pronged advance to move on the assembly and capture it. A column from the southeast under Brig.-Gen. George Crook would move first. Another would move east from Montana under Col. John Gibbon. The third, under General Terry (which included the superseded Custer and the 7th Cavalry), would move westward from Fort Lincoln, pick up the Yellowstone River and follow it to the mouth of Rosebud Creek before it moved southwest to meet the other two columns.

General Crook's column was checked at the Battle of the Rosebud (June 17, 1876), and withdrew back to Fort Fetterman. Meanwhile, General Terry and Colonel Gibbon planned to link up on the Little Bighorn River on June 26. Terry dispatched Custer with the 7th Cavalry (no attachments other than its pack train) on a reconnaissance in force. After a forced march, Custer reached the Little Bighorn on June 25. At noon he divided his regiment (less than six-hundred strong) into three battalion groupings. Major Reno with three companies (troops) moved across the river and upstream with orders to attack the Indian village from the south. Out to Reno's left, Captain Benteen with another three companies was sent on a scout to cover the left flank and "to pitch into" any Indians encountered. Custer took five companies to advance downstream on the east side of the river, leaving one company to guard the pack train. On the west side of the river, Reno ran head on into a superior force of Indians and was driven back across the river where he set up a defensive perimeter. Reno was joined by Benteen later in the day and their combined units held out through June 25–26, suffering over one hundred casualties. In the meantime Custer, continuing his advance northward, was attacked from several directions when the bulk of his command was opposite the east flank of the village. His force was subsequently encircled. In an hour or so Custer and all his men were killed in the famous "Last Stand" or "massacre," depending on a point of view: "When the white man wins, it is a battle; if the Indian wins, it is a massacre."[1] In the final event, on June 27, Terry and Gibbon arrived in time to save Reno and Benteen.

Note: Starting at this point italics are used, not to show a leader's thoughts (as in preceding cases), but to represent comments on critical matters or events which bear on the outcome of the Battle of Little Bighorn.

If one is to see clearly the impact of decisions and events leading up to the battle, it will be wise to get an overview of those events from June 19 to June 25, the day of battle. General Terry, the commander of the Department of Dakota, was now commanding two columns: his own (including Custer) and that of Colonel Gibbon moving eastward from Montana. Terry's mission, by June 21, was unchanged: to bring the Sioux Nation to battle on his terms and either force it to capitulate (meaning going back to the control of Indian agencies) or face annihilation. There is no doubt that Terry would not hesitate to attack if he could catch the Indians between his two converging columns. To do this it is obvious that he had to have a continuing flow of timely intelligence of the location and movements of the Sioux tribes, wary and highly mobile forces who carried their logistical support with them in the form of their portable villages.

By June 19 Terry had gotten word that Major Reno had returned from a reconnaissance with six companies of the 7th Cavalry and made contact with Colonel Gibbon's column now encamped on the north bank of the Yellowstone at a point opposite the confluence of Rosebud Creek with the river. Terry's reaction to Reno's report was twofold. He sent an order to Reno to remain where he was and Terry's column would move to rendezvous with him. The general's other reaction was extreme irritation. Reno had exceeded his orders and instead of going up the Powder River and descending the Tongue River to the Yellowstone he had gone on west and scouted up the Rosebud, a clear violation of his orders. Custer, hearing the news of Reno's reconnaissance, had an even more violent reaction. He was angry in the extreme, but for a different reason. He thought that Reno should have followed the great Indian trail discovered going up the Rosebud and, if at all possible, fallen on the Indians and smashed them. That the latter action would have been a further violation of Reno's orders seems not to have occurred to Custer.

Regardless of Terry's and Custer's reaction to Reno's scout, two things were evident, the first factual, the second a logical deduction. Fact: Reno's scouts had found a huge Indian trail a half-mile wide, made by thousands of lodgepoles, and an abandoned village of 360 lodges, indicating the presence of at least 800 warriors. Deduction: from this and other intelligence the Sioux and allies were moving toward an assembly in the valley of the Little Bighorn. Terry's deductions and intentions are clear in the extract from this telegram he sent his boss, General Sheridan, on June 21:

> No Indians have been met with as yet; but traces of a large and recent camp have been discovered twenty or thirty miles up the Rosebud. Gibbon's column will move this morning on the north side of the Yellowstone for the mouth of the Bighorn . . . Custer will go up the Rosebud tomorrow with his whole regiment and thence to the headwaters and thence down the Little Horn . . . I only hope that one of the two columns will find the Indians.

That last sentence is important for it contains the essence of the conviction of Terry and his commanders that each major force could handle the situation on its own or at least for the time it would take for the approaching force to link up. *The difficulties of conducting convergent operations against a mobile enemy over vast and rugged expanses of terrain without timely communication seems, incredibly, to have gone unappreciated at the highest levels of command: Sheridan's (in far-off Chicago), Terry's, or Gibbon's.*

In the afternoon of that same day, June 21, Terry held his final command conference before Custer's departure with the 7th. We will never know the details of just what was said in this meeting aboard the *Far West*, for Custer would soon be silent forever and the accounts by participants who did survive are contradictory and marred by attempts to justify actions that followed. In any case we can be sure that the following items were critical to the conference:

1. Terry's strategy was reviewed: his aim was to get the Indians between his two detachments and bring them to bay.
2. If the Indians were allowed to escape into the Big Horn Mountains, the Army's plans would be foiled and operations would have to start all over again.
3. Custer should move up the Rosebud until he found which way the great trail led. If that trail turned west (over the divide between the Rosebud and the Little Bighorn) Custer should not follow it, instead he should proceed south for about twenty miles—maintaining a vigilant reconnaissance to his left (east)—then turn west and move up the Little Bighorn valley (northward) toward Gibbon.
4. It appears that Terry failed to provide for coordinating the general movement of the link-up forces (Terry's and Gibbon's columns), thus leaving that undefined requirement to Custer whose mission was actually a reconnaissance in force.
5. Despite the insistence of reliable Indian scouts that the hostile warriors could not number less than 5,000 the general consensus of the officers was that there were not more than 1,000 to 1,500 warriors. It is believed that only Custer put the latter estimate that high.[2]
6. The strength and capability of Custer's regiment to go out on such a mission without reinforcement was questioned. Accordingly it seems that Terry wanted to explore the possibility of attaching Major Brisbin's battalion of the 2nd Cavalry to Custer's command, but that was declined by Custer who said that his regiment could handle any Indians they might encounter and the extra battalion (whose companies could have increased Custer's force by a third) would then not be needed. To the proposal of attaching the platoon of Gatling guns to the 7th, Custer again declined on the grounds that the guns could not keep up with his horsemen in the rugged terrain they must cover and hence would not be an asset but a liability.

The conference ended apparently without anyone questioning the details of just how all this would result in the army's "catching" the Indians. *The only reliable evidence of the discussion of details points to Custer's rejection of the two reinforce-*

ments. In the case of the Gatlings he must have been justified. The Gatling attached to Reno's reconnaissance had failed to keep up; the guns were drawn by "condemned horses," ones unsuitable for cavalry mounts. As for Custer's refusal of Brisbin's battalion, that is another story: there is little doubt that his real reason was making sure that any upcoming battle with the Indians was going to be a 7th Cavalry show.

However, the conference was not without tangible results. On the morning of the day after the conference—that is June 22, the day of Custer's departure with his regiment— Terry sent this written order to Custer. It is reproduced in full because of its significance to what followed in the next three days:

> Camp at Mouth of Rosebud River,
> Montana Territory,
> June 22d, 1876
>
> Lieutenant-Colonel Custer,
> 7th Cavalry.

Colonel:

The Brigadier-General Commanding directs that, as soon as your regiment can be made ready for the march, you will proceed up the Rosebud in pursuit of the Indians whose trail was discovered by Major Reno a few days since. It is, of course, impossible to give you any definite instructions in regard to this movement, and were it not impossible to do so the Department Commander places too much confidence in your zeal, energy, and ability to wish to impose upon you precise orders which might hamper your action when nearly in contact with the enemy. He will, however, indicate to you his own views of what your action should be, and he desires that you should conform to them unless you shall see sufficient reasons for departing from them. He thinks that you should proceed up the Rosebud until you ascertain definitely the direction in which the trail above spoken of leads. Should it be found (as it appears almost certain that it will be found) to turn towards the Little Horn, he thinks that you should still proceed southward, perhaps as far as the headwaters of the Tongue, and then turn towards the Little Horn, feeling constantly, however, to your left, so as to preclude the possibility of the escape of the Indians to the south or southeast by passing around your left flank. The column of Colonel Gibbon is now in motion for the mouth of the Big Horn. As soon as it reaches that point it will cross the Yellowstone and move up at least as far as the forks of the Big and Little Horns. Of course its future movements must be controlled by circumstances as they arise, but it is hoped that the Indians, if upon the Little Horn, may be so nearly inclosed by the two columns that their escape will be impossible.

The Department Commander desires that on your way up the Rosebud you should thoroughly examine the upper part of Tulloch's Creek, and that you should endeavor to send a scout through to Colonel Gibbon's column, with information of the result of your examination. The lower part of this creek will be examined by a detachment from Colonel Gibbon's command. The supply steamer will be pushed up the Big Horn as far as the forks if the river is found to be navigable for that distance, and the Department Commander, who will accompany the column of Colonel Gibbon, desires you to report to him there no later than the expiration of the time for which your troops are rationed, unless in the meantime you receive further orders.

> Very respectfully, your obedient servant,
> E. W. Smith
> Captain 18th Infantry
> Acting Assistant Adjutant General

Much discussion—scholarly or otherwise—has arisen from interpretations of this order. Custerphobes say it was a set of orders which was subsequently disobeyed. Custerphiles maintain that the document was a "letter of instructions" and, as such, left much open to Custer's discretion. I see nothing to be gained by traipsing through this vale of disputation in the company of learned men who never had to write, receive, or execute an order in the field. *It seems to me that since Custer himself referred to the communication as an order,[3] that it was delivered to him over the signature of Terry's adjutant, and that the recipient knew it to be genuine, how could he have regarded it as anything but an order confirming in writing what had been gone over verbally at the conference the day before?* Perhaps I wallow in ignorance, but I have never heard of a commander who had his adjutant or adjutant-general draw up a set of billets-doux, kindly hints, gentle suggestions, or persuasions to a subordinate commander who was getting set to carry out a combat mission just assigned.

At noon on the day that he pocketed Terry's order, Custer stood with Terry and Gibbon as the 7th passed in review. Men and officers were in high spirits and it showed as the long ranks swept by while the band played "Garry Owen." After the twelve companies had cleared the parade ground and wheeled into a column of fours Custer turned to shake hands with the others before mounting up. As he rode off to take his place at the head of the column, Terry called after him, "God bless you!" Gibbon added his shout, "Now, Custer, don't be greedy! Wait for us!"

Custer turned in the saddle and answered over his shoulder, "No, I will not!", and rode away. Which of Gibbon's exhortations Custer was answering we will never know, but it is fascinating to conjecture what he had in mind if he had been answering the latter.

If officers and troopers had been in high spirits at the review, they were soon to find that they would have need of them in the forced march coming up. As it turned out, the first leg of the march was the easiest, but things were going to get tough and tougher as time and dusty miles would tell. Custer led the regiment up Rosebud Creek preceded by two groups of Arikara scouts who scouted each side of the creek far in advance of the command. Ahead of those scouts rode Mitch Bouyer and six Crows who knew the area. Bouyer was a half-breed with a deserved reputation for being one of the best in his business.

The regiment was halted at 4:00 P.M. after covering some sixteen miles, an easy half-day's march. The early halt was largely caused by the necessity to close up the pack train, whose mules were straggling into camp as late as sunset. At that time Custer held an officers' call, the accounts of which have aroused a great deal of speculation because of its unusual nature and the fact it was called at all. Custer normally kept counsel to himself and gave orders only when he felt it necessary. Now he was to take his officers into his confidence while making an obvious effort to win theirs—both uncharacteristic actions of their dashing and self-confident leader. After covering such details as march stages—he said easy ones of twenty-five to thirty-five miles a day—he surprised the gathering with a detailed rationalization of his rejections of the offered Gatling guns and Major Brisbin's battalion. It soon became obvious that this confiding in his officers—so unlike him—was intended, at least in part, to indicate that he was looking for a quick and brilliant victory, an action whose success would wipe out the cloud that had hovered over him after the temporary loss of his regimental command when Grant replaced him with Terry as expedition commander. Custer ended with an appeal for cooperation and loyalty, for he intended to track down the Indians if it meant following them as far as their agencies in Nebraska or on the Missouri River, distances far in excess of the time for which the regiment was rationed. After the council broke up and officers were returning to their duties, Lieutenants McIntosh, Wallace, and Godfrey were walking toward their bivouacs, in silence for some time. Then Wallace spoke out.

"Godfrey, I believe General Custer is going to be killed."

"Why, Wallace," Godfrey said, "what makes you think so?"

"Because I have never heard Custer talk in that way before."

Later Godfrey went on his rounds before turning in and came across Mitch Bouyer, who at the request of Half Yellow Face, asked Godfrey if he had fought the Sioux and how many hostiles the regiment expected to catch up with. Godfrey replied that he had fought Sioux and that he guessed the Indians could number as many as a thousand to fifteen hundred.

"Can the regiment handle that many?" Bouyer asked.

"Oh yes, I guess so," Godfrey replied.

After interpreting the lieutenant's answer in sign language, Bouyer turned back to Godfrey.

"Well," Bouyer said, "I can tell you we are going to have a damned big fight."

Before we leave the regiment bedded down in bivouac, one statement made by Custer at his officers' call deserves attention: "I intend to follow the trail until we get the Indians even if it takes us to the Missouri River or Nebraska agencies." This statement should be compared with the last sentence of General Terry's order: . . . "and the Department Commander, who will accompany the column of Colonel Gibbon, desires *you report to him there no later than the expiration of the time for which your troops are rationed*,* unless in the meantime you receive further orders."

If Custer told his officers—as the accounts show—that they could be out after the Indians for a great deal longer time than that for which they were rationed, is that obeying the letter or the spirit of Terry's orders?

The next morning at five o'clock (June 23) Custer mounted up and led the regiment out, his old dashing self, trailed by two color-sergeants, one carrying the regimental

*Italics added.

standard, the other bearing the same headquarters flag that had been Major-General Custer's when commanding his cavalry division during the Civil War. This vain display might have gotten by on a parade ground but was a little out of place for a march or campaign, especially when Lieutenant-Colonel Custer no longer rated a major-general's personal flag. But unlike his conduct at the previous evening's officers' call this was all part of the man's make-up and, as such, accepted by the cavalrymen as matter-of-factly as the morning's sunrise. The column pushed on up the Rosebud where the bluffs rose higher and steeper and where the trail crossed the stream as often, in one leg of the march, as five times in three miles. Five miles out of bivouac the scouts picked up Reno's old trail and, in another three miles, the signs of the large Indian camp reported by Reno.

Three times during the day the column passed old Indian camp grounds and halts were made at each. There were all sorts of speculation about the signs and how old they were, but it appears that none of the Indian scouts was called in to pass on these important matters. As the column wound its way past the bluffs and around ravines, the Indian trail that Custer was following became more heavily marked, out to a width of about 300 yards. The scouts interpreted this one trail as being made by 1,500 lodges indicating a population supporting at least 3,000 warriors. Custer apparently was not impressed with this widening trail because he persisted in believing that it had been made by the same tribal village making successive camps rather than a growing number of groups funneling into a march toward an assembly area.

In all, the regiment made a good thirty-three miles on its second day's march and went into camp around four-thirty in the afternoon.

The following morning (June 24) Custer again led the regiment out at five o'clock, and an hour later the Crow scouts, who had been out for several hours, reported fresh signs of movements by the Sioux. At the time of the report the column was passing through the site of a great Indian village with sure signs that the camps had been arranged in circles. In spite of the fact that these were obviously camps of a number of tribes and the signs all of the same age the cavalry officers were not impressed. In fact, there was such a puzzling naivete among those experienced officers that the great number of wickiups (bushes stuck in the ground with the tops bent in to support covers made by blankets) were taken to be shelters for dogs. Any scout could have told them that they were shelters for transients and not for dogs, which Indians traditionally left to fend for themselves. But it seems that the scouts were not consulted, and as far as Indian numbers were concerned the officers clung to their belief in the earlier estimates that they would not encounter over eight hundred warriors.

That afternoon the regiment ran across another large trail coming up from the south to join the one being followed. The joined trails showed every indication that even a recruit could have read—hoof and travois marks scratching deep runs in the softer ground and scads of pony droppings. All signs were clear: the 7th was catching up to the hostiles who could not be many miles ahead. About the time this evidence had become clear the white scout, George Herendeen, requested permission to ride back to Terry and make a report as had been directed (see the opening sentence of the last paragraph of Terry's order), but Custer did not grant the permission.

It should be noted that in the same sentence the order specified that "you [Custer] should thoroughly examine the upper part of Tulloch's Creek." By this time the command had passed the upper reaches of Tulloch's Creek *without any effort at making a reconnaissance of that area. Thus, in one afternoon, Custer had disregarded two specifications of Terry's order: no scout was sent to report as directed and no "examination" of Tulloch's Creek had been made.*

Yet before this day and the night that followed were over we will observe another departure from Terry's order that will make the two preceding deviations seem like mere "tut-tuts." After packing in another thirty miles the regiment went into camp about 8:00 P.M. In all, the 7th had now covered some seventy-five miles in fifty-six hours and its commander was well ahead of the schedule discussed in the conference on the *Far West*. Custer was re-earning an old sobriquet among the troopers, the "horse killer," but the worst was still to come. Custer had dispatched the Crow scouts to seek out the continuing direction of the great Indian trail. They reported back at 9:00 P.M. to state definitely that the trail had turned right (to the west) and crossed the divide which separates the valley of Rosebud Creek from the valley of the Little Bighorn. Custer was electrified and at once ordered a night march to begin in two hours, at 11:00 P.M. Then, having heard of the Crow's

Nest (a high, rounded hilltop on the crest of the divide from which an observer could see for miles up and down the Little Bighorn valley), he directed Lieutenant Varnum, the officer in charge of scouts, to take Bouyer and Charlie Reynolds, along with several Crow and Arikara scouts, to see if they could locate the Indian village by its campfires that night or by other sightings in the morning.

Having made those decisions and given the orders to carry them out, we see the stark evidence of the third—and by far the most fateful—disobedience of Terry's order which specified: "Should it [the Indian trail] be found . . . to turn towards the Little Horn, he [Terry] thinks that you should still proceed southward, perhaps as far as the headwaters of the Tongue, and then turn towards the Little Horn . . ."

At this juncture it has been conjectured (it remains conjecture) that since Custer had been aching for the opportunity to gain a glorious victory over the Sioux with the glory going to him and the 7th alone, he knew that to delay action would mean having to share the credit with Terry and Gibbon. Additionally, it has been suggested that if he continued on to the south he might encounter General Crook and be absorbed into his command to become a mere subordinate commander who would not get the credit for the larger force's victory (Custer, as well as Terry and Gibbon, did not know of Crook's check and retreat after the Battle of the Rosebud on June 17).

Whatever his motives, Custer's plan went into execution late that night. The night march, with fatigued horses and riders, made excruciatingly slow headway up a little tributary of the Rosebud. It was pitch dark, so black that the troopers had to maintain contact in file by clanging messkits or banging tin cups on their saddles. Needless to say, the resulting uproar would have sounded to a hostile scout like the advance of an army. After about six miles had been crossed in this Laurel-and-Hardy fashion the command was halted at about 2:00 A.M. While the regiment got an uneasy rest for a couple of hours, Custer was able to check out more details with some scouts regarding the hostile strength. Fred Girard, a white scout, told him that the consensus of the scouts was that the number of warriors somewhere in the Little Bighorn valley would total at least 2,500.

At dawn the scouts on the Crow's Nest saw what was to them conclusive evidence of an immense Indian village. Although details could not be seen at the estimated distance of fifteen miles, two things were cited as proof: the smoky haze from innumerable campfires and the movements of a pony herd, described by Charlie Reynolds as "the biggest pony herd any man ever saw." He was seconded by Mitch Bouyer who added, "Biggest village. A heap too big." Lieutenant Varnum's tired eyes could not make out the sightings, but he knew his experienced scouts and trusted them enough to send a messenger to Custer with the news.

At 8:45 on Sunday morning, June 25, Custer again led the regiment forward. After about four miles he halted it and rode on to the Crow's Nest. He spent some time observing the area, but stated flatly that he could not see the scouts' signs of the village. It has been pointed out by Dr. Hofling in *Custer and the Little Big Horn* that it *was* possible that Custer did not see the indications "for conditions had changed. The scouts had made their observations in the early morning, when the earth was not warmed by the sun. Now, at 10:30 or so, there was a shimmering haze over the valley. [But] Bouyer assured him that the village was the largest ever seen on the plains."[4]

There were other reports when Custer returned to the regiment. Two small war parties, sighted at some distance, had seen the regiment and ridden away toward the village. Herendeen reported seeing a warrior only hundreds of yards away who was obviously scouting the regiment. Then a sergeant from F Company and two men had ridden back to search for missing provisions and had found a warrior helping himself to hardtack. The hostile brave mounted up and took off when he sighted the soldiers. By now it should have been clear to the officers as well as the scouts that the Indian village would soon know of the regiment's location and its approach march.

At an officers' call following his return from the Crow's Nest, Custer told the assembly that the regiment must attack now or the Indians would escape. This was not a piece of advice, it was a tactical decision followed by orders. Custer's decision to move at once into an attack has been criticized— not without reason—as the error from which all that followed that day could be traced. From a purely tactical viewpoint, the criticism seems justified. The time for the 7th to exploit surprise had passed, hence an all out attack held no promise of overrunning the Indian camp as the 7th had done in the Battle of the Washita. Thus, sound tactical sense would have held that the regiment be kept under tight central control until the enemy strength and dispositions were clarified and, if indicated, a new course of action could be adopted.

There is the reverse side of the coin: what was known to Custer at the time and what were the influences operating on him? First, he knew that he had lost the chance of surprise, but he also knew—in his sublime confidence in his regiment and himself—that no body of Indians could stand up to a charge of the 7th Cavalry. Further, in spite of his intelligence of the Indian trail signs and scout reports, he knew that a large Indian encampment could be scattered as easily as a small one. That is probably why he sent his scouts on ahead to stampede the pony herds. Without their horses the warriors would be easy prey for cavalry attacks on the village. Thus, Custer could have discounted large numbers of Indians due to overconfidence. Finally, Custer might well have been a man whose mind was not functioning clearly because of the strain he was under. His military career had been under a cloud ever since he had incurred the President's wrath, and now was perhaps his last chance to redeem himself with a resounding victory. On the other hand, if he let the Sioux escape, that failure would end his military career, and he knew of no other future for him.

Sound or not, the decision was made to attack and that decision was to form the base for all the actions that followed.

After ordering the scouts to attack the pony herds Custer took measures to assure the security of the pack train. Captain McDougall's B Company was assigned the task and it was reinforced by seven men from each of the other companies. Altogether the pack train guard totaled 130 men, a fifth of the regiment's strength.

At noon on June 25 Custer led the regiment over the divide and descended into the valley of the Little Bighorn. After moving less than a mile toward the mouth of Sundance Creek (now Reno Creek), Custer halted and gave the orders which divided the command into three battalions. Reno was given command of three companies (A, G, and M), and three others (H, D, and K) were placed under Benteen. The five remaining companies (C, E, F, I, and L) were retained under Custer's control.

Benteen was then detached with orders to move out to the left to cover the left flank (after crossing the Little

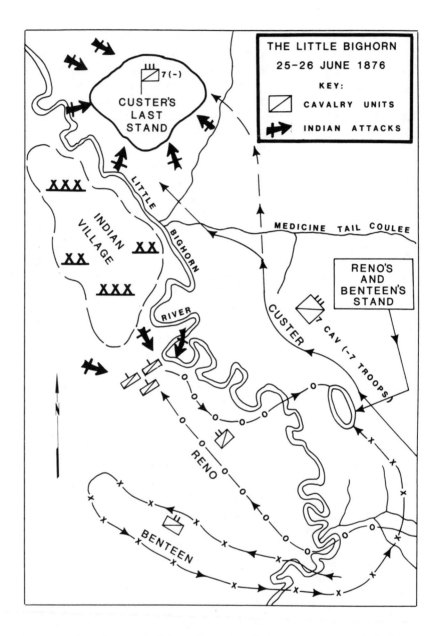

Bighorn) and to "pitch into" any Indians encountered. Subsequently orders were sent to Benteen by courier to reconnoiter as far as the second line of bluffs (to the west), and if no Indians were found "to go into the valley."

Meanwhile Reno's command was to remain with the regiment and, as it developed, Reno would receive further orders.

The division of the command into four parts, including the pack train, was, of course, the first result of the decision to attack. From this point on, all maneuver of the regiment would have to depend on this organization for combat—right or wrong, sound or unsound. In this kind of fluid situation there could be no "point of return."

By 12:15 Benteen's battalion was out of sight of the main column, which continued to march roughly northward and parallel to the river. When the valley widened Reno crossed to the west side of the stream and his column moved parallel with Custer's and abreast of it. The two columns continued to move in this manner until Custer motioned Reno to cross back and move on alongside his column.

They made a temporary halt at a point which has been known as the Lone Warrior Tepee. Custer and Reno could now see several miles into the valley, though the great village was still obscured by hills and tree lines. About this time Fred Girard rode up and shouted, "There go your Indians, running like devils!" What he was reporting was his sighting of a group of about forty warriors riding away to the north on the near (east) side of the river. Whether this sighting was confused with a dust cloud that had been raised in the direction which Custer and Reno had been observing (up the west side of the river where the Indian village was supposed to be) is not clear. In any event Custer's officers, apparently infused with Custer's *idée fixe* of preventing the escape of the village, were enthusiastic at the prospect of action. Custer evidently decided to speed up his attack even if the rest of his command had not come up.

His first order was that the scouts pursue the hostiles in the direction of the dust cloud. They refused to go, apparently convinced of the vast numbers of the Sioux. Custer derided them for cowardice, "If any man of you is not brave, I will take away his weapons and make a woman of him." There were replies in sign language but no movement, so Custer decided to send Reno to attack with his battalion in the direction of the dust cloud and, it was hoped, the village. There was disagreement over the wording of the verbal order and how it was delivered—by Custer or by Lieutenant Cooke, his adjutant—but Reno was ordered, in effect, to "pursue and charge the Indians where you find them, *and you will be supported by the whole outfit.*"*

This order was given about 2:15 and Reno moved across the river at a ford, accompanied by about twenty scouts. He trotted forward about three miles until what had begun as a kind of fox hunt turned into a real fight.

Reno, spurring forward into what he thought was the pursuit of warriors retreating toward their village, was accompanied for a short while by Capt. Myles Keogh, one of Custer's company commanders, and Lieutenant Cooke. They had neither the authority nor sound reason for attaching themselves to Reno's command and, as it has been pointed out, it would have been better for Custer and all concerned if they had stayed with Custer the whole time. The two watched Reno's spirited advance long enough to see that all was going well, then rode back to Custer to report that "fact," a perfectly true report for what little they had seen. But they had not stuck around long enough to see what really happened, a common enough occurrence in anyone's war. With that message reinforcing his made-up mind, Custer cantered his column on northward, following the river's course but out of sight of it at times due to the line of bluffs fronting the river.

Reno had meanwhile sent a trooper with a message to Custer that he had the enemy in front of them in great strength. In continuing his advance Reno deployed his three companies with two in line followed by the third in reserve. Soon he found that he was not pursuing a dust cloud, and that, if anything, the cloud was coming at his pounding troopers. Then everything seemed to happen at once. Reno's scouts disappeared from his left flank (it has been said they left to carry out their role of stampeding the enemy's horses) leaving it unprotected. Then hordes of hostiles began to appear on his left flank and rear. Reno lost the initiative. Although no losses had been suffered and his men were within a few hundred yards of the village, Reno dismounted his men into a skirmish line and sent the horse-holders, each with his four, to a wooded bend in the river to the right rear. In about twenty minutes the dismounted line began to disintegrate and Reno let it withdraw to the "shelter" of the wooded bend. At this time, unbelievable as it seems, Reno's command had lost only two or three men killed in spite of the exchange of fire

*Italics added.

between the two sides. As the line fell back the swarms of Indians were reinforced from the village until an estimated five hundred warriors were circling around the dismounted cavalrymen. The Indian tactics, to say the least, were more adapted to the situation than Reno's. They circled at a trot or gallop outside and inside carbine range seeking their chance to pounce. When that chance came, its effects were incredible.

Reno's command, properly organized and with good fire discipline, could have held out for hours. But the fire control and organization of the position never developed. The uncontrolled expenditure of ammunition began to tell while the Indians were beginning to close in from several directions, finally to infiltrate the woods from the east bank of the river. Reno, seeing that his right could be turned and the men cut off from their horses, considered a retreat. He decided on it and gave the order to mount. There was no bugle call and some troopers got the word only when they saw others running for their horses. A great deal of what has been called "disorder" ensued, and the situation increasingly resembled that well-known maneuver known as "getting the hell out of there." Reno has been called a coward for this action, but there are a good many things to be said on each side of the charge. One thing, however, is certain: what may have begun as an orderly withdrawal turned into a mounted rout. While the troops were starting to form to mount up, a party of Sioux broke into the timber and poured a volley into the cavalrymen at point-blank range. Troopers were hit, and the scout Bloody Knife was struck by a bullet between the eyes, splattering blood and brains in Reno's face. This may have unnerved Reno, who led the mounted troops out of the woods in a beeline for the ford on the east side, leaving behind two lieutenants and about fifteen unwounded men. As the troops started out in a column of fours the Indians fell back in surprise, thinking they were being counterattacked. They quickly recovered and began pouring their fire into the flanks of the column. This became an ordeal by fire as the troopers became fugitives trying to gallop away from the screaming warriors, who soon made a gauntlet out of the rout. Here Reno's command suffered its real losses, a common occurrence in rout and pursuit. Reno had not made any attempt to cover the withdrawal which became a desperate run for the ford. The bulk of the panicked cavalrymen made it across the ford and up the steep bluff beyond to the heights now known as Reno Hill. The Sioux, for reasons not known, did not pursue across the river, and Reno's exhausted troopers were allowed to collapse on the hilltop at about 4:00 P.M.

There may be argument, pro and con, ad nauseam, about the alleged incompetent employment of Reno's command and his "panicking" at critical turns in his battle, *but what deserves consideration is Custer's failure to support Reno in some manner or to withdraw him to the east side of the river before he (Reno) got too involved.* Instead of consigning Reno's command to an indeterminate future, why didn't Custer at least establish observation posts with couriers to keep him informed about Reno's attack? And the story about Custer appearing on a height across the river and waving his hat at Reno to signal him forward in his attack can be dismissed as pure drivel. For a commander to wave his hat, from a bluff a mile or more away, at a battalion commander who is in the act of leading a cavalry attack which is kicking up clouds of dust, is—to put it mildly—stretching one's imagination. *The question remains unanswered: why did not Custer support Reno as he had promised?*

While Reno was fighting his battle and leading his disastrous retreat, Custer was leading his five companies into epic and legend. There are so many unknowns, so many variables, about the route he took and the orders he may or may not have given that it is purely daunting to try to reconstruct the details of Custer's advance and subsequent actions. It can be worse than daunting; it may be so far off target as to be criminally misleading. Let us, then, stick to the *events that had to have happened.*

Custer and his five companies covered about twelve miles, after splitting away from Reno, before coming opposite the Indian village across the river. What followed has been put succinctly by Marshall: "What we know for certain is that Custer charged deliberately into a neatly rigged trap, though it is likely that the trap came about empirically rather than through preconceived design, there being no centralized Indian leadership."[5] What is not so certain is Marshall's assumption that Custer ran into an ambush in the shape of an inverted L and that the Indians set up a blocking force to prevent him entering the lower (northern) end of the village.

It would appear that Custer's strung-out force was stopped by fire from the front and quickly attacked from west, north, and east until the five companies were nearly encircled. Then a band of Sioux charged the rear companies, already dismounted, and completed the encirclement. The Indian strength has been estimated at anywhere from 1,800 to 9,000, but 3,000 seems to be a reasonable figure in the lower range. If that is so, Custer's force was fighting against 13-to-1 odds, giving the Indians somewhat of an edge.

The return fire from the troopers of the rearward companies was heavy enough at first to check the Sioux attack from the south. There was a rush from the cavalrymen down the ravines toward the river, which was then checked in its turn by fire from dismounted Indians. The soldiers then withdrew, backing up the hill. Jack Red Cloud, son of Chief Red Cloud, has given a typical Indian account of that action and the final phase of Custer's stand: "The Sioux kept circling around Custer and as his men came down the ridge we shot them. Then the rest dismounted and gathered in a bunch, kneeling down and shooting from behind their horses."[6] The "bunch" was probably the true Last Stand, the site now marked by the enclosed headstones at Custer Battlefield National Monument.

The duration of the action, measured from the encirclement until its tragic end, has been estimated variously at from forty minutes to two hours. If the latter period is accepted, the fight was over by 5:30, which would have been before Reno started to move toward the scene. Whenever the end came, the Sioux overran the field, killing every soldier who showed signs of life. Then the bodies were stripped and the uniforms thrown into a pile which was set afire while the Sioux did a war dance around the flames. About 225 soldiers and a few civilians died. One must say "about" 225 because of the army's sloppy record-keeping.

Custer's body was stripped but unmarred, unlike the others which were scalped or mutilated in other ways. He could have died from either of two bullet wounds, one in the left breast, the other in the head. It has been said that the Sioux did not mutilate Custer's body because they respected his qualities as a warrior. That assertion has been contradicted by the claim that the Indians would not have recognized Custer because "Yellow Hair," as they called him, had his long locks cut short early in the campaign.

This brief venture into the Custer myth and its attendant controversy has been far from a joyful task, and I wish to step outside the circle of controversy when I say that I am convinced that Custer died a hero's death. If I could leave my own version of an epitaph it would be to use these two lines of Shakespeare's:

> Nothing in his life
> Became him like the leaving it

It may seem anticlimatical to add the account of Reno and Benteen, but it should be briefly told so that one can try to keep the whole picture in perspective.

First Benteen. His reconnaissance produced only negative intelligence; not an Indian had been encountered. Some time after he had come back to the main trail (about 2:20 P.M.) Benteen met a galloping courier, Sgt. Daniel Kanipe, bearing a verbal message to McDougall, the commander of the pack train. Kanipe wanted to give his message to Benteen, a not-unnatural tendency of couriers in battle situations, but Benteen sent him on to McDougall to deliver the word to "rush the train forward."

In less than a quarter of an hour, when his column had reached a spot about a mile south of Reno Hill, Benteen was met by Trumpeter John Martin who handed the captain the scrawled (now famous) message:

Benteen—
Come on. Big village. Be quick
bring packs.
P.S. Bring pacs

Benteen read it and asked Martin, "Where's the general?" Martin answered that Custer had run across Indians in a ravine leading to the river. When queried about the Indians, Martin replied he thought they were "skedaddling." After consulting Captain Weir, commander of D Company, who had no comment, Benteen did not act on the order. Benteen may well have been puzzled by the message which must have referred to ammunition packs. He could see the pack train coming on, at its regular slow pace, about a mile behind him. He chose to ride on into the Little Bighorn valley where he could see to the north.

The first thing he saw was the small group of Reno's abandoned troopers on the opposite (west) side of the river, fighting a dismounted action against a mass of Indians. He next saw several Arikara scouts leading some captured horses. They informed Benteen that the bulk of Reno's command was on a hill to the right. Benteen led his column up the hill to meet a distraught Reno.

"For God's sake, Benteen, halt your command and help me. I've lost half my men." By actual count he had lost 3 officers and 40 men, and had with him about 105 effectives. Benteen asked where Custer was, and Reno told him that Custer had gone northward (downstream) with five companies and he had had no word from him.

Benteen had his men divide their ammunition with Reno's, so that every soldier ended up with more than half his regular load. In looking around for the enemy, all that could be seen were a few scattered warriors over a thousand yards away. The united commands were now in no immediate danger, so what followed is difficult to understand. There were reports of firing downstream, yet neither moved to take any action. *Benteen's failure to act is the more remarkable for three reasons.* He was the dominant, unshaken personality. His command was intact and his horses recently watered. And, most important, he had Custer's written order to come forward. *What he did do was to place himself under Major Reno's command.* The latter, though scared and shaken, still had two-thirds of his command, now reinforced by Benteen's battalion. He had fought through the Civil War and had seen heavy fighting. *Yet he too stayed put.*

Two hours before, Captain Weir had asked Reno's permission to move forward, but he was refused. Sometime short of 5:00 P.M. Weir repeated his request, and was again refused. Weir decided to have a look for himself and rode northward. He was followed by his company (D) which was temporarily under command of Lieutenant Edgerly, who mistakenly thought that Weir had been given permission to move the company. They moved about a mile and a half to a promontory (now Weir's Point) where there was a view of the battlefield about two miles to the north. A heavy cloud of dust and smoke cut off most of Weir's vision but he could see Indians riding around and shooting into the ground. At about 5:30, Weir's company closed on the hilltop and, at about the same time, the pack train started arriving on Reno Hill.

Reno delayed his advance until a little after 6:00 P.M., then moved the command to join Weir's company. No sooner had the command closed around Weir Point than masses of

Indians were seen advancing toward them. By now all sounds of firing from the north had ceased, but the air in the battlefield area was still filled with dust and smoke. After a hasty consultation, Reno and Benteen decided that Reno Hill was, for several reasons, the more defensible position, so the command withdrew to that hill and set up its defensive perimeter.

The saucer-shaped top of the hill afforded a central area in which the wounded and the pack mules and their burdens could be placed. The Indians began an all-around series of attacks that lasted for three hours until dark. The command held out against ferocious attacks by Sioux who were burning with their triumphs over Custer and over Reno in his first battle. In this period, eighteen soldiers were killed and forty-six wounded. With nightfall came blessed relief. Most of the Sioux withdrew to their village to celebrate with feasting and dancing. But rest was denied the soldiers on the hill until rifle pits were started—there were few tools and many had to resort to messkits, spoons, and knives—redeployments made, and pickets posted.

At dawn the returning Indians renewed their attacks, but the command held its own until mid-afternoon when the hostiles started withdrawing. Later in the afternoon, the whole Indian village could be seen moving up the valley. Not until the command was relieved on the morning of June 27 by Terry and Gibbon was it learned that the Sioux had moved southward toward the Bighorn Mountains because of the advance of the Terry-Gibbon columns.

Let us review our goals. First, we stand to lose perspective if we proceed down the narrow alley of: "what did Custer do wrong and what should he have done?" Instead, our goals are to see where the leaders' (Custer, Reno, Benteen) judgment can be evaluated *and* what may be learned from it.

Secondly, it would also be beneficial to rid ourselves of another fallacy—that the Little Bighorn stands out as a series of glaring errors. The same thing may be said of the battle as J. F. C. Fuller said of Waterloo: "It has been so thoroughly investigated and criticized that the errors committed in it are apt to appear exceptional and glaring."[7]

If we peer through the fog of war—which has only partially cleared—we can find a number of key questions that should lead to useful answers. That number, however, can be reduced from a baker's dozen to four main "judgment points."

Why did Custer decide to attack when surprise was lost and the size of the Indian village was apparently not clear to him?

Why did Custer divide his regiment into four groupings in order to execute his attack?

Why did not Custer keep his "promise" to Reno?

Why did Reno and Benteen fail to move to Custer's support?

Regarding Custer's decision to attack, it has been pointed out that the decision formed the basis of all that followed. Tactically it seems to have been unsound, but extenuating circumstances, mostly bad for Custer, must have influenced his thinking and judging of the situation. As for his judging the size of the village (and the number of warriors it would support), if Custer chose not to accept at face value the scouts' estimates he may be said to have been making his own intelligence estimate of the situation. And when he spent a reasonable amount of time at the Crow's Nest trying to confirm—it has been said that he used his field glasses—the scouts' sightings of an immense village and pony herds, he probably did not see anything. Whether this was due to atmospheric conditions, we may never know. Then too, it should be remembered that Lieutenant Varnum also failed to see anything, and he was looking (through tired eyes?) at the same time the scouts were making their observations.

The question of dividing his command has occasioned more criticism than any other action Custer took before and during the battle. It is easy to say, because it *is* a valid criticism, that Custer should have kept the regiment grouped under his centralized control until the valley of the Little Big-horn had been adequately reconnoitered. Granted; but may he have been thinking that he was doing that initially when he kept Reno's battalion with the rest of the regiment? It will be recalled that Custer kept Reno's command moving parallel to his own for quite some time, and, in the meantime, he detached Benteen (with roughly a fourth of his command) to make a reconnaissance to the west while simultaneously protecting the regiment's left flank. Only when Custer ordered Reno to split away and attack northward did he make the final, fatal division of the regiment. When that commitment had been made, the clearest course of action was to follow and support Reno, which brings us to the question of Custer's promise "that the rest of the outfit will support you."

Everything hinges on the words "promise" and "support." There has been much fuzzy thinking in regard to the meaning of the latter at this point in the action—regrettably even among military critics who should know better. Support does not necessarily mean that one part of a command will come to the aid of another by physically placing itself alongside or behind the supported unit. It can mean that a supporting unit will maneuver or engage the enemy in a manner that will relieve enemy pressure on the supported unit so that it can accomplish its mission. Custer may well have believed that if he could maneuver so as to attack the Indian village from the east or north he would not only destroy the village and the Indian force in it but also would, by so doing, come to Reno's support. Consequently, as it has been observed, it is possible that Custer rode to his death thinking that he was on his way to keeping his promise.

Lastly, there is the matter of the failure of both Reno and Benteen to move northward in support of Custer after Reno had retreated to his hill and had been united with Benteen. It has been noted that Reno's command, following its disastrous retreat through the woods and across the river, collapsed on the hilltop exhausted and ineffective for further combat. This was no doubt true, but the question arises: How long would it have taken to get Reno's shaken command reorganized and back into shape as a fighting force? Reno and Benteen were united some time around 4:00 P.M., but it was not until after 6:00 P.M. that the two battalions, now nominally under Reno's command, moved out toward Weir Point. That allows two hours during which there was more than enough time to reorganize, reissue ammunition—which was done—and prepare to move out northward. Yet, as we have seen, Reno and Benteen did nothing about moving out. Reno had six companies in the united command (before the pack train's reinforced company arrived between 5:30 and 6:00 P.M.), or half the regiment, which was a force numerically stronger than Custer's, yet both leaders chose to remain inactive.

If one acknowledges that Reno was a badly shaken man whose combat effectiveness was questionable after his disaster, then what about Benteen? The latter has been described as cool and courageous throughout the day as well as being the dominant personality in the united command, so this leads to other questions about his judgment. Benteen was handed Lieutenant Cooke's message (actually an order from Custer over his adjutant's signature) by Trumpeter Martin about 3:00 P.M. (Benteen's time as given at Reno's court of inquiry), and had it in his possession for the rest of the time. So one may wonder why Benteen did not take one of two courses of action. He could have shown the order to Reno to emphasize a recommendation that Reno lead the command forward. Or, if it is accepted that Reno's original command was so exhausted that it could not be restored to combat effectiveness, why could not Benteen have taken it on himself to move out with his three companies? This would not have been an act of insubordination in the sense of leaving Reno even without his permission, for Benteen had his regimental commander's written order to "come on—be quick," which was still in effect.

Despite all the investigations, inquiries, and analyses, these three figures, Custer, Reno, and Benteen, seem to remain enigmatic at this distance of over a hundred years. Are there really critical points where their respective judgments can be questioned? What do you think?

Part Four

PRESENCE

Lannes at
Ratisbon, 1809

Brazenose at
Lungtungpen, 1899

PRESENCE

You know we French stormed Ratisbon
  A mile or so away
On a little mound, Napoleon
  Stood on our storming-day;
    . . . . . .
    My plans
That soar, to earth may fall,
Let once my army-leader Lannes
  Waver at yonder wall,—
    —Browning, *Incident of the French Camp*

In April, 1967, an action officer in the Office of the Chief of Staff of the Army was handed the four volumes that were the final product of the *ARC Study: Art and Requirements of Command*. Although the study raised no great waves of action or reaction at the time, it did in its quiet way represent a leap of the imagination in exploiting a wide and deep reservoir of leadership experience. For the first time in our military history an incisive effort had been made to learn firsthand from the commanders themselves the lessons they had learned the hard way in the hard ways of war. The study was launched "on the premise that high-level tactical command . . . is a highly personalized art as well as a clearly defined professional discipline." And though its immediate goals were "directed toward identifying and analyzing the command-control support requirements of senior commanders,"[1] it affords a once-in-a-lifetime opportunity for us, as observers of the leader's art, to gain unobscured insight into the attribute of presence.

Volume II of the study—"Generalship"—represents the firsthand findings from experience that are its major and most valuable product. The basis for this effort was a detailed questionnaire which was returned by more than eighty respondents. The number seems of no significance when considered by itself, but what is remarkable is the fact that every one of those queried had held long and high-level tactical command in World War II; high-level meaning command of an army, corps, division, or regiment. Question 4.5 is of particular interest, not only for its subject, but for the consensus of the responses: "In this step [the following-up by the commander of his own orders], how important was face-to-face contact with subordinates?"[2]

238

To Rally

THE CONSENSUS WAS "all-important." But of particular value are these typical comments:

"Most important especially when [a] unit had been having tough going."

"I regard it as vital."

"Absolutely, Number 1."

"The most important factor of all."

"Most important. Spreads confidence."

"Invaluable."

"Essential to highest morale and confidence."[3]

Since these combat commanders were all of one mind in regard to the matter of physical presence, just why did they consider that an indispensable attribute? The answer, in terms of common sense as well as the findings of the study, is that *presence* was the only wholly reliable way that the commander could assure himself that his orders were being carried out in an effective and timely manner.

In fairness to the reader I should point out that the responding leaders considered the use of presence as a matter of routine, as well as a means of handling "emergencies."

We are concerned in this book with emergencies and not with matters of routine. Upon examination, in the former there are two ways in which the leader's use of presence can bring events under his control: to rally and to inspire. What does

239

the term "to rally" mean in this context? Simply defined it means *that the leader uses personal example and force of character to bring order out of potential chaos during a critical turn of events;* further, he uses them *as a means of assuring that the rallied unit will go on to accomplish its mission.* Admittedly, defining "rallying" is a simple matter, but doing it under the stress of battle is not so simple a thing.

In our next case we will see a leader in the act of rallying units whose morale was on the verge of being shattered; had that morale collapsed the mission of an army would have been jeopardized.

There are two major characters in the action, and events will unfold through their eyes. First, Marshal Jean Lannes, Napoleon's great advance guard leader whose skill and dash assured French victories in such campaigns as Marengo, Jena, and Friedland. The other, Marcellin de Marbot, at the time a captain of cavalry and veteran aide-de-camp to Lannes.

In great part we are indebted to Marbot's *Memoirs* for their wealth of detail and quality of "you-are-thereness." I go to the trouble of mentioning Marbot not only because of my debt to him, but also because he has been, on occasion, the butt of commentators who tend to dwell on his Gallic enthusiasm for embellishing exploits in which he played a part. However that may be, Marbot is a delight to read, and the incident which makes up the climax of the upcoming action is by no means Marbot's imagination at work. The story of the storming of Ratisbon—and our focus of interest on it— can be found in any authoritative source which goes into detail in the account of Napoleonic battles. Then too, Marbot's participation in the incident calls for a final caveat. If his actions appear to be excessive for those of an aide, one should realize that the duties of an aide to Napoleonic generals demanded much more than would be the case today. These hand-picked officers were anything but glorified body-servants or brilliantly uniformed couriers. They were expected to carry their commander's orders—often verbal in the heat of battle—and once they were delivered, the aide would often remain to observe the orders being put into execution. He was further expected to return not only with the subordinate commander's reply but also with a detailed situation report for his chief. On occasion he could be directed to guide units into action or even lead them if the situation called for it. All this under extreme pressure and in constant danger.

Over the Wall and Through the Gate

In the dusk of the April day they had watched the leading
infantry battalions of Gudin's division halt in place to allow
the heavy cavalry of Nansouty's and St. Sulpice's brigades make
their passage of lines. The grateful infantry, exhausted after
hours of forced marches and a half-day slugging match with
the Austrians, sank to the ground where they had taken their
last steps, too tired even to curse the cuirassiers for raising
the dust as they passed, too tired to exchange the usual insults that were bantered back and forth whenever French
cavalry rode past French infantry. The big men on the tall
horses were tired, too, as were their mounts, and the squadrons moved at a walk even though they would be deploying
in minutes to attack the Austrian cavalry which had come forward to cover the retreat of their beaten infantry. In the fading twilight the steel cuirasses and helmets no longer flashed
as they had in the late afternoon sun, for their glitter had
been dulled by the dust which had settled over the once-
colorful columns. The dark blue sleeves of their under-
jackets now seemed a dull black, and the scarlet epaulets and
shoulder linings had turned a dusty maroon. The only
uniform fittings that had kept their luster were the long
black horsehair plumes of their steel helmets.

The weary infantrymen would not have looked up long
enough to share Captain Marbot's biased interest in the soldiers of his own arm, nor would his commander, Marshal
Lannes, spare the passing cavalry a glance. The commander
of the Provisional Corps had thirty thousand men of his own
who were his chief concern now as he strained his eyes to
study his map in the failing light. The marshal and his aide
had dismounted at the roadside long enough to spread the
map on the top of the rock wall that separated the orchard
from the dusty road, and Marbot's momentary distraction with
the cavalrymen had caused the marshal to look up at him
with one of his penetrating glances, this time one of irritation.

"Look here, Marbot, since you have given so greatly of
your attention to studying this map, be so kind as to inform
me of the distance from our location to the walls of Ratisbon," Lannes said.

Marbot did not need the Marshal's keen stare to tell him
he had put himself on the spot by being caught like a school-
boy staring out a classroom window. He had served on Lannes'

staff in Spain in enough campaigns to know how the quick-tempered "Roland of the French Army" could punish a wool-gathering aide. But Marbot's hussar's luck was working for him, and two things combined to save him. His quick memory told him that it was about fourteen kilometers from Alt Eg-glofsheim to the city, and the marshal had inadvertently kept the tip of his forefinger on the road junction a stone's throw from the orchard.

"I make it to be fifteen kilometers, *Monsieur le Maréchal*," Marbot answered without hesitation.

Lannes grunted, made a crumpled roll of the map, and thrust it into Marbot's hands.

"Here," he said, "have the staff mount up. We'll go forward far enough to get a look at what happens when these *grosse-bottes** meet their enemy."

"Yes Sir, but I thought you intended to go into Alt Eg-glofsheim to meet the Emperor," Marbot said.

"He'll not be there yet, and besides, how could I rec-ommend continuing to advance my infantry until I know what happens to the Austrian cavalry who are covering the with-drawal of their infantry?"

Marbot started to suggest posting couriers to watch the cavalry action, but quickly closed his mouth with the reali-zation that he was about to say a foolish thing. Would the finest advance guard commander in the *Grande Armée*—or in all Europe—be contented with receiving messages when he could be assessing the outcome of a combat for himself? He ran through the trees toward his horse, calling out to the oth-ers to mount up and follow.

The wall in front of the Bavarian farmhouse made an improvised gallery for Lannes and his staff to observe the deployment of the heavy cavalry. Junior aides and orderlies perched on the far reaches of the wall like farm boys at a fair, while the marshal and senior officers stood behind it and braced their elbows on the top ledge. Lannes handed his field glass back to Marbot, it was getting too dark to focus on any distant object. Already the twilight was being reinforced by the light of the rising moon, so that the deployed lines of horsemen could be seen as dark masses on the flat plain that stretched all the way to Ratisbon and the banks of the Dan-ube. The green shoots of the young wheat and barley, now

---

*Literally "big boots," soldier slang for the heavy cavalry of the Guard or the cuirassiers.

only visible as a lighter-shadowed background, would soon be ground to a damp pulp under thousands of hooves.

"I see that our light cavalry has withdrawn to the flanks just in time. Safer there for hussars and chasseurs I suppose," Lannes said with a side glance at Marbot.

The aide had been through this chaffing too many times to take it in any way other than it was intended—the marshal's bluff way of showing his gentler side to his veteran staff officers. And when it was Marbot's turn it always took the form of an old infantryman bantering with a young cavalryman; it was an old game and the aide always played well his side of the court.

"Of course the marshal realizes that the flanks of our 'heavies' must be protected. As you see, the enemy's light cavalry is doing the same, so they must be countered," Marbot replied.

"Oh, of course, of course. But look now, don't I see the Austrian cuirassiers moving forward?" The marshal's tone was serious now, all business, as Marbot recognized.

"Yes, and General Nansouty's squadrons advance to meet them. St. Sulpice follows in support, his Bavarians on the right and Würtembergers on the left. What a sight it should have been, had we only some daylight left."

"But, my God, so slowly! Is this what Nansouty calls a cavalry charge?"

"Sir, the horses are too worn to work them up from a walk to a trot, then to a gallop. Unless I'm mistaken, Nansouty will be able to charge only at the trot."

Marbot was not mistaken. The shadowy massed lines of the French cuirassiers broke into a trot and smashed into their oncoming Austrian counterparts. The melee that followed was as eerie as it was majestic, as thousands of armored horsemen crashed into each other. The shouts of the cavalrymen were almost drowned by the ringing blows of sabers against steel helmets and cuirasses. The night was actually lighted at times by sparks flying from the clash of steel against steel. It soon became impossible for the observers to distinguish friend from foe as more lines of opposing squadrons charged into the fray. Now the plain seemed filled with rearing, whirling horsemen—demons' shadows in the dim half-light of the moon. But Lannes and the others could see that the rearmost squadrons of the French cavalry had come to a halt, standing fast, short of the melee.

"St. Sulpice is playing his game well. No need for him to

commit any of his brigade into that brawl, and he knows that some must be held back to pursue if Nansouty can win his battle," Lannes said.

"That must be it, Sir, and Nansouty's men have a double advantage over the Austrians in that action," Marbot said.

"Oh, and what do you find those to be?"

"Our heavies are better swordsmen and they have double cuirasses, front and back, while the Austrians are protected only in front."

"So you are saying that, in that hand-to-hand fighting, the advantage goes to him who can strike at the rear of his opponent when his back is exposed."

"Exactly, Sir. In that sort of a melee everyone is circling about trying to get in a killing stroke, and our troopers need not worry when their backs are exposed."

"Thank you, Marbot. It won't take long to see if you have sized up the situation accurately."

Marbot's words were proven sound for the second time that evening. Such a violent combat could be sustained for only a matter of minutes. In that short time French swordsmanship and complete armor did end the fight. The Austrians, realizing the heavy losses they were taking, pulled out of the battle, wheeled and tried to flee the field. Marbot's words about exposed Austrian backs came true with a vengeance, as he tells it in his *Memoirs*: "When they [the Austrians] had wheeled about, they understood still better what a disadvantage it is not to have a cuirass behind as well as in front. The flight became a butchery as our cuirassiers pursued the enemy, and for the space of half a league [a mile and a half] the ground was piled with killed and wounded cuirassiers."

The marshal stayed long enough to see St. Sulpice launch his brigade in pursuit of the broken Austrian cavalry, then, satisfied, he gave the order to his staff to mount up and follow him back to Alt Egglofsheim. As the group started to find its way down the moonlit road, Lannes summed it up as they rode.

"What we have seen is an omen, if not a beacon. If there are any unbroken Austrian battalions between us and Ratisbon they could be overrun in no time. If only the Emperor can be convinced of that we can have the Archduke Charles's army in our pocket."

His were words that could make up prophecies, yet it must be noted that his statements contained two significant "ifs."

Lannes was accompanied by Marbot and one other aide, the young De Viry, when he made his way toward the *Maison,* at the center of Imperial Headquarters. The three had left their horses with orderlies at the edge of the great encampment, and followed on foot after their guide, one of the senior aides-de-camp. They passed the circle of tents that housed Marshal Berthier's army staff, past sentries who snapped to Present Arms when they caught sight of the crossed batons on Lannes' gold-fringed epaulets, on to the huge tent with the green drapes that was the heart of the *Maison,* the Emperor's secretarial cabinet and personal staff.

Lannes quickened his step when he saw Marshal Masséna standing outside the front entrance to the anteroom. The two marshals greeted each other warmly, Masséna's dark eyes sparkling in his Italian face. He grasped both of Lannes' hands in his and gave a smiling nod to the two aides.

"Well, IVth Corps seems to be following you as usual, *mon cher* Jean, you who seem to make a profession of leading advance guards," Masséna said.

"I do as I'm told, like the rest of you, that's all," Lannes said with the quick grin that lighted his scarred face.

"And here comes our 'teller of what to do'—no less than the Prince of Neuchâtel himself," Masséna said as he turned toward the brilliantly uniformed figure coming out of the entrance. This was Louis Alexandre Berthier, Marshal of the Empire, Prince of Neuchâtel, and Chief of the Army Staff. He was hatless, his thick curly hair tousled as always. He was resplendent in full-dress foot uniform with his dark blue, knee-length coat glittering with gold braid and crossed by a broad scarlet shoulder sash. He was frowning and biting the nails of his left hand, and with his right he was waving a dismissal to a green-coated valet.

"That'll be all for now, Constant, His majesty won't need you until this conference is over," Berthier said.

When he became aware of Lannes' and Masséna's glances the frown disappeared, and a jolly, joking Berthier emerged. He was all smiles as he greeted the other two marshals.

"Why are you two looking so serious? You've got everything going your way, haven't you?" Without giving either a chance to reply, he went on as though he had not already spoken.

"The Emperor is with Bacler d'Albe at the map table. He'll see us in just a moment."

As he spoke, a small dark man with a handsome, smooth-

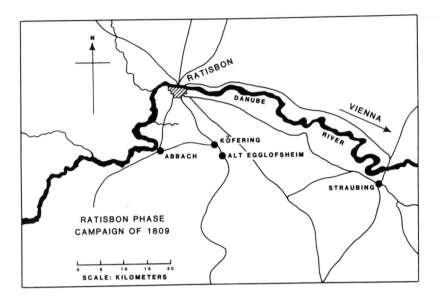

RATISBON PHASE
CAMPAIGN OF 1809

shaven face emerged from the inner room and passed silently behind Berthier, giving a pleasant nod to the group as he passed.

"So, d'Albe has finished the evening situation map-posting. I'll see if we can—"

He was interrupted by a sharp voice from within the tent, one that crackled with command.

"Berthier, Berthier, get in here, and bring the others with you. We haven't got the rest of the night to dawdle over greetings and the like!"

The Prince of Neuchâtel spun on his heel like a sergeant-major, his short, stocky body muscling to attention, and marched through the anteroom into the "sanctuary of genius." Lannes and Masséna followed, trailed by their aides who quickly aligned themselves against a tent wall.

Napoleon, still clasping a pair of compasses in his right hand, turned from the map on the table at room's center, and faced the marshals. The five-foot-six figure in the dull green uniform coat of a colonel of chasseurs was half in shadow from the light of the table lamps, but the face was in full light. Marbot had seen his Emperor at a distance in the field and less often close up on occasions such as this, and he never ceased to wonder at the piercing glare of the great grey eyes which seemed to hypnotize anyone on whom they were focused. Their glance swept around the room, and as it passed over Marbot's face an icy tingle ran down his spine. Suddenly the Emperor's facial muscles flexed, and a quick smile enveloped them all, so that they seemed to relax in its warmth.

"Let us to it, gentlemen. As you see here we have reached this line stretching from Abbach on the north to the east of this village of Alt Egglofsheim. The Austrians are beaten at all points, and the latest reports indicate no organized, large-scale capability of resistance. And I've just had the word of the heavy cavalry's battle. Do you take it to be as successful as Nansouty's courier would have us believe, Lannes?"

"I witnessed it myself, your majesty, a complete victory in every sense. I stayed long enough to see St. Sulpice's thirty-four squadrons launched in pursuit. And, if you will permit, that fact brings me to my point: I believe that we can destroy the Austrian army between this present line and the Danube, but only if we keep moving," Lannes said.

The grey eyes turned expressionless as they looked into those of Lannes. Then they were turned on Masséna and Berthier.

"What say you two, can we continue with a night advance?"

Masséna's alert face was a portrait of mixed dismay and anger.

"Since you ask, Sire, every infantryman in every corps is drunk with exhaustion. When their formations are halted, they drop to the ground, senseless with sleep. We can't pursue with an army of corpses," Masséna said.

"He is right, your majesty, every report that has come in within the last two hours would confirm that," Berthier added.

"Is that it then, Masséna?" Napoleon asked.

"No, Sire, that is not the whole picture. We are still far from Ratisbon and the Danube, with neither time nor means to prepare a night attack. I don't have to tell you what confusion could ensue—with mixed-up units and intermingled commands and all that goes with it. And an enemy who has fought us as stubbornly as this today, might still be capable of a fight. That is the rest of the picture," Masséna said.

The Emperor started to speak to Lannes when an aide of Berthier's stepped through the anteroom and slipped a rolled paper into his chief's hand.

"Excuse it, Sire, but General Mouton has admitted this aide with an urgent dispatch," Berthier broke in.

"Go ahead, Alexandre, if it bears on our council here."

"General St. Sulpice reports sweeping everything in front of his advance as far as Köfering. In that area he overran two Austrian grenadier battalions which he says were the last organized resistance he found. And there is a postscript which tops off the whole affair."

"Well, go on, go on," Napoleon said.

"St. Sulpice says that he came within a hair's breadth of capturing the Archduke Charles himself."

"If you're telling me that my cavalry leader *almost* captured the enemy army's commander, that is pure dramatics, and not a military report," Napoleon's tone was scornful.

"Your majesty is correct, of course, but the incident does show the extent of the cavalry pursuit," Berthier said.

Napoleon looked at Lannes who seemed about to burst out of his marshal's coat.

"Sire, is this talk of exhaustion, of puny distances, of confusion in night attacks—is this the spirit of Lodi, of Arcola, of Friedland? Thou* can see for thyself what the heavy cavalry—*exhausted* heavy cavalry—can accomplish with drive and leadership. Wouldst thou listen to this drivel about sleepy men? True, my men are tired, they've gone farther than any other infantry, but I can make them go on. Why can't the others?"

Napoleon's swift glance caught Masséna's Italian temper bristling, and the once-jovial Berthier was showing signs of temper.

"You have the esprit, I know, Jean. But cool that Gascon temper, and face reality with me. Masséna and Berthier are right, I must admit. And I *could* order a continuation of the attack, but I will not."

Lannes gave a shrug that spoke sentences of resignation. Napoleon went on for a tense quarter of an hour, the stream of orders pouring out until the marshals were wearied just listening as the secretaries took it all down. The Emperor paced back and forth, hands clasped behind his back, as he glanced from the map to a perspiring Berthier. Then he was done. Lannes and Masséna knew from long experience that there would be no formal dismissal, so motioning their aides to follow, they slipped quietly out of the tent.

"There you are, Jean, and no bad feelings, I hope." Masséna said with his head cocked to the left in the gesture that he used to show interest or sympathy.

---

*Lannes was the only marshal who dared use the familiar "tu" in addressing Napoleon.

"Of course not, Andre, it's all quite simple in spite of all that detail that Berthier has to master. You swing your IVth Corps eastward toward Straubing and capture the bridges near there and intercept any Austrians who try to escape down either side of the Danube," Lannes said.

"And you and Davout and Lefebvre continue to advance on Ratisbon."

"That's it, and as usual, at first light. With any luck we'll be joining forces again and soon," Lannes said.

"What do you mean, 'with luck.' " Doesn't our Emperor say that all his generals must be lucky? I'll see you in Vienna, my friend."

He left Lannes staring after him for a space of seconds before he started for the dismounting point.

Three of Lannes' aides-de-camp—Marbot, de Viry, and Labédoyère—had dismounted and were observing the walls of Ratisbon from a point where the Straubing road ascends a slope southeast of the town. Labédoyère handed his field glass back to Marbot.

"From even two kilometers I can see that those old medieval walls could never withstand the fire of siege cannon for long, don't you agree, Marcellin?" Labédoyère asked.

"Agreed, but hardly the point," Marbot said.

"How do you mean?"

"We've ridden within musket shot of those walls and have drawn enough fire to know that those walls are still defended in strength by infantry and artillery, enough to make it really rough on any assaulting force."

"Then you still think we'll assault the town rather than besiege it?"

"I'll wager that that's the subject being discussed by our marshal and the Emperor right now," Marbot said, gesturing toward the knot of horsemen on a low hillock a hundred meters to his right.

"That's hardly a betting matter. How about your two louis against mine that there'll be no assault?" Labédoyère challenged.

"Done, if I'm saying that there will be a storming—no siege," Marbot said.

"Done then. Will you hold the money, de Viry?" Labédoyère asked. "And now are we agreed on the report to the marshal of the results of our little reconnaissance, Marcellin?"

"I see little to report other than an estimate of the Austrian garrison's strength. As for the rest, anyone with a field glass can see for himself," Marbot said and made a sweep of his arm that took in the town walls as far as the eye could see.

The noon sun beat down bringing to the spring day the promise of a hot afternoon. The crumbling walls of the town, decaying after centuries of standing guard, shimmered under heat rays reflected from the old ramparts. An occasional glint was reflected from a bayonet or musket barrel, showing the presence of watchful Austrian infantry manning the walls. Yet despite their dilapidated condition the walls rose to a height of ten meters above the dry ditch that had served as a moat in medieval times. The ditch itself was as deep as the walls were high, its outer side almost cliff-like in its steep slope. Marbot's fascination with the rich greenness of the wide ditch bottom had been quickly quashed by young de Viry, whose eye had been quicker than the older aide's. "Those are really vegetable gardens, kept by the town folk living just inside the walls," de Viry said, laughing at Marbot's embarrassment. The approaches to the ditch from the French side would have to be made across the wide promenade that encircled the town and bordered the dry ditch for its entire length. From their position on the forward slope the aides could see the battalions of Morand's division moving up in dense columns to positions short of the promenade, just out of range of Austrian muskets. Labédoyère exclaimed and pointed to the artillery guns being towed at a walk through the wide intervals between the dark blue masses of the infantry columns.

"There go the twelve-pounders forward, they're foot artillery from our corps. That doesn't make my money look any too safe," he said.

"We'll see soon enough," de Viry said. "Look, they're going into position now."

As the aides watched, the gun teams pulled ahead of the halted infantry and swung from column into line, each eight-man team preparing for action as it arrived at its designated place. When all eight guns of the battery had signalled readiness, the first ranging rounds began booming out.

"Ranging in on that house there, that one that extends from the walls halfway across the ditch," Marbot said.

"Unlucky people to have built in that place," de Viry said, "but why that house as the target? Why not breach the wall itself at some point?"

Labédoyère's reply carried the lofty tone of the veteran condescending to correct an errant recruit.

"In the first place those walls are far too thick to be breached by field guns. Now, if you'll watch, you'll see that the walls of that house, even though they are made of stone, will soon crumble. See, right there, those rounds striking at the base of the house!"

Powdery grey blossoms of smoke marked the strikes of the round shot against the lower wall of the house. Round after round battered the ditch side of the house until its wall began to fall apart and its debris began tumbling into the ditch. De Viry's embarrassed nod showed he had heard but had still not understood the senior aide's meaning.

"Now, see here," Labédoyère went on, "those broken stones and mortar will soon pile up enough to fill part of the ditch and form an incline that could make a base for a storming party's assault."

"Ah," Marbot broke in, "so you do admit then that there will be a storming—and no siege! Hand over my money, de Viry."

"Oh no you don't," Labédoyère put himself between Marbot and the younger aide, "I'll admit nothing until we hear our marshal himself announce the orders."

"Very well then, let's back to business. I was going to submit an estimate of at least five Austrian battalions holding the town that I got in great part from General Gudin's senior aide. After all, that division learned the hard way this morning after having made a half-dozen attacks and failing to penetrate the walls in each."

"Agreed," Labédoyère said, "and we'd better be getting over there within voice range of the marshal. He may call on us any time now. Have you anything to add, de Viry?"

"Well, no, but it occurs to me that if the Emperor had heeded Marshal Lannes' recommendation last night all of this bloody work would never have to be. We'd be inside those walls instead of an Austrian rear guard."

"Would you listen to our little general now," Labédoyère said, "and while you're wishing why didn't you wish that Colonel Coutard with his 65th of the Line had never surrendered the town to the Austrians three days ago! What about that, my young crystal-gazer?"

Marbot sighed, then set the example as he swung into the saddle.

"All right, you two. What's to be gained by all this child's gabble? If you'd open your eyes instead of your mouths, you'd see that we're being summoned."

The Emperor's eyes were sparkling as he watched the battery's salvos taking their effect on the rapidly crumbling walls of the house. While he was enrapt in his artillery observations—the old gunner back again behind the Toulon batteries or overseeing Marmount's guns at Marengo—none dared attempt to distract his attention. None until Lannes, chafing to get away to his task, spoke up with the familiarity that never failed to shock the household staff.

"If thou hast naught else to say, I ask confirmation of my mission."

Napoleon spoke without taking his eye from his field glass.

"I know I should have listened to you at last night's council, but now that's water under the bridge—Ratisbon's bridge that has carried Archduke Charles' escaping army. And we've been over all the rest of the matter this morning. To sit down here in front of these walls and dig in siege works, batteries, mines and all that would be fatal to my purpose, so near the end of this campaign."

The Emperor handed his field glass to an aide, and directed his attention to Lannes who knew it would only delay attaining his object if he were to make Napoleon's monologue a discussion.

"Yet," Napoleon went on, "you know as well as I that I cannot turn away from an Austrian-held Ratisbon and march down the Danube to take Vienna. If I did, Charles could recross the river by Ratisbon bridge and cut my lines of communications. On the other hand, if I am checked here by a siege or any other kind of delay, Prussia and those other German states could join actively in Austria's cause."

He shifted his seat in the saddle, and looked back again at the artillery battery and its target. His irritation showed in his indecision about whether to continue his ponderings or simply to refocus his attention on the artillery fires. After a few seconds he turned his eyes on Lannes.

"It's a good thing you're on horseback, you know," Napoleon said.

"Why, Sire, I don't understand," Lannes said.

"If you were standing, it would be on one foot and then the other. Very well, you will have the orders you've been waiting for. I put the whole matter in your hands. You take Ratisbon, however you will, and now!"

"I thank your majesty, and have I leave to go and make preparations?"

"To make preparations, indeed. Do you think your Emperor is blind? I see that you have ordered up Morand's division, and right under my eyes. Yes, go, and report when you are ready to—"

Napoleon's face contorted, and his unfinished sentence was cut short with his muffled cry of pain.

"I'm hit, Jean," he managed to gasp under his breath, "don't alarm the others."

Napoleon was leaning forward, supporting his right shoulder against his horse's neck. Lannes was off his horse in a flash, running to the Emperor's side. He freed his chief's boot from the stirrup, got his arms around him, and lowered him to the ground, where he held Napoleon erect by pulling his right arm around his shoulders.

"Where, Sire, where?" Lannes asked.

"My right foot—the ankle."

Before the words were out, Napoleon and Lannes were surrounded by Berthier, General Mouton, and a dozen aides and staff officers. Lannes had gotten the Emperor to sit on the ground and stretch out his legs. The marshal looked up at the circle of stricken faces, and snapped his orders at them.

"Mouton, get the others back from here, and send for Doctor Larrey. Alexandre, help his majesty sit up while I get his boot off. Duroc, get some cloaks or blankets together and make a cot to put him on," Lannes ordered.

Lannes grasped the heel and toe of the Emperor's right boot, and pulled firmly and as gently as he could. Napoleon's face was as expressionless as he could manage, but Lannes saw that he was biting his lower lip to stifle an outcry. When the foot of the boot was free of the ankle the boot slid off smoothly. Lannes and Berthier saw the oozing of blood just forward of the ankle bone. When the silk stocking had been peeled off, the two could see that the bullet had spent its force when it had penetrated the boot. While they were uncovering the wound, Larrey, the surgeon-general, arrived and quickly finished his examination.

"Well, Dominique, what is it? What do you say about it?" Napoleon demanded.

"Sire, it is only a scratch of a flesh wound. The bullet was spent, and no wonder, at this distance. It must have been one of those Austrian Tyrolese sharpshooters taking an off-chance that his rifle shot could reach the command group here. I will dress it, and you must stay off your feet. There will be a lot of muscular pain, that's all," Larrey said.

"Well, get on with it. Mouton, I must get mounted at once. Have Marengo brought back," Napoleon said.

The word of the Emperor's wounding had spread like wildfire through the army, and already soldiers were running up to the imperial cavalry demanding news of the Emperor's condition. The hillock threatened to become smothered under masses of excited soldiers, alarmed by confusion and rumor. When his grey Arabian was ready, Napoleon was assisted into the saddle and was on his way to show himself to his troops. As he left he called back to Lannes.

"Get on with it, Jean. Don't wait to make a report, go when you're ready. Everything will be all right as soon as the troops see me riding."

Lannes was already in the saddle, needing no further word to start him on his mission.

When the marshal and his three aides dismounted behind the long storage building at the near edge of the promenade they found that Lannes' preparatory orders had been carried out to the last detail. The first storming party was organized and ready; fifty hand-picked volunteers from grenadier companies were stretched on the ground in the shelter of the stone building, their scaling ladders lying between the leading files. Other ladders were being unloaded from carts rounded up from the surrounding farm villages. Morand was at Lannes' side as he dismounted, and made his report.

"Excellent, Louis," Lannes said, his grin showing his pleasure, "let's get them on their feet and ready to move out."

When the storming column had fallen in, Lannes faced the file leaders at its head, and raised his voice so that even the supporting companies behind the grenadiers could hear him.

"You know you've got to move fast to get across that hundred and fifty meters of open ground before you get to the ditch. Remember that you will need ladders to get down into the ditch and more ladders to get up the walls. You must find footing for them in the rubble that the artillery made of that house. No cheering, now, there'll be time for that later. Be off with you, lads, and God go with you!"

Lannes and Marbot watched from the corner of the building as the closely packed column swung into the open and started across the promenade. The last files had scarcely cleared the building when the column was met by volleys of musketry and a storm of grapeshot. The leading files carrying the ladders broke into a run, the rest of the party following on their heels. Men began to drop until the storming column's path was marked by a trail of dead and wounded. Lannes watched a handful of leaders, fewer than twenty in all, disappear over the side of the ditch and saw the ramparts obscured by clouds of powder smoke. He thrust aside the field glass Marbot had held out to him. He needed no glass to see the ramp of rubble that was the storming party's first goal. In the seconds that followed, the first of the walking wounded made their way back to the shelter of the stone building, blood-stained and beaten men. Even worse, in Lannes' sight, was that the inclined pile of rubble had been undisturbed by the feet of any French soldier; not a man had made it across the ditch, for all had been mowed down by nearly point-blank fire from the Austrian infantry on the ramparts.

Morand knew as well as Lannes that no time should be wasted in dispatching a second storming column. The sight of the wounded and the tales of Austrian firepower that would follow would wreak havoc on the morale of the supporting infantry. Morand and Colonel Valterre of the 30th of the Line had the next group poised, ready to charge forward. Lannes made no address to the men, they had already heard his send-off to their predecessors. He simply waved them on with his blessing. Again he watched from the corner of the building as the next fifty volunteers dashed across the promenade. And again he saw the slaughter as the wreckage of the column made it into the ditch, never to reappear on the rubble against the far wall. This time even fewer wounded returned with their stories of the hail of bullets and cannon shot that had almost annihilated their column.

Morand's third call for volunteers—"from any company"—was met with a gloomy silence. Lannes' attempt to support Morand with his own call met with the same silence.

My God, Lannes thought, *here we still stand, in full view of the Emperor and the whole army, an utter failure with not a single Frenchman reaching that wall, let alone scaling it.*

His racing thoughts were interrupted by Morand's plea.

"Sir, these battalions of Colonel Valterre's 30th stand ready to charge if you will only give the order." Morand's desperation showed in every line of his livid face. Here was a renowned soldier, one of the "three immortals," ready to go down before Austrian bullets rather than face the disgrace of failure in the eyes of the army and the Emperor. Lannes knew that as well as he knew he drew breath. That was why his voice was almost gentle in his answer.

"I know I could give that order, Louis, but you know I will not. You know only too well the difference between *élan*

Marshal Lannes at Ratisbon, from a drawing by John W. Thomason, Jr.

and simple obedience. We will go next with volunteers or we will not go at all. Now, I'll try once more with them," Lannes said.

He turned to face the columns drawn up in the rear of the building, and put his innermost thoughts into his shouted words.

"Do I have to tell you men that your Emperor and the rest of the army are watching you? No, you know that as well as I. Then, will it be said by them that the soldiers of this division refused to volunteer because they had seen their comrades fail?"

Lannes paused, waiting to hear the shouts of men pressing forward to take their places in the next storming party. Instead he was met with the same stubborn silence. The men in the front ranks were staring at the ground to avoid the blazing eyes of their marshal. Lannes felt the silence that had fallen across the massed battalions and over the whole plain and the army behind it. Even the Austrian ramparts were silent, as though the infantry there would share the scene with their enemy. The silence lasted for seconds that seemed to stretch into hours. Suddenly it was shattered by Lannes.

"*Eh bien,* I will let you see that I was a grenadier before I was a marshal, and still am one!" He snatched a ladder from an astonished grenadier, and heaving it to his shoulder, marched around the corner of the building toward the corpse-littered promenade.

An astounded Marbot and de Viry dashed after him. When they caught up to him, Marbot grabbed at the front end of the ladder while de Viry tried to seize the other end. Lannes swung the ladder away from them and raged at them:

"Let be! If you will follow, do so, but I am carrying this ladder."

Marbot dared to place himself two paces ahead of his chief before he spoke.

"*Monsieur le Maréchal,* do you want us disgraced, and that we will be if you were to get the slightest wound while carrying that ladder—and as long as one of your aides was left alive."

Lannes marched stubbornly on, as if he had not heard a word. Marbot and de Viry, seeing that the time for words had passed, grabbed for the ladder again. This time the younger men succeeded in wrenching the ladder from their marshal's grasp, even though he continued to resist. As the

three men came to a halt they realized that the plain was resounding with the cheers of Morand's division. At the sight
of a marshal of France, struggling with his aides-de-camp over
the leading of an assault, Morand's battalions had begun to
voice their esprit and the shouts of aroused men had run
through the whole division.

When the three got back to the building they were almost
overwhelmed with officers and soldiers who had rushed forward to seize ladders and join in the next assault. Morand
and his senior officers restored order, and as the men returned to their ranks, they began their selection of the next
fifty. It was not a simple task, for every man was now a volunteer, but in moments the best officers and the tallest grenadiers had been chosen and formed into a new column. While
this was being done, Lannes had time for a calmer exchange
with Marbot and de Viry.

"So now, fire-eaters, the cork has been drawn, and the
wine must be drunk, bitter though it may be," Lannes said.

"Sir, we have earned the right to lead this next storming
party, and we would continue to deserve disgrace if we were
thought to have put on a show just to turn the job over to
someone else," Marbot said.

The marshal took off his great cocked hat with its white
fringe, red cockade, and gold loop, and wiped his brow before fixing both aides with a stare.

"Very well then, Marbot, you may lead, accompanied by
de Viry and Labédoyère. I suppose I should also send all my
staff, so that I alone will be my own headquarters after all
have been lost. And, Marbot, you had better have a plan after
what we've seen this afternoon," Lannes said.

"Sir, I already have a plan based on what we've seen happen to those other two assaults. They failed because they were
storming columns, not parties. They presented a mass, a target to the Austrians that couldn't be missed. What's more, the
ladder men were all in front, getting tangled up with each
other and slowing up those behind them." Marbot almost
stuttered in his haste to get out his lessons from the situation.

"But how do you propose to remedy all that?" Lannes
asked.

"If General Morand will designate a staff officer to dispatch my groups that will follow, de Viry and I will take off
with the first ladder. The other ladders should follow at twenty-
pace intervals, everyone moving at a run," Marbot said.

"And after that, what? How do you intend to get at the walls?"

"When we reach the ditch all the ladders should be placed against the near side of the ditch, two paces apart. After the leading files have descended they will take every other ladder, climb the pile of rubble, and place those ladders against the ramparts a half-meter apart."

The marshal gave his approval and saw that Morand's officers and men understood Marbot's plan. Finally, the details were settled and Lannes sent them out by saying,

"Off with you, lads, and Ratisbon is taken!"

At those words, Marbot and de Viry led out, darting around the building, and crossing the promenade at a dead run. They slung their ladder down the rear wall of the ditch and slid rather than climbed down it. The Austrians, bewildered by the sight of running pairs of men who presented only small fleeting targets, loosed off renewed volleys. But the musket is not an accurate weapon even against men standing in ranks beyond fifty paces, and now its ineffectiveness showed immediately. All of Marbot's officers and the fifty grenadiers reached and crossed the ditch without the loss of a man. The rearmost grenadiers acted as *tirailleurs,* blazing away at the Austrians on the ramparts.

Marbot and de Viry, now carrying separate ladders, ran stumblingly up the heaped rubble and got their ladders seated and leaned against the wall. Marbot was the first to ascend his ladder up the wall, double a man's height from the top of the rubble to the ramparts. Labédoyère was climbing the ladder next to Marbot's, only a forearm's length away, when he felt his ladder's bottom end begin to slide out from the wall.

"Marcellin, give me your hand. My ladder is slipping!" Labédoyère shouted.

Marbot heard his cry in spite of the muskets banging away overhead. He grasped the aide's left hand in his right, and together they reached the rampart. For a second or two they were standing there in full view of the Emperor and the army. Even at a distance of hundreds of meters they could hear across the plain the cheers coming from scores of thousands. One cannot doubt the sincerity of Marbot's words when he says in his *Memoirs:* "It was one of the finest days of my life."

In a moment the two were joined by the other officers and the fifty grenadiers. The Austrian infantry had disappeared into the streets below, and Marbot could look back over the wall and see the columns of supporting battalions swarming into the ditch and placing more ladders against the walls. The impossible had been made possible, and the French were in Ratisbon, but Marbot and his storming party had still to carry out the rest of Marshal Lannes' orders: "Get to the Straubing gate and open it to the marshal who will be leading the battalions which have been designated to penetrate the town and seize the bridge before the Austrians can destroy it." The gate was scarcely more than a hundred meters distant from the point where Marbot and his men had scaled the wall. But what enemy force was there between them and the gate?

As soon as Marbot and his little group were down in the street nearest the wall, he divided the fifty grenadiers into two sections and assigned officers to each. His orders were brief:

"Each section to a side of the street, keeping in double file and hugging the houses. I will lead the right section, and both sections will guide on me."

Their advance was cautious but steady, and as they moved down the street and around the first corner they found no signs of Austrian soldiers. The streets and even the houses, as far as Marbot could tell, were deserted; no doubt the town-folk living near the walls had fled at the sounds of heavy firing. Marbot was leading them down the closest street that paralleled the wall. It was a narrow thoroughfare, and Marbot could see it curving to the left, out of his sight for the next thirty meters. He covered that distance at a quick pace until he was able to see around the curve into the tiny *platz* where the streets met under a wide archway. What he saw across the little square brought him to an abrupt halt. Marbot had seen more than his share of strange sights this day, but what confronted him now made him freeze in place.

Under the arch that extended to the Straubing gate and in front of the gate itself an Austrian infantry battalion, a thousand strong, was massed in close order facing the gate. Every man in the formation was facing the gate, obviously deployed there to counterattack any French assault on the gate. Even the battalion commander who had posted himself near the center of the rear rank was facing in the same direction. Marbot was quick to note another incredible detail—no sentries had been posted over the gate or on top of the wall!

Marbot silently signalled his two sections to halt and form into double rank across the street they had just come up. The rattle of the grenadiers' arms and the sound of boots on the cobblestones must have alarmed the Austrian commander, who faced around toward the French with a startled oath. His sharp cry, in turn, alerted his officers who faced the rear ranks about and had them level their muskets. Labédoyère gave a similar command to the French grenadiers, and Marbot found himself facing the Austrian major at a distance of three paces, each commander looking into ranks of levelled muskets, cocked and ready to fire.

Sacrebleu! Marbot cursed to himself. *What a hell of a thing to happen after all we've been through today. This is indeed a situation calling for "military tact." One thing is certain—this Austrian can see only the front rank of my party, and he doesn't know what is behind it. This leaves but one thing to do.*

He had been carrying his unsheathed hussar's saber; he snapped to attention and saluted the Austrian with it. The major's eyes grew even rounder at the amazing sight of a brilliantly uniformed French cavalry officer saluting him in front of two ranks of grenadiers with levelled muskets. His right hand came slowly to the salute as though it was being raised by an unseen force.

"The major speaks French?" Marbot asked.

He did.

"Then I must ask that your men lay down their arms. I lead the advance guard of Marshal Lannes' corps of thirty thousand men, and the town is in our hands. The corps of Marshals Davout and Lefebvre have already reached the bridge and captured it. You have no choice but to accept the terms of an honorable surrender," Marbot said.

The Austrian's face was a study in dismay and disbelief. As he struggled with his conscience and a sense of the inevitable, Marbot's quick eye took in another fact—the white-coated Austrian infantrymen's uniforms were as clean as if on parade, and the major's glistening, gold-topped boots showed no traces of dust. Clearly this was a battalion that had not yet been committed to action, and as such must have no knowledge of the tactical situation. This was confirmed when the major decided that Marbot had indeed summed up the situation with accuracy. He gave the command to ground arms, and then in a torrent of German explained the situation to his men.

His words were heeded by the companies in front—those

which had been the rearmost before the confrontation—who passed forward their muskets to be grounded by the front rank. But three companies, now in the rear and nearest the gate, began shouting refusals to surrender. The Austrian commander sent officers to subdue the commotion and restore order when a new disaster threatened to wreck Marbot's "tactful" victory.

The fiery Labédoyère had jumped to the conclusion that Marbot had let things get out of hand and that the Austrians were going to resort to a last-ditch fight. He sprang at the Austrian major and grabbed him by the throat. When the Austrian pushed him back in order to defend himself, Labédoyère threatened to run him through with his drawn saber. Marbot knocked the blade aside with a swing of his saber while de Viry put his arms around Labédoyère from behind, pinioning him until he could be calmed down.

Order restored, the surrender went on without further incident until all the Austrian muskets had been piled and the battalion had marched away under its own officers, guided by a French officer with a file of grenadiers.

Hardly had the Austrians cleared the square when Marbot and the others were treated to the sound of French axes battering at the outer side of the gate.

"It sounds like our marshal has a rude way of announcing his entry. But things would go smoother if we were to open the gate ourselves, don't you think?" de Viry asked Marbot.

When Marbot could make himself heard, the battering on the other side stopped, and the grenadiers were able to unchain the great bars and slide them aside until the gates swung inward. Marshal Lannes, sword in hand, stood facing his aides while double files of infantry swirled past him through the gateway. Marbot ran forward to make his report, and Lannes motioned him to the far side of the square in order to get out of the way of the columns of infantry pouring through the square. Lannes listened with his usual intentness until Marbot had finished the story of his bluff and the Austrian surrender. The marshal's face lit up with a grin at the thought of a thousand Austrians being duped into surrender by a storming party one-twentieth of their strength.

"So now, Marbot, you have no twinges of conscience after telling such tall tales—you with three army corps behind you, indeed. *Merveilleux!*"

"None, Sir, especially when one remembers that you and Marshal Murat took the Spitz bridge five years ago from the Austrians without a shot fired—and with some of the same kind of persuasion."

"*Bien touché,* we will not pursue that point further, at least not now. But now I want you to find Major Saint-Mars and have him bring his guides along. He can find me, I'm taking that street over there that should lead to the town center. You can catch up with me, along with Saint-Mars. I'll take the other aides with me, for now," Lannes said, taking off across the square with his swift stride.

Labédoyère and de Viry started to follow the marshal when Marbot stepped in front of them.

"Just one moment, old friends, but we have a small matter to settle before you join the marshal. Monsieur de Viry, I believe you are carrying four gold louis which belong to me," Marbot said.

"Ah yes, I believe I am," de Viry said, reaching inside his pelisse for his purse, "if, of course, Monsieur Labédoyère has no questions about the total coming to four louis."

"I think not, de Viry. Even a man who confuses sieges with assaults can add two and two," Marbot said. "Is that not true, Labédoyère?"

Marbot never got his answer. Labédoyère was already halfway across the square, hastening to catch up with his marshal.

Inspiration

ONE OF THE MOST widely known admonitions of World War II was not given by a superior officer to a subordinate. Yet the reversed warning made a great deal of sense: "General, do you have to draw fire while you are inspiring us?" This, an obvious misuse of *presence*, often fetched results that were as undersirable as they were opposite to the intent.

In its most pragmatic sense *inspiration* must, to be effective, produce the results the leader sought before he arrived on the spot where he thought his presence would turn the trick. And perhaps "turning the trick" is the key to finding a criterion, a simple definition: *The leader's presence should be used only when it can be seen as a requisite for moving men to actions that are essential to accomplishing the mission.* In more soldierly terms, don't do it unless you are sure that you are the one who is needed on the spot to get the job done. If the latter terms seem to imply something short of the heroic, just recall that the leader has no more immunity to enemy action than has the newest replacement; and the dead or seriously wounded leader is of no more use to his command than a dead replacement.

Thus, calculation ought to govern a leader's use of inspiration rather than impulse, no matter how heroic the aim. The exposure of the self to physical danger should, to produce the desired end, be resorted to only when there is a reasonable probability of success.

In our next example the leader has chosen to expose himself in two ways, as we shall see. For me it is a dramatic instance that shows the use of presence as inspiration. I have not been able to find an equal to it.

The Taking of Lungtungpen*
by
Rudyard Kipling

My friend Private Mulvaney told me this, sitting on the parapet of the road to Dagshai, when we were hunting butterflies together. He had theories about the Army, and colored clay pipes perfectly. He said that the young soldier is the best to work with, "on account of the surpassing innocence of the child."

"Now, listen!" said Mulvaney, throwing himself full length on the wall in the sun. "I'm a born scutt of the barrack room! The Army's meat an' drink to me, because I'm one of the few that can't quit it. I've put in seventeen years, an' the pipeclay's in the marrow of me. If I could have kept out of one big drink a month, I would have been an honorary lieutenant by this time—a nuisance to my betters, a laughin' stock to my equals, and a curse to meself. Bein' what I am, I'm Private Mulvaney, with no good-conduct pay and a devourin' thirst. Always barrin' my little friend Bobs Bahadur,** I know as much about the Army as most men."

I said something here.

"Wolseley be shot! Between you an' me an' that butterfly net, he's a ramblin', incoherent sort of a devil with one eye on the Queen and the Court, an' the other on his blessed self—everlastin'ly playing Caesar and Alexander rolled into a lump. Now Bobs is a sensible little man. With Bobs and a few three-year-olds, I'd sweep any army off the earth into a towel, and throw it away afterward. Faith, I'm not jokin'! 'Tis the boys—the raw boys—that don't know what a bullet means, and wouldn't care if they did—that do the work. They're crammed with bull-meat till they fairly romps with good livin'; and then, if they don't fight, they blow each other's heads off.

---

*Reprinted from *Soldiers Three* by permission of Doubleday & Co.
**Bobs Bahadur—Field Marshal Lord Roberts, this five-foot-three idol was known by his soldier nickname "Bobs," and was the most popular of Victorian generals; the Bahadur was a title of respect, traceable to the ancient Asiatic title of knight or lord.

'Tis the truth I'm tellin' you. They should be kept on water and rice in the hot weather; but there'd be a mutiny if 'twas done.

"Did you ever hear how Private Mulvaney took the town of Lungtungpen? I thought not! 'Twas the Lieutenant got the credit; but 'twas me planned the scheme. A little before I was invalided from Burma, me and four-an'-twenty young ones under a Lieutenant Brazenose, was ruining our digestions trying to catch dacoits.* And such double-ended devils I never knew! 'Tis only a dah** and a Snider*** that makes a dacoit. Without them, he's a peaceful cultivator, and felony for to shoot. We hunted, and we hunted, and took fever and elephants now and again; but no dacoits. Eventually, we puckarowed one man. 'Treat him tenderly,' says the Lieutenant. So I took him away into the jungle, with the Burmese interpreter and my cleaning-rod. Says I to the man, 'My peaceful squireen," says I, 'you squat on your hunkers and demonstrate to my friend here, where your friends are when they're at home?' With that I introduced him to the cleaning-rod, and he commenced to jabber; the interpreter interpreting in betweens, and me helpin' the Intelligence Department with my cleaning-rod when the man misremembered.

"Presently, I learn that, across the river, about nine miles away, was a town just drippin' with dahs, and bows and arrows, and dacoits, and elephants, and jingles.**** 'Good!' says I; 'this office will now close!'

"That night, I went to the Lieutenant and communicates my information. I never thought much of Lieutenant Brazenose till that night. He was stiff with books and theories, and all manner of trimming's of no manner of use. 'Town did you say?' says he. 'According to the theories of War, we should wait for reinforcements.'—'Faith!' thinks I, 'we'd better dig our graves then;' for the nearest troops was up to their stocks in the marshes out Mimbu way. 'But,' says the Lieutenant, 'since it's a special case, I'll make an exception. We'll visit this Lungtungpen tonight.'

"The boys were fairly wild with delight when I told 'em; and, by this and that, they went through the jungle like buck-rabbits. About midnight we come to the stream which I had

*Dacoit—Burmese or Indian robbers, killers, thieves.
**Dah—a machete-like knife used for slashing vegetation or fighting.
***Snider—at the time the obsolete British Army rifle musket converted to a breech-loader.
****Jingle—the jingal, a bell-mouthed, heavy musket fired from a support.

clean forgot to mention to my officer. I was on ahead with four boys, and I thought that the Lieutenant might want to theorize. 'Stop boys,' says I. 'Strip to the buff, and swim in where glory waits!'—'But I can't swim,' says two of them. 'To think I should live to hear that from a boy with a board-school education!' says I. 'Take a lump of timber, and me and Conolly here will ferry you over, you young ladies!'

"We got an old tree-trunk, and pushed off with the kits and the rifles on it. The night was chokin' dark, and just as we was fairly embarked, I heard the Lieutenant behind me callin' out. 'There's a bit of a nullah here, sir,' says I, 'But I can feel the bottom already.' So I could, for I was not a yard from the bank.

" 'Bit of a nullah! Bit of an estuary!' says the Lieutenant. 'Go on, you mad Irishman! Strip boys,' I heard him laugh; and the boys began strippin' and rolling a log into the water to put their kits on. So me and Conolly struck out through the warm water with our log, and the rest came on behind.

"That stream was miles wide! Ortheris, on the rear-rank log, whispers we had got into the Thames below Sheerness by mistake. 'Keep on swimmin' you little blackguard,' says I, 'an Irriwaddy.'—'Silence, men!' sings out the Lieutenant. So we swam on into the black dark, with our chests on the logs, trustin' in the Saints and the luck of the British Army.

"Eventually, we hit ground—a bit of sand—and a man. I put my heel on the back of him. He skreeched and ran.

" 'Now we've done it!' says Lieutenant Brazenose. 'Where the devil is Lungtungpen?' There was about a minute and a half to wait. The boys laid a hold of their rifles and some tried to put their belts on; we was marching with fixed bayonets of course. Then we knew where Lungtungpen was; for we had hit the river-wall of it in the dark, and the whole town blazed with them messin' jingles and Sniders like a cat's back on a frosty night. They was firin' all ways at once; but over our heads into the stream.

" 'Have you got your rifles?' says Brazenose. 'Got 'em!' says Ortheris. 'I've got that thief Mulvaney's for all my back-pay, an' she'll kick my heart sick with that blunderin' long stock of hers.'—'Go on!' yells Brazenose, whippin' his sword out. 'Go on and take the town! And the Lord have mercy on our souls!'

"Then the boys gave one devastatin' howl, and pranced into the dark, feelin' for the town, and blindin' and' stiffin' like Cavalry Riding Masters when the grass pricked their bare legs. I hammered with the butt at some bamboo-thing that felt weak, and the rest came and hammered contagious, while the jingles was jingling, and ferocious yells from inside was splittin' our ears. We was too close under the wall for them to hurt us.

"Eventually, the thing, whatever it was, broke; and the six-an'-twenty of us tumbled, one after the other, naked as we was born, into the town of Lungtungpen. There was a melee of sumptuous kind for a while; but whether they took us, all white and wet, for a new breed of devil, or a new kind of dacoit, I don't know. They ran as though we was both, and we went into them, bayonet and butt, shriekin' with laughin'. There was torches in the streets, and I saw little Ortheris rubbin' his shoulder every time he loosed my long-stock Martini; and Brazenose walkin' into the gang with his sword, like Diomedes of the Golden Collar—barring he hadn't a stitch of clothin' on him. We discovered elephants with dacoits under their bellies, and, what with one thing and other, we was busy till mornin' takin' possession of the town of Lungtungpen.

"Then we halted and formed up, the women howlin' in the houses and the Lieutenant blushin' pink in the light of the mornin' sun. 'Twas the most indecent parade I ever took a hand in. Five-an'-twenty privates and an officer of the Line in review order, and not as much as would dust a fife between 'em all in the way of clothin'! Eight of us had their belts and pouches on; but the rest had gone in with a handful of cartridges and the skin God gave them. They was as naked as Venus.

"'Number off from the right!' says the Lieutenant. 'Odd numbers fall out to dress; even numbers patrol the town till relieved by the dressing party.' Let me tell you, patrollin' a town with nothin' on is an experience. I patrolled for ten minutes, and begad, before 'twas over, I blushed. The women laughed so. I never blushed before or since; but I blushed all over my carcass then. Ortheris didn't patrol. He says only, 'Portsmouth Barracks and the Hard of a Sunday.' Then he lay down and rolled any ways with laughin'.

"When we was all dressed, we counted the dead—seventy-five dacoits besides the wounded. We took five elephants, a hundred and seventy Sniders, two hundred dahs, and a lot of other burglarious truck. Not a man of us was

Private Mulvaney

hurt—except maybe the Lieutenant, and he from the shock of his decency.

"The Headman of Lungtungpen, who surrendered himself asked the interpreter—'If the English fight like that with their clothes off, what in the world do they do with their clothes on?' Ortheris began rollin' his eyes and crackin' his fingers and dancin' a step-dance for to impress the Headman. He ran to his house; an' we spent the rest of the day carryin' the Lieutenant on our shoulders round the town, and playin' with the Burmese babies—fat, little, brown little devils, as pretty as pictures.

"When I was invalided for the dysentery to India, I says to the Lieutenant, 'Sir,' says I, 'you've the makin' in you of a great man; but if you'll let an old soldier speak, you're too fond of theorizing.' He shook hands with me and says, "Hit high, hit low, there's no pleasing you, Mulvaney. You've seen me waltzing through Lungtungpen like a Red Indian without the warpaint, and you say I'm too fond of theorizing?'—'Sir,' says I, for I loved the boy; 'I would waltz with you in that condition through Hell, and so would the rest of the men!' Then I went downstream in the flat and left him my blessin'. May the Saints carry him where he should go, for he was a fine upstandin' young officer."

So saying, Mulvaney took up his butterfly-net, and returned to the barracks.

•

Part Five

ENERGY

von Lettow-Vorbeck
at **Tanga,** 1914

ENERGY

Beware of rashness, but with energy and sleepless vigilance
go forward and give us victories.
　　　　　　　—Lincoln, *Letter to Major-General Hooker*

A review of the attributes of courage, will, intellect, and presence shows
that each must be supported by a vigorous physique which can produce
and sustain the energy the leader needs for forceful action. When General
Grant was asked what he thought were the qualities that most sustained
him throughout his Civil War campaigns, he replied that health and energy
should head the list. In his words, they gave him "the power to endure
anything."

In that light it appears sound to consider energy as the "life support"
for the other four attributes. It then becomes evident that energy per se
has no value until it is coupled with a desirable quality. This has been illustrated fittingly in the advice (apochryphal, but useful) supposedly given
to officers of the German General Staff concerning the selection and as-
signment of army officers:

"Observe first that sort of officer, the brilliant and the lazy. There is
command material there that must not be overlooked.

"Next, consider the brilliant and energetic. These combined qualities
make for an excellent chief of staff, chief of the operations section or intelligence section.

"Thirdly, one may encounter the stupid and the lazy. This sort may
be retained as line officers, for they will not rise to positions of great responsibility, and they can perform all kinds of dull duties.

"Finally, one may discover the combination of the stupid and the energetic. When this kind is discovered, get rid of him immediately. There
can be no greater danger to the armies of our Fatherland!"

Or anyone else's fatherland. Since we are fortunate in our survey in
not having to consider stupidity (with the possible exception of its popping
up as an element of the dynamic frustration), we may now observe an un-
common combination of the leader's attributes in action all being supported by the leader's energy. In this case there should be but a wee challenge to the reader's perception in identifying all six battlefield dynamics
being countered by the five attributes.

272

Energy

The Junker, the Governor, the British, and the Killer Bees

IT WAS THE evening of August 3, 1914 when the Governor of German East Africa began to feel his world falling apart. The realization came suddenly and in a most ungentle way while he was trying to steel himself to face down the arrogant junker who was the commandant of the colony's crack *Schutz-truppe*. The Prussian's artful gesture of defiance—placing his monocle in the eye wounded during the Herero uprising—had made things no easier for Governor Schnee. He had handed the commandant the Reuters dispatch that confirmed the state of war between Germany, France and Russia, and stated that England's declaration of war on the Central Powers was expected momentarily. It was when the Commandant laid aside the dispatch that the confrontation came to a head. The soldier's reaction showed a thorough lack of understanding of the role he was expected to play under the Governor's policies.

"Good," Lieutenant-Colonel von Lettow-Vorbeck said, "I shall alert the *Schutztruppe* to stand by for my next directive."

"What sort of directive?" the Governor asked.

"I have already sent you my strategic estimate, Excellency, so that you realize how we can assist the Fatherland in a war with the British, and that is by tying up all the British

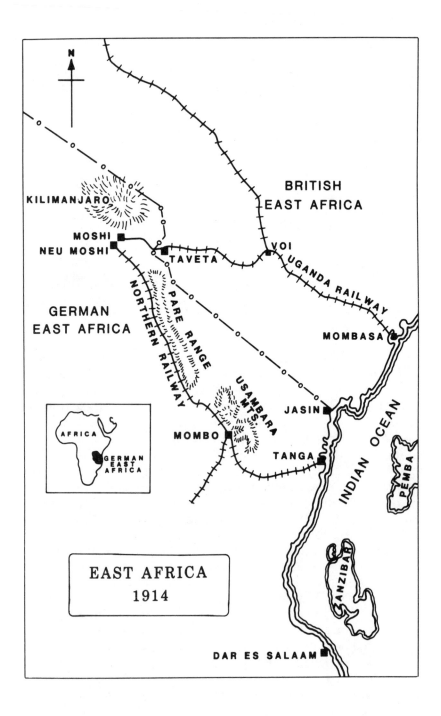

EAST AFRICA
1914

forces we can in Africa. That effort can only be launched effectively against the enemy by striking where it will be felt the most."

"You mean that it is actually your intention to attack the British?" the Governor stammered out his amazement at this affront to his avowed policy of neutrality.

"But of course, Doctor Schnee. And, as I have pointed out, the area where we must strike is through the great gap between Mount Kilimanjaro and the Pare Range, that is via Moshi and Taveta, in order to cut the Uganda Railway that forms British East Africa's vital link from the port of Mombasa to the interior. When we have done that we shall have seized the initiative, thus forcing the British to react, and that reaction will have to come through British forces that otherwise could be employed in Europe."

Halfway through Lettow-Vorbeck's curt military summation, the Governor was out of his chair and pacing behind his desk, his face sweating from more than the African heat.

"I think, Colonel, that it is time that you are oriented in regard to this government's positions on African questions. To put it in words that you will understand, I did not send for you to hear military estimates or plans. You are here to listen to *my* orders and for no other reason."

"With all respect, Your Excellency, it is no longer a case of colonial government giving orders to its commandant. My channel of command runs through the commander of colonial troops in Berlin, and through him to the High Command."

"Aren't you forgetting, Colonel, that I, as Governor of this colony, am also the commander-in-chief of its military forces? I have had my staff draw up plans which will ensure that German East Africa will maintain a neutral status. Accordingly, in order to guarantee the security of the capital, I order you to evacuate Dar es Salaam by noon tomorrow and move your troops to the interior."

"I don't see what good purpose that would serve. You and that staff can't possibly believe that German citizens would be guaranteed their safety by removing the only means of protecting them. So, Excellency, I must ask what objectives you seek by acting in this manner?"

The Governor's effort at self-control was becoming more obvious with each pace. He did not look around at Lettow-Vorbeck as he took up the challenge.

"Look, I, as Governor, have no obligation to answer that. Now, if I have to, I am capable of relieving you of command of the *Schutztruppe* and placing you under arrest. I trust I make that clear."

Lettow-Vorbeck's rugged face was expressionless as he fixed the Governor with his good eye.

"I must ask—what do you intend to do to secure the capital and the other ports?"

"I'll answer that with my question. Are you the military servant of this government or not?"

"Very well, Excellency, if I evacuate Dar es Salaam, and if I must move my troops from here and to the other coastal garrisons, I require concurrence in concentrating them at New Moshi in the Kilimanjaro area."

The Governor smiled, but it was a taut, humorless smile.

"You know that I know New Moshi is too close to the frontier of British East Africa, too close in the sense of making the sort of provocation that I've been trying to avoid. Now, for once and for all, you will move your troops to the interior—and far from the frontier. Is that order clear enough for you, Colonel?"

"Quite, Excellency."

The click of the commandant's heels came precisely as his saluting hand touched his forehead.

"But hold on, Lettow-Vorbeck. We are gentlemen, you and I, and we shall not part without a drink to settle this in a seemly fashion. In all things I hope you'll understand that what I have said here this evening has been in the interests of our colony."

"While I, Excellency, have spoken in the interests of the Fatherland."

Who was this upstart commander who had taken it upon himself to set aims for German strategy in East Africa? And what were the military forces he could count on to carry out those aims?

Lt.-Col. Paul Emil von Lettow-Vorbeck has been characterized as the archetype of the Prussian junker. That sort of characterization might serve to describe Lettow (for that is what we may call him) at a passing glance—blond hair cropped close to the skull in the Prussian fashion, steely blue eyes set beneath rugged brows, a fierce beak of a nose and a narrow mustache over a thin-lipped mouth—yet that glance would

General von Lettow-Vorbeck

miss the real man within. The incisive mind that went straight to the core of a problem was wedded to a Spartan self-discipline that enabled his lean body to endure all the hardships that would have to be faced in the four years of fighting his enemies in some of the roughest terrain in the world.

At the age of forty-four, in 1914, Lettow had come to his post in Africa with twenty-five years of service that provided unmatched credentials for command of the colony's military. After graduation from the military school at Kassel and postings to regimental duties, he served alongside the British in Peking during the Boxer Rebellion, where he gained an impression of "the clumsiness with which English troops were moved and led in battle"—a prophetic insight into the battle where we will see Lettow in action against them. His first experience with operations in Africa came while on detached service with pre-Boer War forces in South Africa under the famed commando leader Louis Botha. Lettow's introduction to African bush fighting followed in 1904 when he was assigned in South West Africa as adjutant to General von Trotha. In the German service of that time and area of operations, the adjutant was not a paper shuffler; he was a chief of personal staff who was required to serve as the occasion demanded as a line officer. It was during the latter kind of duty that Lettow was wounded in the eye and chest while fighting the Hereros. During that campaign, the Hereros had combined with their allies, the Hottentots, to give white colonials their greatest headache since the Zulu Wars.

Initially the Germans learned the hard way, for they found themselves pitted against skillful bush fighters whose operations were masterminded by cunning tacticians. These uncharted and desolate wastes, which varied from savannas to rockbound hills to endless miles of dense thorn growths, the *nyika* or the *bundu*, formed the bitter background in which the young Lettow saw at firsthand something his brother officers failed to appreciate—that small groups of highly motivated men, inured to and familiar with the terrain, could tie up much larger European-trained and organized forces. The Africans could survive and fight where European troop movements became "walking hospitals." Moreover, the native guerrilla fighters could find water in deserts where white men dropped from thirst, and they could move more swiftly through the brush than their enemies could follow on horseback.

There were lessons to be learned in that hard school, and Lettow went on to learn them from the enemy. Like Henry Bouquet a century and a half earlier, Lettow was not too proud to learn from either unfriendly or friendly natives. He soon picked up the basics of bush fighting: how not to be led by a "fleeing" enemy into an ambush; how to meet night attacks with the bayonet instead of with wild firing; to realize that organized units were most vulnerable when in the act of breaking camp; and to develop a healthy respect for the crude weapons of the bush fighter—be they muzzle-loading muskets, spears, or poisoned arrows. When Lettow came back for a tour of duty in Germany he was beyond doubt the Kaiser's most skilled officer in conducting guerrilla warfare in African terrain.

When Lettow returned to take command of the defense forces in German East Africa (later Tanganyika, then Tanzania) he had no sooner reported to the Governor than he was off into the up-country on his first inspection of his *Schutztruppe* companies. He went north from Dar es Salaam by ship to the port of Tanga, then overland to the Usambara Mountains where he met Capt. Tom von Prince, the famed *"Bwana Sakarani,"* the Man Who Is Drunk With Fighting. This walking legend had been a classmate of Lettow's at Kassel. He had been born an Englishman, Thomas Prince, had been refused a commission in the British Army, and had turned to the Prussian service. After years of savage fighting against the rebellious Hehes, Prince had been awarded the teutonic "Von," and had settled down as a retired farmer in the up-country. He would prove an invaluable subordinate in the coming days when the chips were down.

Lettow's survey of troops and terrain took over half a year, during which he had ample time to think of his upcoming role; his busy mind was fully aware of the war threatening in Europe. By the time he returned to the capital his strategy had been clearly formed. He had no illusions about the strategic capabilities of his fourteen companies (totaling 216 officers and 2,450 askaris) in the vastness of German East Africa, a territory three times the size of the Fatherland. So he sat down and thought it out. As soon as war would be declared, the Royal Navy would cut off any reinforcement from Germany, while the British and Belgians would be able, at will, to build up forces and supplies until their numerical superiority would be unquestioned. *But there was the key—that numerical superiority.* Why should not he, Lettow, see that those numbers grew and grew? Obviously he would be outnumbered at the start by at least two or three to one. Why not employ the *Schutztruppe* (augmented by porters, native police, rifle clubs, and what have you) tactically in a guerrilla war to force the British to a buildup that would require at least ten to one odds just to stand off Lettow's raids? And ten (or more) to one odds would mean tying up British men and guns away from the European theater where they would have greatly increased the threat to German arms. It was clear to Lettow that he should take the offensive, using guerrilla tactics, so that he could "grip the enemy by the throat and force him to employ his forces for self-defense."

The question of where that jugular would be most vulnerable was the factor that had brought Lettow into his confrontation with Governor Schnee. The answer was as clear to Lettow as it was repulsive to Schnee: it was the "Taveta Gap," south of Kilimanjaro. A British force coming from Voi (at the critical junction of the Uganda Railway and the Voi-Moshi Line) would have the best chance of invading German East Africa through that pass in order to strike at the German Northern Railway and into the interior in conjunction with other forces invading through coastal ports like Tanga or Jasin. Now, if Lettow could win guerrilla-type victories over such invading, European-type forces ("victories" that could be won by bogging down or harassing organized forces would be just as effective as winning pitched battles), he could also mount a series of raids to cut that vital artery, the Uganda Railway. We have seen the Governor's reaction to that strategy, but Lettow plunged ahead in the fall of 1914 to win out eventually over the Governor and to concentrate his companies at New Moshi and along the Northern Railway. What were these companies that made up the *Schutztruppe*?

In the first place they were the finest bush fighting force, native or European, in East Africa. Clearly the askaris (native soldiers) of the *Schutztruppe* were not trained into an elite overnight. The Germans, having learned from their wars subjugating the hostile tribes, began to hand-pick the officer cadres that would lead the askaris. Selection boards took only the best qualified, and their African service counted for double when computing pensions. Leadership counted first, followed by intelligence and character, and the medical exam was the toughest in the German Army. In the end, a colonial officer corps without parallel led the companies which had been recruited from selected bush fighters. The recruits were selected from tribes with great martial traditions, and the pay, privileges, and attendant prestige allowed the German recruiters to pick and choose. As an example of the incentives, the pay scales were twice what the British had set for their askaris.

The end products were combat units with native mobility, trained and equipped to fight in either European-style or bush warfare. The basic unit was the company, a small independent command of seven or eight German officers and NCOs and 150 to 200 askaris. The company had two machine gun teams, and could be reinforced with porters and *ruga-ruga*, tribal irregulars. The company was not bound into a rigid battalion or regimental structure—there were no such administrative or tactical headquarters—instead, when necessary, a provisional *abteilung* could direct two or more companies. There were no supply links or lines, each company being self-sufficient and able to operate indefinitely on its own. In short, the *Schutztruppe* company was a mobile combat team ideally adaptable to guerrilla warfare. There were, however, in Lettow's eyes, two serious shortcomings in some companies: the low level of rifle marksmanship and the obsolete rifle with which German colonial infantry had been armed. The first Lettow could strive to overcome with higher standards of training. The second was, for the time being, an incurable headache. The single-shot, Model 71, .450-caliber Mausers were dubbed an enemy "secret weapon" by Lettow because their clouds of black powder smoke were an instant giveaway of the firer's position. Eventually Lettow was able to get six companies armed with modern magazine rifles (many through the courtesy of the British Army), but at war's opening in 1914, eight companies had to fight under this serious handicap.

Although the African sun was beating down on the galvanized iron of the verandah roof, the light upland breeze kept things pleasantly cool for Lettow and his bearded companion. Lettow eased back in his straight-backed chair and handed the sheaf of telegrams to von Prince.

"There you are," Lettow said, "all in order by date, so help yourself to a light bit of history."

"Why do you say 'light,' Colonel?" von Prince asked.

"Light in the sense of comic opera, if you will. But read on, we don't have all afternoon, and I have troop trains to dispatch, as you know. Go ahead and read them aloud, that will be a good review for both of us."

Von Prince's white teeth gleamed in his black beard as he picked up the telegram on top.

"This one, dated the twenty-fifth of October, is from your pal, the Governor. Can you imagine that fool in his dream world? The war has been going on for three months in Europe, and he still dashes about mouthing neutrality. Well—"

"Well, get on with it, or you'll be sitting here in New Moshi by yourself," Lettow said.

"His Excellency says—'Stop military occupation of Tanga, town and harbor, because not defensible. Send telegraphic information about such new circumstances as make in your opinion the occupation of Tanga necessary.' That sounds direct enough. Then this one is your answer, correct?" von Prince said.

"Of course, sent the next day."

"I like this part—'Use of Tanga lodgings seemed advisable in view of healthy climate. Dar es Salaam was until now used for accommodating First Rifles. Please wire whether despite this Tanga should be evacuated.' So—Tanga lodgings indeed!"

"I thought you'd appreciate that part about the healthy climate. The next one you have there should be the Governor's reply, of the twenty-seventh of October."

"So it is—'Stationing in Tanga approved with proviso that forces must be evacuated inconspicuously immediately when warships appear. Executive power remains with district commissioner.' And so that was what prompted you to go to Tanga and talk with District Commissioner Auracher, right?"

"Correct. I had to go in person in order to remind Auracher that he was still a lieutenant in the reserve and, further, that his responsibility to the Army in time of war superseded his civil administrative duties," Lettow said.

"Was that enough to bring him around?"

"Yes, but it remained for me to order him to start helping to prepare the defenses of Tanga, and under no circumstances was he to hand the town over to the enemy—unless he wanted to face a court-martial. Oh, he came around all right, especially when I assured him that I would take full responsibility for his actions."

Von Prince started to unfold the next telegram when a German unteroffizier ran up the verandah steps, banged to a halt, and saluted Lettow.

"Herr Oberst-leutnant, Captain von Hammerstein's train from Tanga will be at the station in fifteen minutes. Shall I say that you wish him and the other officers to report to you here?"

"Thank you, Baumer, tell them instead to meet me at the station-master's office. And tell the adjutant to have my operations map set up there," Lettow ordered.

The Commandant was on his feet, as lithe and quick as a cat. He showed one of his rare, thin-lipped smiles to von Prince.

"Come on, Tom. What I've got to say to these officers will bring you up to date faster and better than reading telegrams."

All of the nine *Schutztruppe* officers on the station platform were well acquainted with von Prince, so Lettow wasted no time on formalities. There were no such luxuries as chairs in the tiny shack that represented the New Moshi terminus of the Northern Railway, so the group stood in a half-circle around Lettow with the map propped on the easel.

"A couple of you know most of my plans, others only fragments, which means that I will bring us all into the picture in order that we carry on the operation from here on a common ground.

"First, our intelligence picture. I have confirmation which shows that the British expeditionary force from India—what they call 'Force B'—reached Mombasa, then sailed from there on 1 November en route to Tanga, obviously the first British objective. We don't know their whole order of battle, but we do know that there are two brigades comprising as many as eight to ten battalions—a force I estimate to number at least six thousand infantry.

"There can be no doubt that the enemy seeks to seize Tanga, then advance up our Northern Railway toward New Moshi. If they can reach this point, Force B would link up with other Indian Army units moving up the Uganda Railway through Voi and Taveta toward Moshi. Yes, von Hammerstein, what is it?"

"Colonel, is it possible that the other British force is already on the way up the Uganda Railway?" the captain asked.

"No such intelligence has been confirmed. What we do know—and what is critical to understand here and now—is that the 17th Field Company in Tanga succeeded in beating back the first enemy landing force this morning. Next, you all know that I started troop trains moving the *Schutztruppe* companies down this railway to Tanga, beginning the day before yesterday after I received District Commissioner—I should say, Lieutenant—Auracher's telegram that the captain of the British cruiser *Fox* had entered Tanga harbor and demanded the surrender of the town. Auracher stalled him off, and when he got back to Tanga from the cruiser, hauled down the white flag the Governor had ordered flown, and replaced it with the Imperial colors. Then, I'm told, he went home, put on his uniform, and went to join the 17th Company.

"But enough of that. Know that within eighteen hours we can have all thousand of our men in Tanga, that is, by four tomorrow morning. I will stay here until I see the last train loaded, and I will come into Tanga on that. I see you smiling, Captain von Prince. What have I done to make you so cheerful?"

Von Prince returned Lettow's piercing stare without losing his broad smile.

"Sir, I have cause to be glad to be going into this fight with you, but I was thinking now about this toy railway with its eight engines pulling those little coaches 190 miles with askaris bulging out every window—and every man wearing a grin you could see in the dark," von Prince said.

"A trip on a train is the delight of their lives even though they know it means going into battle. Since you've mentioned it, you all should know that we are working every official and man of the Northern Railway right around the clock. Now, no more interruptions, gentlemen. Time is precious, and I want to end this conference by bringing you up to date on what has happened to the 17th and its reinforcements in Tanga.

"Early this morning a British force had completed disembarking on the east side of Ras Kasone and sent what has been estimated to be two battalions against Tanga. Our 17th Company was dug in in prepared positions east of the railway yard. The company, reinforced with reservists and police, numbered about two hundred and twenty men with four machine guns. They waited until the enemy had struggled through the bush and the plantations to within a hundred yards, then they opened fire. Even their old Model 71s were effective, and I must add that the marksmanship records of the 17th, one of the best in the *Schutztruppe*, paid off handsomely. The enemy attack was halted, then cut to pieces. The Indian soldiers panicked and fell back, and at least a dozen of their officers were killed while trying to rally them. The two enemy battalions—identified later as the 13th Rajputs and the 61st Pioneers—broke and ran when our 17th counter-attacked. Their estimated losses were over three hundred killed and wounded, and the rest ran like stampeded cattle back to their landing beach near the Red House.

"I want the word passed through all your companies about the splendid conduct of the men of the 17th. It will be the best reward they can have to know that the *Schutztruppe* can take on and defeat with ease any number of these Indian and British insects. Yes—*Wahindi ni wadudu!**

"Now, to your companies. I'll see you tomorrow morning in Tanga."

Lettow swung off the engine cab step, and felt his boots scrape solid ground. He ignored the outstretched helping hand of the railway official, and called for his bicycle. It was already being handed out the door of the first coach by two askaris. Lettow reached up and took the bicycle, grunting his thanks in Swahili. In the bright African moonlight he could not miss the astounded looks on both black soldiers' faces. Then he remembered his blackened face, a precaution he had taken after boarding the train. What had gone through those askaris' minds when they saw their *Schutztruppe* Commandant revealed as a black man there in the moonlight would one day make a wonderful story to relate to the officers' mess, but there was no time for such thoughts now. He wheeled his bicycle down the crushed rock of the railway shoulder and swung into the seat just as he heard Major Kraut, his second-in-command, and his assistant crunch down the embankment to halt beside him.

"I've stopped the train at the three-mile marker, we'll have to make it into Tanga from here on our own. What time do you make it?" Lettow said.

"I have four minutes past three," Major Kraut said, "we should meet Captain Baumstark on our way, if he's on time."

"You won't have to worry about him. That's probably him coming now," Lettow said.

The captain's stocky figure emerged from the shadow of the palms at the edge of a clearing. He put down his bicycle and reported to Lettow.

"I've pulled the 17th back to the west side of town. Didn't

*"The Indians are insects"—"insect" representing one of the vilest insults in Swahili.

have enough strength to hold the whole place, not knowing where and in what strength the enemy could be coming at us next."

"A sound move, Captain," Lettow said. "What security measures have you taken around the town?"

"I have outposted the east side of Tanga, mostly along the railway, and there are patrols operating between outposts. And the last thing I did before coming to meet you was to put the 6th Field Company—they had just arrived—in a forward position near the railway station to cover the south flank and to man the post at the railway embankment," Baumstark said.

"Excellent, but we don't know anything of the enemy beyond our outposts, do we? I'm going to have a look for myself. In the meantime, Captain Baumstark, there could be no better guide than you to lead the troops from this train into their assembly areas on this side of town. See that their company officers start unloading the train now. I'll see you later at your command post," Lettow ordered.

"Sir," Major Kraut was quick to speak because Lettow was already back on his bicycle, "I must make two recommendations. Anything might happen to you at night in the town. Let me and a patrol go ahead on reconnaissance. You should stay here and get some rest. You have not had a wink of sleep for at least thirty hours."

"Since when, Major, have I had my officers do my reconnoitering for me? As for sleeping, this is hardly the time for it, with an enemy who outnumbers us at least six-to-one and who are getting set to launch a new attack. No, you and your adjutant come with me. We're wasting the one resource that can never be replaced—time."

The major knew better than to argue with the Prussian disciplinarian. He and the adjutant mounted up in silence.

Tanga was deserted. The silent streets bordered by the European houses—stark white under the African moon in contrast to the black shadows of gardens and their borders of trees—echoed only to the soft swish of their bicycle tires. The three rode on in silent file through the town, turning northward until they came to the harbor. Lettow paused long enough to watch the glare of lights around the British transports where the din of activity was loud enough to carry across the harbor to Lettow and his companions a half-mile away.

He spoke in a lowered voice to Kraut, his teeth gleaming in his blackened face.

"God, I suppose they can afford to be noisy. The fools had already given Baumstark a good twenty-four hours notice before their first attack. What I wouldn't give for those two old 1873 field guns! Even those could raise a bit of hell with that unloading going on out there. Any word on those guns yet?"

"Only that they had to hold them in New Moshi until all the troop trains had been dispatched," Kraut said.

Lettow only grunted, but that spoke a world of disgust. He mounted, and they turned eastward on the Hospital Road that led out to Ras Kasone. They parked their bicycles at the dark Government Hospital, and continued eastward on foot along the beach. They plodded along in silence, pausing now and then for Lettow to stare out toward the cruiser *Fox* and the lighters milling around the transports. After a half-mile of such patrolling, Lettow turned back toward the hospital. In all their reconnaissance, through and around Tanga as well as along the beach, they had not come across a single enemy soldier. In a matter of minutes, Lettow was to learn they had been inside enemy lines even before they had left the hospital.

They retrieved their bicycles and were riding back toward town. As before, they moved in silence. When Lettow rounded a bend to head westward, he skidded to a halt at a sharp challenge from the shadows. The voice sounded military, but the language was strange. Lettow's reaction was instantaneous.

"*Stambuli!*" He bellowed in his loudest parade-ground manner, using the *Schutztruppe* countersign.

The only reply was a crashing through the brush as the Indian sentry fled into the blackness. Lettow picked up his bicycle, shrugged, and they rode on toward the railway station and Baumstark's command post.

It was growing light when Lettow laid aside the Governor's telegram. Lieutenant Auracher had given it to him an hour before, but he had thrust it into a pocket of his jacket, too busy at the time giving final deployment orders to company commanders. Now, he found himself mid-way between dismay and righteous indignation.

"You are forbidden," it read, "to subject Tanga, and the

defenseless subjects of the town, to the rigors of war. Even should the enemy land in force, there must be no resistance. Tanga must be saved from bombardment . . ."

My God, Lettow thought, *the "defenseless subjects" are long gone, and "the rigors of war" are here. Does Schnee think that I'm going to let the British walk into Tanga, and then move, as they please, up the Northern Railway or into the interior?*

Later, he was to voice his thoughts in somber detail when he wrote in *My Reminiscences of East Africa:* "Already my method of waging active war had met with disapproval. If on top of that we were to suffer a severe defeat the confidence of the troops would probably be gone, and it was certain that my superiors would place insuperable difficulties in the way of my exercising command [less formally—the Governor would fire him, and that would be an end to military operations] . . . But there was nothing [else] for it; to gain all we must risk all."

He repocketed the telegram, and went back to the operations map that had been set up in the railway station waiting room. Major Kraut, a box of map pins in his left hand, was marking the company positions with blue pins and what was known of the enemy with red.

"Are you ready to give this a final going over before you disappear again?" the major's question was posed in a familiar tone that no one else dared use with Lettow.

"You sound like a mother hen. Really, did you ever fail to know my whereabouts?" Lettow asked with a straight face.

"I know better than to try and answer that. Well, to make a recapitulation, here is where you had the 6th Field Company move—on about an eight hundred meter front along the railway cutting to cover the east side of the town."

"I know they're stretched thin, but they've got the Gewehr 98 Mausers, and so with the best of magazine rifles and their good marksmanship scores, the 6th will hold that position," Lettow said.

"Baumstark's *abteilung,*" Kraut went on, "made up of the 16th and 17th Companies, will cover the front to the right of the 6th, as well as our right flank, using the railway embankments wherever possible."

"And that leaves us with only the 13th Company and von Prince's units as force reserve?" Lettow asked.

"Yes, and since the 13th and von Prince's 7th and 8th

Schutzen Companies* are our only troops who have traded shots with the British, before yesterday, you should find them a reliable reserve."

"I'd feel more comfortable if I knew when we could expect the 4th and 9th Companies to arrive. And what about the two field guns?"

"All we know," Kraut said, "is that the two companies, and the guns, are somewhere en route."

"*Wunderbar*," Lettow growled, "and you realize that even with the 4th and the 9th we will still be able to face the British with only a thousand rifles. That against what we now estimate to be over six thousand Indians and British."

"True, but why don't you count our other firepower?" Kraut asked.

"Yes, of course, the machine guns. You're right to count them in. We've got our best men on the machine-gun teams, and it remains for us to see how hard training will pay off. Any more word on the British?"

"Our observers see many more units unloading than yesterday. They probably used only two battalions in that initial attack, but now by dependable count the battalions unloading indicate that Aitken may be going to employ his whole force. And that appears to indicate that your estimate of six thousand may have been too low," Kraut said.

"I'll worry about that when we see them coming. I'm off now. I'll be out there checking on the 6th, the 16th, the 17th, and then the reserves, in that order."

"Things are quiet, a good time for you to catch a nap. There's plenty of time."

"Not while we're still organizing our defense. I'll be keeping in touch by telephone."

By midmorning the boiling humidity of the coastal plain had begun to build up. Most of the *Schutztruppe* companies had relaxed for three months in the mountain breezes of the up-country along the Northern Railway, and now the officers and askaris were paying for it as they tried to get used to the tropical heat. Here, five degrees south of the equator, it was eternal summer with one of the most humid atmospheres in the world.

---

*Sharpshooter companies made up of colonial German volunteers, many from rifle clubs.

Lettow ignored the searing sun, or made a good pretense of it, as he made his way from platoon to platoon and to the machine gun teams. There were fields of fire to be verified for the riflemen, traverse limits and overlapping fires for the machine guns. There were company ammunition reserves and resupply measures to be checked. Lettow had to be shown all the essentials, even using the field telephone to call back to his command post—not always to talk with Major Kraut, but to verify that wire communications were in order.

At last, satisfied, he returned to his command post at noon for a final prebattle conference with his commanders. He had traded his tropical helmet for the slouch hat with the upturned side brim that was to become a distinguishing mark for the war years. His face was still caked with blacking that had begun to crack and peel. Two bandoliers crossed his chest over his dusty uniform jacket, and he had rested his rifle in a corner of the room before he had opened the conference. Now, he was concluding his summation before he sent them back to their units.

"See that your men get all the rest in the shade that they can. They're going to have a long wait. The enemy may have started his advance about ten this morning, but they still don't realize what kind of a hell they have to move through. They will be hours struggling through the bush, the undergrowth of the rubber plantations, and the sisal crops, and don't forget the dense thorn-brush.

"Remember that we know how to fight in the bush. They don't. We know how to maneuver here on our ground, and they don't. Our troops are fighting on their kind of land, and the enemy is not. Now, back to your commands, and remind your men that God is with us."

Lettow yielded at last to Kraut's insistent appeals and stretched out on a field cot for a catnap. It seemed to Kraut that he had scarcely gotten back to his map and messages before Lettow walked back in, looking at his wristwatch.

"I have ten minutes after one. Same with you?" Lettow asked.

"You know it is. We synchronized our watches when you started that last conference," Kraut said.

"Now, *I'm* being the old woman. Any reports of importance?"

"Not any particular one, but there is a sameness to what the observers are reporting. The Indians and the British keep trying to maintain a general line as they advance, but the bush is too much for them. They are trying to use some kind of open order, but they don't know how to control squads and platoons in the mangrove swamps, the plantations, or the thorn scrub. What's more, squads of sepoys are collapsing from heat exhaustion."

"Poor devils. All this after weeks of rolling in their own puke, jammed aboard those transports for 2,500 miles in the heat of the Indian Ocean. But all the evil things that have happened to those Indians make it easier for our men."

Lettow had to wait for over two hours, pacing the rooms of his command post and chain-smoking in the way that was to become his habit before battle. The smoking was the only sign of his restlessness. His face and bearing showed an otherwise outward calm. One-thirty passed, then two o'clock, and still no word of forces in contact. At two-thirty the rattle of intermittent rifle firing could be heard, and Lettow soon realized that *Schutztruppe* snipers, firing from skillfully concealed positions in the baobab trees and coco palms, were picking off enemy officers and NCOs.

Three o'clock had passed when Lettow could tell it in his own words, "an askari reported to me in his simple, smart way: '*Adui tayari.*' (The enemy is ready.) Those two short words I shall never forget."

As the reports of the enemy's coming within rifle range increased, Lettow could no longer keep the lid on his boiling impatience. He hurried down to the 6th Company where he could see things at firsthand. After settling down to share the company commander's observation post, the situation in front of the 6th gave him cause for renewing his confidence in his troops. The dit-a-dit-dit of the 6th's Maxims took up a measured rhythm as the machine gunners showed off their training in firing carefully controlled bursts. They were joined by the rifles of the platoons, firing first in volleys, then in fire-at-will as the platoon leaders gave their commands for taking up individual, aimed fire. All across the front of the 6th the results were uniformly disastrous for the sepoys of the 63rd Palmacottah Light Infantry, the Indian battalion that had been unlucky enough to be advancing in the center of the 6th Company's sector. Those Indian soldiers who were left standing after the first German volleys and machine-gun rakings turned and took to flight in a body back toward their landing beach, many throwing down their rifles as they ran.

Lettow turned his attention toward the left center of the 6th's sector where the Indian 13th Rajputs and 61st Pioneers were repeating their performance of the day before in their first engagement against the 17th Company. The two battalions were panicking and joining in wild flight to the rear, in parallel fashion with the 63rd Palmacottah Light Infantry. For a flash of time all that could be seen to the front of the 6th were glimpses of the khaki turbans and cutaway jackets of the fleeing Indians. The cry passed from squad to squad as the askaris took up the shout—*"Wahindi ni wadudu!"*

Lettow was leaving to observe the defenses on the right flank when a phone call from Kraut caught up with him before he got away from the 6th Company's command O.P.

"Things may be going well in front of the 6th," Kraut said, "but you had better get back here. You can't be at the center and on both flanks at once, and you're needed here because I see the need for command decisions coming up soon."

"Things not going as well on the flanks then. Is that it?" Lettow asked.

"Not well at all, and there is too much to tell you over the phone. You will have to see the situation on the map to follow it all."

"I'm on my way."

Major Kraut's tense face had told Lettow, more than mere words could, that his attention was badly needed at the map.

"So they have gotten around the 6th's left flank and into the town. They must be a different kind of soldier than what I saw in front of the 6th," Lettow said, grinding out his cigarette and fixing his monocle in his left eye.

"That's right, these are Gurkhas of the Kashmir Rifles, and they've already sliced up a few of our men with their *kukris*. But what's more important, the Gurkhas have gotten around the Customs House and reached the Hotel Deutscher Kaiser where they've hauled down our flag and run up the Union Jack," Kraut said.

"And on our force right flank—what is happening there?"

"The British battalion, the L.N.L., you know, the Loyal North Lancashires, have broken through across the railway cutting, and some elements have managed to link up with the Gurkhas, and they seemed to be able to adapt to street fighting."

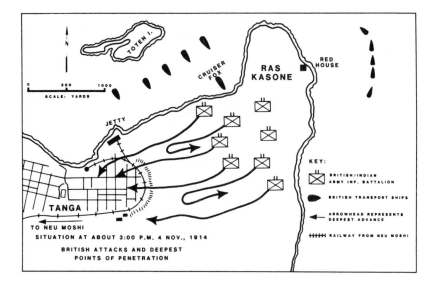

SITUATION AT ABOUT 3:00 P.M. 4 NOV., 1914

BRITISH ATTACKS AND DEEPEST
POINTS OF PENETRATION

"My, aren't we bursting with good tidings! If that is all of the situation report, give me one piece of good news—I hope that our phone line to von Prince is still working."

Kraut took the field phone from an *unteroffizier,* gave its crank a turn, and handed the handset to Lettow who got his good news in the form of von Prince answering in person.

"Quickly," Lettow said, "how much do you know of the situation in our center—in the town itself."

Von Prince's voice carried the calm tone of the veteran bush fighter.

"I've had a few pot shots myself at Gurkhas and British near that little square this side of the office buildings. They are trying to make up enough assault teams to get through the center of town. But I've moved up my machine guns and am getting ready to deploy my—"

"If you're ready, go ahead and do it," Lettow cut in, "commit everything you have. It's up to you to restore the center and kick those bastards out of Tanga."

"If you hadn't said that, I'd have thought I was on the wrong line. We are moving out, Herr Oberst-Leutnant."

Tense moments passed before Lettow got the first of welcome reports from flank units and von Prince's command post. The 7th and 8th *Schutzen* Companies tore into the town with blazing machine guns and rifles. The German volunteers had been chafing at being held back in reserve, and now they sprang into action with a vengeance. Firing from roof-tops, windows, and down alleys and streets, they over-whelmed the enemy assault teams before they could renew their attack. They drove the Gurkhas and the L.N.L. back toward the railway cutting, and though they had not yet turned the situation around, von Prince's riflemen and machine-gun-ners had saved the German center.

Now that his line in and east of Tanga was holding, Let-tow could turn his attention to his right flank—and none too soon. Baumstark's two companies had been forced back by a new penetration of the railway cutting on the south side of Tanga. Baumstark had committed his reserve platoons in a counterattack, but some of the new askaris who were seeing their first action had begun to falter and were taking cover. In minutes Lettow had raced to the scene.

It took only a glance for him to see that if positive action was not taken on the spot the young askaris would panic and that contagion could spread throughout both companies; the result could mean only disaster for the force's flank.

Lettow marched through the coco palms to the clearing where he would be in full view of his askaris—and the en-emy. Turning his back to the British, Lettow faced the cowed men gaping at him from behind the palms, and began to mock them.

"Are these the great warriors of the Wahehe and the Angoni? And are there other little children here from the Wanyamezi and the Wagogo? What would the chiefs of those warrior tribes say of these little men who hide behind trees in fear of their enemies?" Lettow's derisive voice reverberated through the trees, and for seconds there was silence.

The tension was broken by Captain von Hammerstein who was striding toward Lettow. An askari near the captain's right got up and took a step toward the rear. Von Hammer-stein reached in his map case, fetched out a half-empty wine bottle, and hurled it at the soldier. The bottle caught him alongside the head, and sent him reeling. There were bursts of laughter as askaris got sheepishly to their feet, picked up their rifles, and began to form into skirmish line under their squad leaders. The bizarre episode, coming at the moment of Lettow's shaming them, was all it took to restore order and get the counterattack moving.

It was near 4:30 when Lettow got back to his C.P. for an update on the overall situation. This time the intelligence reports lacked the note of pending disaster to Lettow's force, but things remained in a precarious state when he reviewed the whole picture in his mind.

The British, he thought, *attacked initially on about a thousand-meter front with something like ten battalions. We have routed at least four and have caused severe casualties in at least three others. But they almost took the town from me, and only now has my reserve under von Prince restored the center. That center seems to be holding, but—and there is the greatest "but"—that leaves me no force reserve, no reserves at all. The 4th and 9th Companies have still not shown up, and the only maneuverable unit that I can possibly use is the 13th Company.*

He looked back at the map, this time focusing his attention on Kraut's red map pins marking the enemy's battalions in his center and left flank.

"Look here," he said to Kraut," the British have never been able to plug the gap the Palmacottah Light Infantry left when we routed them. Am I correct, and are those pins still showing our latest intelligence on the L.N.L. and the 101st Bombay Grenadiers?"

"You are right in both cases."

"Then that 101st has been trying, as I see it, to shift to its right in an effort to close the gap left by the Palmacottahs. That leaves the 101st's left flank, and the whole British force's left flank, extended and wide open."

"My God, you're right. I see what you mean."

"Well, then take this down."

Lettow's orders directed the immediate move of the 13th to swing wide around the British left and cut in on it with enfilading fire from the flank. He reinforced it with two machine guns in the expectation that the four guns would be sufficient to wreak havoc with the 101st Grenadiers.

His expectation was realized beyond anything he had dared imagine. The four machine guns were rushed into their new positions, and within minutes their interlaced fires were slaughtering the Indians. These sepoys were made of better stuff than those who had turned and run in midafternoon. These Indians stood and fought, and within the next quarter-hour it became evident that those brave men had fought back for nothing. It might have been better—certainly less of a bloody debacle—if they had run. Within minutes the methodical German gunners had reduced the battalion to company strength, and the 101st as an effective fighting unit could be wiped from the map.

While the 13th Company was throwing everything it had in straining to keep up the momentum of its counterattack, the gods of war began to smile on Lettow. The overdue 4th Company arrived, and Lettow had it brought forward at the double and thrown in on the left of the 13th. The two companies swung forward together, and the new impetus to the German counterattack doomed the forces on the British left. Lettow watched the collapse of the British flank units, and when he could see those battalions fold and stream away to their rear he was able to ascertain without doubt the beginning of a general withdrawal by the whole enemy force.

He grabbed the nearest field phone and got an excited Major Kraut on the other end.

"My God, the reports coming in!" Kraut was shouting so loudly that Lettow had to hold the handset away from his ear. "They're beaten! They're falling back everywhere!"

"If you'll stop shouting, Georg, you would find out that I'm aware of all that, and that I'm calling to give an order, not to listen to dramatics." Lettow's voice was sharp but calm. The chastened major answered that he was ready to acknowledge.

"Order a general advance—a bayonet attack all across the front. I will be at this observation post if you need to reach me."

In the minutes that followed the transmission of Lettow's order, the rattling din of rifle and machine gun fire gave way to a pandemonium made up of whistle blasts, tribal war cries, and bugle calls as the *Schutztruppe* companies swept forward to get at their enemy with the bayonet. The British retirement that had begun as an attempt at orderly disengagement began to dissolve into a rout. Then something happened to deliver the coup de grâce to an already ruined British cause.

It was the native custom to hang their beehives on tree limbs, and a number of hives had been struck by random bullets. The infuriated bees poured forth to launch an attack of their own against the unfortunate Indians and British. Charles Miller in *Battle for the Bundu** makes the comparison

*Macmillan, 1974.

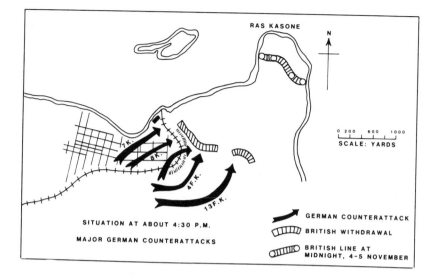

RAS KASONE

N

0 200   600   1000
SCALE: YARDS

SITUATION AT ABOUT 4:30 P.M.

MAJOR GERMAN COUNTERATTACKS

GERMAN COUNTERATTACK

BRITISH WITHDRAWAL

BRITISH LINE AT
MIDNIGHT, 4–5 NOVEMBER

that African bees "were to European bees what a leopard is to a tabby cat." Whatever their comparative ferocity, it is certain that each bee wielded his own bayonet, and in no time sepoys and British Tommies were seen dancing wildly about, throwing rifles aside to roll and writhe on the ground, or were leaping up to dash away in an effort to outrun their assailants. It was anything but funny to the participants; many faces, arms, and legs were swollen to twice their normal size. A British signalman managed to take down a message while under attack by the bees, and had to have over three hundred stings removed from his head; he was awarded the Distinguished Conduct Medal, no doubt an award that must have set a record for uniqueness in the history of the British Army. But the bees, however neutral their status before having their homes shot from beneath them, showed a savage impartiality in their assaults. The four machine guns of the 13th were out of action while the crews made frantic displacements to new positions. Lettow gained an unwanted notoriety that persisted for years among the British survivors: the bee attack had been a diabolical contrivance, master-minded by the German commander, that released the bee attack through trip wires that sprang open the lids of the hives. The myth was entirely unfounded, as Lettow never ceased to maintain.

When things had finally buzzed to an uneasy quiet in the bee zone, Lettow could survey the battlefield, bees and ter-

Native wild beehives at Tanga

rain permitting, to find that his victory was complete. Force B's rout had ended only at the water's edge, and by sundown the British were taking cover behind a defensive perimeter around the beachhead. There was no need for Lettow to try an assault on the beachhead, which he could not have managed in any event. It became clear on the following morning (November 5) that the whole thrust of Force B's activity was now directed toward evacuating all the unwounded to the safety of the transports, following which the force would steam back to Mombasa, a battered monument to—in the words of one historian—"a fruitful lesson on how not to start a colonial campaign."

Major-General Aitken, commanding Force B, left behind at Ras Kasone more than his wrecked career. In their haste to reembark the British abandoned on the beaches sixteen machine guns, enough rifles to rearm three of Lettow's companies, 600,000 rounds of ammunition, all their field telephones, and enough clothing and blankets to last the

Schutztruppe for the rest of the war. In addition, the British losses in casualties were shocking: 800 dead, 500 wounded, and an indeterminate toll of missing. On the other hand, Lettow's triumph had not come without its costs: 15 Europeans and 54 askaris; and worst of all, von Prince was killed in a Tanga street while leading his men, an incalculable personal loss to Lettow.

Yet this tremendous bag of captured materiel and supplies was nothing compared to, in Lettow's words, "the enemy's loss in *moral* [sic]; after being so soundly thrashed by a force one-eighth their own strength, the British and Indians almost began to believe in spirits and spooks."

All true, but Tanga was to establish three things that were beyond measures such as materiel and military morale. These factors can be considered in their ascending order of significance. Lettow had become a colonial hero, and Governor Schnee had to swallow the bitter medicine that would change his policy of neutrality as well as his plans for influencing Lettow's operations. Secondly, even the neutralists in a hitherto-divided colony were caught up in the patriotic spirit that swept across German East Africa, putting the colony squarely behind Lettow's cause for resisting invasion and providing him with volunteers and lasting material support. Lastly, Tanga gave Lettow the resounding send-off that he needed to launch and carry on a grueling four-year war of attrition and guerrilla operations; the war wherein he accomplished his deduced mission of tying up (keeping troops away from the war in Europe) over 130,000 Allied troops, mostly British and Indian Army, from November, 1914, to November, 1918.

General von Lettow-Vorbeck surrendered to the British on November 25, 1918, but only after he had been convinced that Germany had acknowledged defeat in the armistice of November 11, 1918, and the surrender of his forces had become obligatory. As Charles Miller has so aptly described the surrender: it was a "capitulation of an army that had not lost to an army that had not won."

Only in the last two decades has Lettow received belated recognition as the father of twentieth-century guerrilla warfare involving large-scale operations (no apologies to T. E. Lawrence). Lettow's right to such a title is being substantiated in a growing bibliography of no mean quality.

This chapter was designed to demonstrate the essentiality of personal energy as a force required to give life to one or more attributes of a leader. When one follows Lettow's actions, beginning with his supervision of troop movements (190 miles from Tanga) until the end of the battle three days later, one witnesses an incredible output of energy that enabled this leader to win his battle under a host of pressures. However, Tanga was not selected as a means of focusing on energy per se; it was selected because the leader's energy can be seen providing continual support to all the other attributes.

Yet Lettow should not be elevated to the status of a "better" leader simply because he appears to embody elements of five attributes. Such leaders appear once in an era and become stamped as "great captains" (Napoleon, Caesar, and Alexander are examples) and there are neither better leaders nor great captains in this book. There are only men whose actions have epitomized an attribute of leadership.

Lettow and his battle were chosen because they were representative of the leaders and battles in this study. By now the reader will have observed also that "decisive battles" do not appear in these pages. The omission has been deliberate so that the reader's insight would not be diverted by generations of writers who have concentrated on household words and great events. If this omission has helped the reader's vision, that alone should be reward for this work.

Epilogue

Whereas there are for all men two ways of improvement, to wit
by one's own disasters or those of others, the former is the more
vivid, the latter is the less harmful.

—Polybius

Bismarck is alleged to have stated the idea in blunter form:
"Fools say they learn by experience; I would learn from the
experience of others." In any event, no reasonable man wants
to learn the hard way, and that is what this journey through
time has been about: *ideas illuminated by the experience of others.*
The "others" have been men who used certain attributes to
develop, each in his own way, an art of leadership. The journey we have taken to look at that art in its formative stages
has reached four continents and covered a span of almost
twenty-two centuries. Any yet there have been only eleven
stops en route, and one of those in a fictional setting. The
matter of a limited number of stops—case histories—may
arouse some criticism.

The more perceptive critics (those, of course, who think
as I do) might think that a sampling of ten factual cases is
not sufficient to convey the impact of the art over a period
of 2,200 years. There are two responses to that criticism. First,
when confronted with the task of scanning 1,500 battles for
examples of an art in practice, one soon finds that one must
adopt an eclectic method. Second, common sense will reveal

that a protracted parade of examples, no matter how colorful, will in time tire the reader and "lose the name of action."

Yet the argument for examining a more extensive "spread"
of leaders and battles is most persuasive, especially if the reader
can be shown more leaders in a variety of situations across a
broad range of history. However, before we venture further
afield it would be helpful if we could get an over-the-shoul-
der glance at where we have been and what we have seen.
Table 1 enables us to take that look. The left and center columns are listings of leaders and battles in the order in which
they have appeared in the text. The right-hand columns represent the leader's attributes as they can be deduced from the
depiction of the battle. The quality (or qualities) that went to
make up an attribute are italicized and listed in the order of
their contribution. For example, Scipio's *moral* courage was
shown in his plan to attack a numerically superior enemy and
in the execution of his plan; his *boldness* in conceiving and
making his attack was a manifestation of his will; and his
imagination enabled him to innovate—a clear demonstration
of his intellectual powers. There may be cases where a reader
disagrees with my conclusions regarding either an attribute
or a contributing quality. If so, he has become an ally, for he
has shown the readiness and the ability to make his own evaluation.

Missing from the table is Kipling's Lungtungpen since,
as a fictional case, it may have doubtful validity in an analysis
of our observations. Also, *energy* is not shown as an attribute
because, at this stage, it is evident that it is *essential as a mainstay of the others* and, as such, may be assumed to exist across
the board. We will return to Table 1 when we can make a
final evaluation of our findings. Table 2 presents an extended range of leaders and battles. There are two additions
to this table as an extension of Table 1: a column with dates
and another with brief descriptions of the battles. These additions are aids for identifying a battle's place in history and
its nature. The right side represents this writer's conclusions
regarding the leader's attributes and qualities. One's accep-
tance of these conclusions must, at this point, be based on faith
if we are to complete an evaluation of this book's claim for
finding the bases of an art of leadership. I say "based on faith"
for two reasons: it would take another book merely to show
the reasoning behind the selection and analyses of the leader's actions in each of the twenty-six battles in the table; fur-

Table 1
Conclusions Deducible From the Text

LEADER	BATTLE	ATTRIBUTES/QUALITIES				
		COURAGE	WILL	INTELLECT	PRESENCE	
Morgan	Cowpens	Moral Physical	Boldness	Imagination Flexibility Judgment		
Wayne et al	Stony Point	Physical	Boldness	Flexibility		
Davout	Auerstadt	Moral	Boldness Tenacity	Flexibility	Inspire	
Cortes	Cempoala	Moral	Boldness	Judgment		
Chard & Brom- head	Rorke's Drift	Moral Physical	Tenacity	Flexibility	Inspire	
Scipio	Ilipa	Moral	Boldness	Imagination		
Bouquet	Bushy Run	Moral Physical	Tenacity	Flexibility	Inspire	
Custer	Little Big Horn	Physical			Inspire	
Lannes	Ratisbon	Moral Physical	Boldness	Flexibility	Rally	
Lettow-Vorbeck	Tanga	Moral Physical	Boldness Tenacity	Imagination Flexibility	Rally Inspire	

Table 2
Conclusions Deducible from an Extended Range of Leaders and Battles

Leader(s)	Battle	Date	Description	Attributes and Contributing Qualities
Epaminondas	Leuctra	371 B.C.	Tactical masterpiece defeats Spartans	Courage—Will—Intellect/Moral/ Boldness/Imagination
Philip II of Macedon	Chaeronea	338 B.C.	Macedonian system conquers Greece	Courage—Will—Intellect/Moral/ Tenacity/Flexibility
Alexander the Great	Arbela	331 B.C.	Alexander conquers Persian Empire	Courage—Will—Intellect— Presence/Moral-physical/Bold- ness/Flexibility/Inspire
Hannibal	Cannae	216 B.C.	Classical masterpiece of annihilation	Courage—Will—Intellect/Moral/ Boldness/Imagination-innovation
Julius Caesar	Ilerda	49 B.C.	Bloodless tactical triumph over the Pompeians	Courage—Intellect/Moral/ Imagination-judgment-flexibility
Narses the Eunuch	Taginae	552 A.D.	Justinian's general conquering Italy	Courage—Intellect/Moral/ Imagination-flexibility
William the Conqueror	Hastings	1066	Norman conquest of England	Courage—Will—Intellect/Moral- physical/Boldness/Flexibility
Richard the Lion-Hearted	Arsouf	1191	Third Crusade victory over Saracens	Courage—Will—Presence/Moral- physical/Tenacity/Inspire
Sabuti & Batu	Sajo (or Mohi)	1241	Mongol invasion of Central Europe	Courage—Will—Intellect/Moral/ Boldness/Imagination-flexibility
Henry V of England	Agincourt	1415	English archers/men-at-arms defeat French chivalry	Courage—Will/Moral-physical/ Boldness-tenacity

	Battle	Year	Description	Attributes
Gonzalo de Cordoba	Garigliano	1503	Spanish surprise attack on the French	Courage—Will—Intellect—Presence/Moral/Boldness/Imagination/Inspire
Gustavus Adolphus	Breitenfeld	1631	Protestant victory over Catholics, Thirty Years War	Courage—Will—Intellect/Moral/Tenacity/Flexibility
Johan Baner	Wittstock	1636	Swedish victory over Saxon-Imperial Army	Courage—Will—Intellect/Moral/Boldness-tenacity/Imagination
Frederick the Great	Rossbach	1757	Prussian victory over French, Seven Years War	Courage—Will—Intellect/Moral/Boldness/judgment-flexibility
Napoleon	Lodi	1796	Charge to seize bridge held by Austrians	Courage—Will—Presence/Moral-physical/Boldness/Rally-inspire
Napoleon	Castiglione	1796	Swift maneuver defeats Austrian strategic thrusts	Courage—Will—Intellect/Moral/Boldness/judgment-flexibility
Napoleon	Austerlitz	1805	Tactical gem—defeats Austrians & Russians	Courage—Will—Intellect/Moral/Boldness/imagination-flexibility
Wellington	Salamanca	1812	Outmaneuvers French to gain surprise	Courage—Will—Intellect/Moral/Boldness-tenacity/judgment-flexibility
Stonewall Jackson	Valley Campaign	1862	Strategic/tactical masterpiece of maneuver	Courage—Will—Intellect/Moral/Boldness/Imagination-judgment-flexibility
Lee & Jackson	Chancellorsville	1863	Masters of maneuver gain surprise	Courage—Will—Intellect/Moral/Boldness/Imagination-judgment
Grant	Vicksburg Campaign	1863	Swift maneuver and rapid strikes separate the Confederacy	Courage—Will—Intellect/Moral/Boldness/Imagination-flexibility

Table 2 (continued)

Conclusions Deducible from an Extended Range of Leaders and Battles

Leader(s)	Battle	Date	Description	Attributes and Contributing Qualities
Hindenburg & Ludendorff	Tannenberg	1914	Masterful maneuver and surprise defeats Russians	Courage—Will—Intellect/Moral/Boldness/Imagination-flexibility
von Below & Hutier	Caporetto	1917	Tactical surprise and exploitation	Intellect/Imagination-flexibility (adaptation of a new tactical system)
Byng & J. F. C. Fuller	Cambrai	1917	Tactical surprise, first use of massed tanks	Will—Intellect/Boldness/Imagination-innovation
Rommel	Mersa Matruh	1942	Bold stroke in following up Gazala victory	Courage—Will—Intellect/Moral/Boldness/Flexibility
Vo Nguyen Giap	Dienbienphu	1954	Vietminh exploit French strategical blunder	Courage—Intellect/Moral/Judgment-flexibility

ther, if a skeptical and undaunted reader wishes to make his own evaluations (or selections) there are annotated sources in the last section of the bibliography which will aid in charting one's own course.

For those faithful who will follow the course of this evaluation, we should consider Tables 1 and 2 as superimposed to form a common ground on which we may move toward further inquiries. Table 3 shows the results of such an inquiry. These numbers are based on a count of the occurrence of certain attributes when all thirty-six cases (Table 1 plus Table 2) have been examined. While the resultant percentages may be interesting, let us lay them aside for a moment as we go on to look at Table 4. Here attributes have been scrutinized with these objectives in mind: to find what combinations have been demonstrated in the thirty-six cases; and to determine the percentage of occurrence of each combination when considering all the case histories.

When we place Tables 3 and 4 side by side we find two related and significant factors emerging. Table 3 shows courage, will, and intellect occurring respectively 94 percent, 86 percent, and 89 percent of the time. Turning to Table 4, we find the combination of the same three attributes occurring in 58 percent of the cases.

Then what is the significance of these findings? In answering this critical question it should be fair to reader and writer alike to review what has been accomplished and also to assess the means of discerning attributes in the leaders of today and tomorrow.

Table 3
Data on Single Attributes as Derived from Tables 1 and 2

Attribute	Number of Times Occurring[a]	Percentage of Occurrence[a]
Courage	34	94%
Will	31	86%
Intellect	32	89%
Presence	10	28%
Energy (assumed in all cases)		100%

a = Out of a total of 36 cases (Table 1 plus Table 2).

Table 4
Combinations of Attributes as Derived from Tables 1 and 2

Combinations	Number of Times Occurring[a]	Percentage of Occurrence[a]
Will—Intellect	1	3%
Courage—Will	1	3%
Courage—Intellect	3	8%
Courage—Presence	1	3%
Courage—Will—Intellect	21	58%
Courage—Will—Presence	2	6%
Courage—Will—Intellect—Presence	7	19%

a = Out of a total of 36 cases (Table 1 plus Table 2).

In the Introduction three goals were set: to show that battles could be won by the minds of leaders who were skilled in their art; to demonstrate that the art of leadership is embodied in the man himself; and to establish the fact that the art is based on certain attributes found in leaders who have proved themselves in battle. The reader was able to see skilled leaders practicing their art and sharpen his insight by seeing actions (and reactions) revealed through the minds and hearts of the leaders.

Moreover, attributes have been defined and the contributing qualities isolated to enable the reader to visualize each as a building-block in the creation of a leader's art. By no means, however, need the scope of historical examples be limited to those depicted in the book. Following the definitions of attributes, any number of selections and evaluations can be made.

It is a less simple task to determine the significance of the related findings from Tables 3 and 4. When one takes a second look at Table 4 one cannot avoid focusing on the triad: courage—will—intellect. It is remarkable enough that it occurs in 58 percent of the cases, but another look reveals that it recurs in the last-listed combination: courage—will—intellect—presence. Thus if we were to "combine the combinations" we would find the triad appearing in 77 percent (58 percent + 19 percent) of the cases—something of a revelation!

Surely such a combination, even if our sampling of case histories seems limited, points the way toward discerning and evaluating desirable attributes in military leaders. When that direction has been made clear, this book will have served yet another purpose: showing a better way of profiting from the experience of others. The better way has been established in these pages; its essence lies in the act of showing rather than telling. The lessons of military history can be stimulating as well as instructive if they are not reeled off as narratives told from an omniscient viewpoint.

When leaders and battles are presented by *showing*, the leader-to-be will learn to examine each historical case through his mind's eye, and ask the following questions:

What and where were the dynamics of battle that confronted the leader?

What attributes of the leader's art did he employ in overcoming his problems?

How should I have acted in the same situation?

Appendixes

Appendix A
Levels of The Conduct of War

This brief review is intended to serve only the theme and aims of this book. If it were not so restricted it would blunder into the crossfire that historians and analysts have raised in their sniping at one another's definitions for a half-dozen generations. That is why only three levels are defined (a fourth is considered but not retained) and exemplified; and then only in the descending order of their relevance to this writing.

TACTICS *is the art of fighting battles*—regardless of the size and extent of the operations of opposing forces. Prior to the First World War, tactics could be seen in action because the commander had a personal view of his battle. As the size of engaged forces increased in hitherto inconceivable proportions, the historians and analysts began to struggle with their definitions of battle and tactics. This was unnecessary. Despite the apparent disproportionate numbers in troops, space, and time the above definition retains its meaning.

Dan Morgan's Battle of Cowpens was over an hour after the first shots were fired. The total forces engaged numbered a little over 2,000 men, roughly the equivalent of two modern U.S. infantry battalions. The whole affair was consummated in an area less than a mile and half deep by three-quarters of a mile wide.

Thirty-four years later Waterloo was fought almost entirely on a Sunday afternoon, and the opposing forces totaled 140,000. The battle raged over a relatively small area about a mile and a half deep by two miles in width.

Almost a century after Waterloo (1815 to 1914), Tannenberg lasted five days and involved 600,000 men. The maneuver of the German and Russian armies took place in an arena 120 miles deep and 90 miles wide. Yet Hindenburg and the enemy army commanders at Tannenberg were fighting a *battle* no less than had Morgan and Tarleton at Cowpens. Thus, opposing commanders in all the cases examined in this book—as well as in over 1,500 battles dating from 1479 B.C. to the present—were attempting to employ their *tactics* to defeat their enemies.

It has been said, with a good deal of soundness, that tactics and its big brother, strategy, may seem to look alike on occasion, but in actual practice they are anything but twins. It may be helpful to see the two as did Sun Tzu in 500 B.C. when he told his audience "all men can see these tactics whereby I conquer, but what none can see is the strategy out of which victory is evolved."

MILITARY STRATEGY, or simply strategy, *is the disposition of military power within a theater of operations in a manner designed to increase the probability of victory.* In other terms, the high command moves its forces to bring enemy forces into situations most favorable for capture or destruction.

The German strategy in the 1941 invasion of Russia wisely foresaw the overwhelming advantages of employing rapidly moving armored forces to bag hundreds of thousands of prisoners vis-à-vis slugging it out in battles with the Russians.

Grant's Vicksburg campaign in 1863 was the implementation of a bold strategy which included Grant abandoning his lines of communication in order to defeat his enemies in five successive battles before he could invest and take Vicksburg. When all that had been accomplished, Grant succeeded in carrying out the ultimate aims of the North's grand strategy: to cut the Confederacy in two, invade the Southern states east of the Mississippi, and destroy its armies or its people's will to carry on the war.

GRAND STRATEGY represents *the highest level at which national (or allied) policies are established and the resources of the nation (or alliance) are mustered and allocated in a manner assured to maximize their potential for achieving the ends of policy, military or political.*

Napoleon's Continental System is an example of grand strategy whereby he attempted to close the ports of Europe to England as a means of bringing her to his terms of non-interference with his imperial aims.

A case in recent times was the joint decision of Roosevelt and Churchill to assign first priority to the American war effort in supporting plans for the Allied invason of Europe.

GRAND TACTICS which took its place between military strategy and battlefield tactics in Napoleon's art of war is mentioned only because his *bataillon carré* system was an important part of that art. We saw Marshal Davout's operations at Auerstadt as an extension of the *bataillon carré's* functioning. The term grand tactics has been favored by some historians for general use, but it is not used by military planners and field commanders in modern armies.

Appendix B
Anthony Wayne's Nicknames

Because Anthony Wayne deservedly won his reputation as an outstanding leader, his two military nicknames require exposition lest they be taken in a disparaging sense. Neither should be seen in a bad light.

Wayne was a leader who believed in setting a personal example in dress as well as on-the-ground leadership in battle. He was a stickler for discipline and training, and to him the uniform symbolized the martial spirit. He wanted his men to look like soldiers and spared no effort or expense in trying to keep them properly clothed and equipped. That he did not consistently succeed was not to his detriment in an army where even the commander-in-chief's constant efforts didn't always spell success in providing for the men.

It was only natural for Wayne to set the example for immaculate dress wherever he commanded. Yet he did not affect show for show's sake. He wanted to look the general, and he succeeded. Hence the sobriquet "Dandy" which followed him from his earlier days in command. But it should be recognized that the soldiers who bandied the name about would volunteer to follow him into the hottest action and the most dangerous assignments.

While Wayne eventually outlived "Dandy," he seems to

have gotten stuck with "Mad Anthony," and there is little that can be done about that except to explain that the "mad" is entirely undeserved if it is interpreted as a badge of rashness. One of Wayne's biographers, Harry Emerson Wildes,* cites the originator of the nickname as a disgruntled chronic deserter, one Jeremy the Rover, who proclaimed Wayne to be "Mad Anthony" when the general did not act to get him released from jail: "He must be mad, or he would help me. Mad Anthony that's what he is!"

Somehow the name took with the soldiers and became indelibly stamped on Wayne. Then, years later, as both Wildes and Stillé affirm it, "Washington Irving, wholly misunderstanding the nickname, jumped to the false conclusion that it was given Wayne because of rashness, recklessness, and unbridled daring, and by so doing not only smirched Wayne's military reputation as a cautious, careful strategist who never took unnecessary chances, but in addition gave him a stigma of mental unbalance which many of Irving's uncritical readers accepted."

Fortunately, in our day Wayne comes through without the stigma, and the nickname now reflects only an appreciation of his "bridled" daring.

Appendix C
Wayne's Order for The
Storming of Stony Point

The order is quoted verbatim from Henry P. Johnston's *The Storming of Stony Point* (James T. White & Co., New York, 1900).

The troops will march at ——O'clock and move by the Right making a short halt at the Creek or run next on this side Clements's. Every Officer and non-commissioned Officer must remain with and be answerable for every man, in their platoons; no soldier will be permitted to quit his ranks on any pretext whatever until a general Halt is made and then to be attended by one of the officers of the Platoon.

When the Head of the Troops arrive in the rear of the Hill Z Fuger [Febiger] will form his Regiment into a Solid Col-

---

Anthony Wayne: Trouble Shooter of the Revolution, Harcourt, Brace and Co., New York, 1941, p. 236.

umn of a half Platoon in front as fast as they come up. Colo. Meggs will form next in Febiger's rear and Major Hull in the rear of Megg's which will form the right column.

Colo. Butler will form a Column on the left of Febiger and Major Murphrey in his Rear.

Every Officer and Soldier are then to fix a piece of white paper in the most conspicuous part of his Hat or Cap as an Insignea to be distinguished from the Enemy.

At the word March Colo. Flury will take charge of One Hundred and fifty determened and picked men, properly Officered, with their Arms unloaded, placing their whole Dependence on the Bay[onet] who will move about twenty paces in front of the Right Column by the Rout 1 and enter the Sally port b. He is to detach an officer and twenty men a little in front whose business will be to secure the sentries and Remove the Abattis and obstruction for the Column to pass through. The Column will follow close in the Rear with sholder'd muskets led by Colo. Febiger and Genl. Wayne in person. When the works are forced—and not before, the Victorious troops as they enter will give the Watch word ["The fort's our own"] with a repeated and loud voice to drive the Enemy from their Works and Guns which will favor the pass of the whole troops. Shou'd the Enemy refuse to Surrender and attempt to make their escape by water or otherwise, effectual means must be used to effect the former and to prevent the Latter.

Colo. Butler will move by the route 2, preceded by One Hundred chosen men with fixed Bayonets, properly officer'd, and Unloaded [muskets] under the command of ———, at the distance of about 20 yards in front of the Column, which will follow under Colo. Butler with shouldered Muskets and enter the Sally port E or d occationally; these Hundred will also detach a proper Officer and twenty men a little in front to Remove the obstruction. As soon as they gain the Works they are also to give and continue the Watch Word which will prevent confusion and mistakes.

Major Murphey will follow Colo. Butler to the first figure 3 when he will divide a little to the Right and left and wait the Attack on the Right which will be his Signal to begin and keep up a perpetual and gauling fire and endeavour to enter between and possess the Work aa.

If any Soldier presumes to take his Musket from his sholder or Attempt to fire or begin the Battle until ordered by his proper Officer, he shall be instantly put to Death by the Officer next him, for the misconduct of one man is not to put the whole Troops in danger or disorder and be suffered to pass with life.

After the troops begin to advance to the Works the strictest Silence must be observed and the closest attention paid to the commands of the Officers.

The General has the fullest Confidence in the bravery and fortitude of the Corps that he has the Happiness to command. The distinguished Honor conferred on every Officer and Soldier who has been drafted into this Corps by His Excellency, Genl. Washington, the Credit of the States they respectively belong to, and their own Reputation will be such powerful motives for each man to distinguish himself that the General cannot have the least doubt of a Glorious Victory; and he hereby most Solemnly engages to Reward the first man who enters the works with Five Hundred Dollars, and will represent the conduct of every Officer and Soldier who distinguishes himself on this occasion in the most favorable point of view to His Excellency, whose greatest pleasure is in rewarding merit.

But shou'd there be any soldier so lost to every feeling of Honor, as to attempt to Retreat one single foot or Skulk in the face of danger, the Officer next to him is immediately to put him to Death,—that he may no longer disgrace the Name of a Soldier or the Corps or State he belongs to.

As General Wayne is determined to share the danger of the Night—so he wishes to participate of the glory of the day in common with his fellow Soldiers.

Appendix D
Napoleon's Bataillon Carré System

The system was apparently conceived early in Napoleon's career as an army commander, and the first evidence of its use showed in his first Italian campaign during the maneuver that resulted in the French victories at Lonato and Castiglione in 1796. The system which later became the bridge between the Emperor's strategy and battlefield tactics was further developed in the first Italian campaign when General Bonaparte used it to parry and defeat the Austrian strategic thrusts into northern Italy (1796–1797).

> Then clearly the *bataillon carré* system, for Napoleon's purposes, tied the strategic plan and the strategic advance to his grand tactics by climaxing the campaign with a decisive concentration against his ultimate objective, the enemy main army. There can be no confusing the use of the *bataillon carré* with minor tactics, since the need for the system had ended when

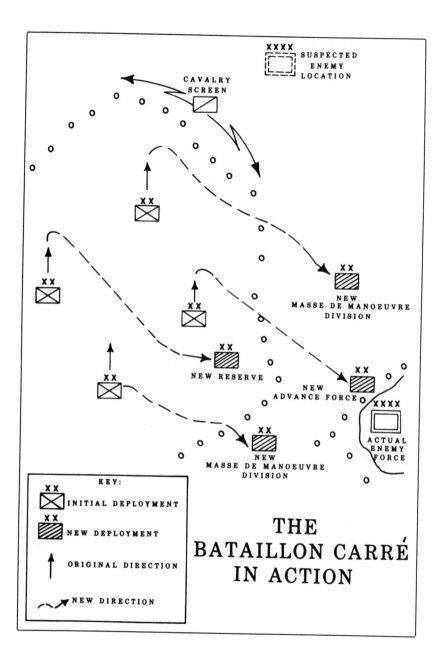

SUSPECTED
ENEMY
LOCATION

CAVALRY
SCREEN

NEW
MASSE DE MANOEUVRE
DIVISION

NEW RESERVE

NEW
ADVANCE FORCE

ACTUAL
ENEMY
FORCE

NEW
MASSE DE MANOEUVRE
DIVISION

KEY:

INITIAL DEPLOYMENT

NEW DEPLOYMENT

ORIGINAL DIRECTION

NEW DIRECTION

THE
BATAILLON CARRÉ
IN ACTION

Napoleon's major elements had concentrated on or near the battlefield.

How did Napoleon, after Castiglione, forge this grand tactic into the sword which was to cut down army after army of France's enemies? In the first place he was acutely aware that Bourcet's magic words "controlled dispersion" provided the real key to the system. This came to be the carefully planned advance of divisions over a road net in a time and space disposition that permitted the concentration of the army in any direction. Thus if the hostile main body were encountered (normally by units of the cavalry screen) on, say, the right flank, the division on the right became the new advance guard and fixing force. Those divisions composing the original front and rear became the *masse de manoeuvre*, marching directly to the support of the advance division. Usually, the new maneuver divisions now had the mission of enveloping one or both of the enemy's flanks. The division marching on the original left now reconstituted the army reserve, having, in effect, to execute a "column right" toward the enemy. The over-all effect was, in Liddell Hart's words, like "a widespread net whose corners are weighted with stones; when one of the enemy's columns impinged on it the net closed in round the point of pressure [Napoleon's fixing force] and the stones crashed together on the intruder." Later, as we shall see, the *bataillon carré* became magnified in scale, as the Emperor replaced divisions with corps.*

Appendix E
Organization and Tactical
Formations of The Roman
Legion, c. 220 B.C.

It would be difficult indeed to find a clearer and more concise description of the organization and basic battle drills than the following excerpt from the Dupuys' *Encyclopedia of Military History***:

> There were four classes of soldiers. The youngest, most agile, and least trained men were the **velites,** or light infantry. Next in age and experience came the **hastati,** who comprised the first line of the legion heavy infantry. The **principes** were

---

*"Forgotten Sword," William J. Wood in *Military Affairs*, Vol. XXXIV, No. 3, Oct. 1970, 77–79 with permission. Copyright 1970 by the American Military Institute. No additional copies may be made without the express permission of the author and of the editor of *Military Affairs*.
**Pages 72–74 from *The Encyclopedia of Military History*. Copyright 1970 by R. Ernest Dupuy and Trevor N. Dupuy. Reprinted by permission of Harper & Row, Publishers, Inc.

veterans, averaging about 30 years of age; the backbone of the army, mature, tough, and experienced, they made up the second line of the legion. The oldest group, the **triarii,** who contributed steadiness to offset the vigor of the more youthful classifications, comprised the third line of heavy infantry.

The basic tactical organization was the **maniple,** roughly the equivalent of a modern company. Each maniple was composed of two **centuries,** or platoons, of 60–80 men each, except that the maniple of the **triarii** was one century only. The **cohort,** comparable to a modern battalion, consisted of 450–570 men (120–160 **velites,** the same number of **hastati** and **principes,** 60–80 **triarii,** and a **turma** of 30 cavalrymen). The cavalry component of the cohort rarely fought with it; the horsemen were usually gathered together in larger cavalry formations.

The legion itself—the equivalent of a modern division—comprised some 4,500–5,000 men, including 300 cavalrymen. For each Roman legion, there was one allied legion, organized identically, except that its cavalry component was usually 600 men. (Some authorities suggest that allied contingents were not organized in this formal manner, but that it was merely Roman policy to support each legion with an approximately equal number of allied troops, whose largest formal organization was the cohort.)

A Roman legion, with its allied counterpart, was the equivalent of a modern army corps, a force of some 9,000–10,000 men, of whom about 900 were cavalry. Two Roman and two allied legions comprised a field army, known as a consular army, commanded by one of Rome's two consuls.

A consular army was usually 18,000–20,000 men, with a combat front of about one and a half miles. Often the two regular consular armies would be joined together, in which case the consuls would alternate in command, usually on a 24-hour basis. In times of war or great danger, however, Rome might have more than the 8 standard legions (4 Roman, 4 allied) under arms. In such cases, if a dictator had been appointed, he would directly command the largest field force, exercising overall control over the others as best he could under the circumstances. Whether or not there was a dictator, additional armies were usually commanded by proconsuls (former consuls), appointed by the Senate, or praetors, elected officials.

Since consuls were elected executive officials, both military and political power lay in their hands; rarely were Roman commanders harassed by directives from home. On the other hand, this system often resulted in mediocre top military leadership. Another drawback to this system was that consuls changed each year; yet in a long-drawn-out war, such as against Hannibal, Roman generals had to keep the field for years on end.

Under the consul or proconsul was a staff of senior officers or quaestors, who took care of administrative and planning tasks delegated by the army commander. The senior officers of the legion were the 6 tribunes—2 for each combat line. In a peculiar arrangement, the 6 tribunes rotated in command of the legion, though later a legate was frequently appointed over the tribunes as legion commander. Below the tribunes were 60 centurions, 2 for each maniple.

The flexibility of the legion lay in the tactical relationship of the maniples within each line, and between the lines of heavy infantry. Each maniple was like a tiny phalanx, with a front of about 20 men, 6 deep, but with the space between men somewhat greater than in the phalanx. Each man occupied space 5 feet square. Between the maniples in each line were intervals of the same frontage as that of a maniple, about 20 yards. The maniples in each line were staggered, with those of the second and third lines each covering intervals in the line to their front. There were approximately 100 yards between each line of heavy infantry.

This cellular, checkerboard type formation had a number of inherent advantages over the phalanx: it could maneuver more easily in rough country, without fear of losing alignment, and without need for concern about gaps appearing in the line—the gaps were built in. If desired, the first line could withdraw through the second, or the second could advance through the first. With its triarii line, the legion had an organic reserve, whether or not the commander consciously used it as such. The intervals were, of course, a potential source of danger, but one that was kept limited by the stationing of other troops immediately behind those of the first two lines. In battle it appears that the lines would close up to form a virtual phalanx, but these could quickly resume their flexible relationship when maneuver became necessary once more.

The hastati and principes were each armed with two sturdy javelins, about 7 feet long, and with a broad-bladed short sword, about 2 feet long. The javelins were usually thrown at the enemy just before contact, with the sword (**gladius**) being wielded at close quarters. The tactical concept would be comparable to modern bayonet attacks preceded by rifle fire. The triarii each carried a 12-foot pike, as well as the gladius. The velites were armed with javelins and darts. To obtain greater diversity in range and effective missile weapons, the Romans sometimes employed foreign mercenaries, such as Balearic slingers and Aegean bowmen.

Notes

Introduction

1. Random House, 1981.
2. Fallows, *National Defense*, p. 171.
3. Robert S. Dudney, "The New Army With New Punch," *U.S. News & World Report* (September 20, 1982), pp. 59–62.
4. *The Random House Dictionary of the English Language* (New York: Random House, 1981), p. 84: definition 9 of art.
5. J. F. C. Fuller, *A Military History of the Western World* (New York: Funk & Wagnalls Company, 1955), I, p. xi.
6. Will and Ariel Durant, *The Lessons of History,* as the Epilogue to the work, *The Story of Civilization* (New York: Simon & Schuster, 1968), p. 81.
7. Carl von Clausewitz, *On War* (London: Routledge and Kegan Paul, 1966), I, p. 49.
8. *Random House Dictionary,* p. 73, def. of apprehension.
9. Clausewitz, op. cit., p. 77.
10. Stephen Vincent Benét, *John Brown's Body* (New York: Heritage Press, 1948), pp. 112–113.

Prologue

1. Kenneth Roberts, *The Battle of Cowpens* (Eastern Acorn Press, Eastern National Park & Monument Association, reprinted 1981), pp. 48–49.
2. Ibid., pp. 72–73.
3. North Callahan, *Daniel Morgan: Ranger of the Revolution* (New York: Holt, Rinehart and Winston, 1961), p. 213. This one sentence is so brilliantly

apt that I found I could not improve on it, so those five words must be credited to Callahan.

4. Mark M. Boatner III, *Encyclopedia of the American Revolution* (New York: David McKay Company, 1976), p. 445.
5. Banastre Tarleton, *A History of the Campaigns of 1780 and 1781 in the Southern Provinces of North America* (Dublin, 1787), pp. 217–218.
6. Edwin C. Bearss, *The Battle of Cowpens: A Documented Narrative and Troop Movement Maps* (Washington, D.C.: National Park Service, 1967), p. 38.
7. Tarleton, op. cit., p. 221.

Part One

1. *Great Books of the Western World (GBWW)* (Chicago: Encyclopaedia Britannica, 1952), 7, p. 35.
2. John Keegan, *The Face of Battle* (New York: The Viking Press, 1976), p. 70.
3. Ardant du Picq, *Battle Studies* (Harrisburg, PA: The Military Service Publishing Company, 1958), pp. 112–131.
4. Keegan, op. cit., p. 74.
5. S. L. A. Marshall, *Men Against Fire* (New York: William Morrow & Co., 1947), p. 50.
6. Ibid., p. 161.
7. *GBWW*, 9, p. 322.
8. *GBWW*, 2, pp. 253–254.
9. See Appendix B for sobriquets of "Mad Anthony Wayne" and "Dandy Wayne."
10. Boatner, op. cit., p. 1065. Also, Charles J. Stillé, *Major General Anthony Wayne and the Pennsylvania Line* (Port Washington, N.Y.: Kennikat Press, 1983), p. 190 and n.
11. Boatner, op. cit., pp. 1092–1093.
12. Ibid., p. 1066; Stillé, op. cit., p. 403.
13. Boatner, op. cit., p. 1066.
14. Bernard Law Montgomery, *A History of Warfare* (New York: World Publishing Company, 1968), pp. 15–16.
15. *GBWW*, 6, p. 397.
16. Conrad H. Lanza, *Napoleon and Modern War: His Military Maxims* (Harrisburg, PA: The Military Service Publishing Company, 1949), p. 81.
17. David G. Chandler, *The Campaigns of Napoleon* (New York: The Macmillan Company, 1966), p. 494.
18. Ibid., p. 494.
19. John G. Gallaher, *The Iron Marshal: A Biography of Louis N. Davout* (Carbondale and Edwardsville, Illinois; Southern Illinois University Press, 1976), p. 130.
20. Frederick N. Maude, *The Jena Campaign, 1806* (London, New York: The Macmillan Company, 1909), p. 172.
21. Chandler, op. cit., p. 488.
22. Ibid., p. 496.

23. V. J. Esposito and J. R. Elting, *A Military History and Atlas of the Napoleonic Wars* (New York: Frederick A. Praeger, 1964), Chapter: "Sketches."

Part Two

1. S. L. A. Marshall, op. cit., pp. 174–175.
2. Lanza, op. cit., p. 103.
3. Ibid., p. 96.
4. David G. Chandler, *The Art of Warfare on Land* (London, New York: The Hamlyn Publishing Group, 1974), p. 7.
5. David G. Chandler, *Atlas of Military Strategy* (New York: Macmillan Publishing Company, 1980), p. 11.
6. Rupert Furneaux, *The Zulu War: Isandhlwana and Rorke's Drift* (Philadelphia and New York: J. B. Lippincott Company, 1963), pp. 43–44.
7. Donald R. Morris, *The Washing of the Spears* (New York: Simon & Schuster, 1965), pp. 408–409.
8. Michael Glover, *Rorke's Drift: A Victorian Epic* (London: Leo Cooper, 1975), p. 97.
9. S. I. Hayakawa, *Use the Right Word* (Pleasantville, N.Y.: The Reader's Digest Association, 1968), p. 689.

Part Three

1. Edgar I. Stewart, *Custer's Luck* (Norman, Okla.: University of Oklahoma Press, 1955), p. ix.
2. Ibid., pp. 242–243.
3. Charles K. Hofling, *Custer and the Little Big Horn: A Psychobiographical Inquiry* (Detroit: Wayne State University Press, 1981), p. 26.
4. Ibid., p. 33.
5. S. L. A. Marshall, *Crimsoned Prairie* (New York: Charles Scribner's Sons, 1972), p. 148.
6. Ibid., p. 155.
7. J. F. C. Fuller, *A Military History of the Western World* (New York: Funk & Wagnalls Company, 1955), II, p. 492.

Part Four

1. Technical Report 1-191, *Art and Requirements of Command (ARC)* by Joel N. Bloom, Adele M. Farber, et al (prepared by the Franklin Institute Research Laboratories for the Office of the Director of Special Studies, Office of the Chief of Staff, Department of the Army, Contract No. DA 49-092-ARO-154, April 1967), I, p. vii.
2. Ibid., II, p. 74.
3. Ibid., pp. 74–75.

Bibliography

These listings include the works I have used in writing this book as well as other writings suggested for further reading. The last section of this bibliography, under *Epilogue*, contains recommended sources for the reader who wishes to pursue his own researches in the field of leadership in war.

Introduction

Benét, Stephen Vincent. *John Brown's Body*. New York: The Heritage Press, 1948.

Clausewitz, Carl von. *On War* (3 Vols.). London: Routledge and Kegan Paul, 1966.

Dudney, Robert S. "The New Army With New Punch," *U.S. News & World Report*, September 20, 1982.

Dupuy, R. E. and T. N. *The Encyclopedia of Military History*. New York: Harper & Row, 1970.

Durant, Will and Ariel. *The Lessons of History* as epilogue to the work, *The Story of Civilization*. New York: Simon & Schuster, 1968.

Fallows, James. *National Defense*. New York: Random House, 1981.

Fuller, J. F. C. *A Military History of the Western World* (3 Vols.). New York: Funk & Wagnals, 1954.

Prologue

Bass, Robert D. *The Green Dragoon: The Lives of Banastre Tarleton and Mary Robinson*. Columbia, S.C.: Sandlapper Press, 1973.

Bearss, Edwin C. *The Battle of Cowpens: A Documented Narrative and Troop Movement Maps.* Washington, D.C.: National Park Service, 1967.

Boatner, Mark M. III. *Encyclopedia of the American Revolution.* New York: David McKay Company, 1976.

Callahan, North. *Daniel Morgan: Ranger of the Revolution.* New York: Holt, Rinehart and Winston, 1961.

Davis, Burke. *The Cowpens—Guilford Court House Campaign.* New York: J. B. Lippincott, 1962.

Graham, James. *The Life of General Daniel Morgan of the Virginia Line of the Army of the United States.* New York, 1859.

Higginbotham, Don. *Daniel Morgan: Revolutionary Rifleman.* Chapel Hill, N.C.: University of North Carolina Press, 1961.

Lee, Henry. *The Campaign of 1781 in the Carolinas.* Spartanburg, S.C.: The Reprint Company, 1975.

Roberts, Kenneth. *The Battle of Cowpens.* New York: Doubleday and Company, 1958.

Sawyer, Winthrop S. *Firearms in American History.* Boston: published by author, 1910.

Tarleton, Banastre. *A History of the Campaigns of 1780 and 1781 in the Southern Provinces of North America.* Dublin, 1787.

Windrow, Martin and Embleton, Gerry. *Military Dress of North America, 1665–1970.* New York: Charles Scribner's Sons, 1973.

Part One

Billias, George Allen (ed.). *George Washington's Generals.* New York, 1964.

Boatner, Mark M. III. *Encyclopedia of the American Revolution.* New York: David McKay Company, 1976.

Boyd, Thomas. *Mad Anthony Wayne.* New York: Charles Scribner's Sons, 1929.

Chandler, David G. *The Campaigns of Napoleon.* New York: The Macmillan Company, 1966.

———. *Dictionary of the Napoleonic Wars.* New York: The Macmillan Company, 1979.

Copeland, Peter F. *Uniforms of the American Revolution.* New York: Dover Publications, 1974.

Davout, Louis N. *Operations du 3ème Corps, 1806–1807: Rapport du Maréchal Davout, Duc d'Auerstädt.* Paris: Calmann Levy, 1896.

Delderfield, R. F. *Napoleon's Marshals.* Philadelphia-New York: Chilton Books, 1962.

Dunn-Pattison, R. P. *Napoleon's Marshals.* London: EP Publishing Limited, 1977.

Esposito, V. J. and Elting, J. R. *A Military History and Atlas of the Napoleonic Wars.* New York: Frederick A. Praeger, 1964.

Freeman, Douglas Southall. *George Washington* (7 Vols.), Vol 5. New York, 1948–1957.

Fuller, J. F. C. *A Military History of the Western World* (3 Vols.). New York: Funk & Wagnalls, 1955.

Gallaher, John G. *The Iron Marshal: A Biography of Louis N. Davout*. Carbondale and Edwardsville, Ill.: Southern Illinois University Press, 1976.

Johnston, Henry P. *The Storming of Stony Point*. New York: James T. White and Company, 1900.

Katcher, Philip. *Armies of the American Wars, 1753–1815*. New York: Hastings House, Publishers, 1975.

Keegan, John. *The Face of Battle*. New York: Viking Press, 1976.

Klinger, R. L. and Wilder, R. A. *Sketch Book '76: The American Soldier 1775–1781*. Union City, Tenn.: Pioneer Press, 1967.

Lanza, Conrad H. *Napoleon and Modern War: His Military Maxims*. Harrisburg, Pa.: Military Service Publishing Company, 1949.

Liddell Hart, B. H. *Strategy*. New York: Frederick A. Praeger, 1957.

Lossing, Benson J. *The Pictorial Field Book of the Revolution*. New York, 1851.

Marshall, S. L. A. *Men Against Fire*. New York: William Morrow & Company, 1947.

Maude, Frederick N. *The Jena Campaign, 1806*. London & New York: The Macmillan Company, 1909.

Montgomery, Bernard Law. *A History of Warfare*. New York & Cleveland: The World Publishing Company, 1968.

Du Picq, Ardant. *Battle Studies*. Harrisburg, Pa.: Military Service Publishing Company, 1958.

Schultz, A. N. (ed.). *Illustrated Drill Manual and Regulations for the American Soldier of the Revolutionary War* (Collector's Edition). Charlotte, N.C.: Sugarcreek Publishing Company, 1976.

Smith, Page. *A New Age Now Begins* (2 Vols.). New York: McGraw-Hill Book Company, 1976.

Stember, Sol. *The Bicentennial Guide to the American Revolution* (3 Vols.). New York: E. P. Dutton, 1974.

Stillé, Charles J. *Major General Anthony Wayne and the Pennsylvania Line in the Continental Army*. Philadelphia, 1893 (re-issued by Kennikat Press, Port Washington, N.Y., 1968).

Ward, Christopher. *The War of the Revolution* (2 Vols.). New York: The Macmillan Company, 1952.

Wildes, H. E. *Anthony Wayne: Trouble Shooter of the Revolution*. New York: Harcourt, Brace and Company, 1941.

Wood, William J. "Forgotten Sword," *Military Affairs*, Vol. XXXIV. No. 3, Oct 1970, pp. 77–82.

Part Two

Bancroft, Hubert Howe. *History of Mexico* (5 Vols.), *Vol I, 1516–1521*. San Francisco: The History Company, Publishers, 1886.

Bernal Diaz del Castillo. *The Discovery and Conquest of Mexico, 1517–1521*. New York: Farrar, Straus and Giroux, 1956.

Blacker, Irwin R. *Cortes and the Aztec Conquest*. New York: Harper & Row, 1965.

———— and Rosen, Harry M. (eds.). *Conquest: Dispatches of Cortes From the New World*. New York: Grosset and Dunlap, 1962.

Colenso, Frances E. *History of the Zulu War and Its Origin*. London: Chapman and Hall, 1880.

Coupland, Reginald. *Zulu Battle Piece—Isandhlwana*. London, 1948.

Furneaux, Rupert. *The Zulu War: Isandhlwana and Rorke's Drift*. Philadelphia and New York: J. B. Lippincott Company, 1963.

Glover, Michael. *Rorke's Drift: A Victorian Epic*. Leo Cooper, 1975.

Harford, Henry. *The Zulu War Journal of Colonel Henry Harford, C. B.* (ed. Daphne Child) Hamden, Conn.: The Shoe String Press, 1980.

Helps, Arthur. *The Life of Hernando Cortes* (2 Vols.). London: Bell and Daldy, 1871.

Laband, J. P. C. and Thompson, P. S. *A Field Guide to the War in Zululand 1879*. Pietermaritzburg, So. Africa: University of Natal Press, 1979.

MacLeish, Archibald. "Conquistador" from *Collected Poems, 1917–1952*. Boston: Houghton Mifflin Company, 1952.

MacNutt, Francis Augustus. *Fernando Cortes and the Conquest of Mexico*. New York and London: G. P. Putnam's Sons, 1909.

Morris, Donald R. *The Washing of the Spears*. New York: Simon and Schuster, 1965.

Prescott, William H. *Conquest of Mexico*. New York: The Book League of America, 1934.

Sedgewick, Henry Dwight. *Cortes the Conqueror*. Indianapolis: The Bobbs Merrill Company, 1927.

Simpson, Lesley Bird (transl. & ed.). *Cortes: The Life of the Conqueror by His Secretary*. Berkeley and Los Angeles: University of California Press, 1965.

Tarassuk, Leonid and Blair, Claude (eds.). *The Complete Encyclopedia of Arms and Weapons*. New York: Simon & Schuster, 1982.

Wise, Terence. *The Conquistadores*. London: Osprey Publishing, 1980.

Part Three

Ambrose, Stephen E. *Crazy Horse and Custer: The Parallel Lives of Two American Warriors*. Garden City, N.Y.: Doubleday and Company, 1975.

Anderson, Niles. *The Battle of Bushy Run*. Harrisburg, Pa.: Pennsylvania Historical and Museum Commission, 1975.

————. "Bushy Run: Decisive Battle in the Wilderness," *The Western Pennsylvania Historical Magazine*, Vol. 46, No. 3, July 1963.

Asprey, Robert B. *War in the Shadows* (2 Vols.). Garden City, N.Y.: Doubleday and Company, 1975.

Balsdon, J. P. V. D. *Romans and Aliens*. Chapel Hill, N.C.: University of North Carolina Press, 1979.

Boatner, Mark M. III. *Encyclopedia of the American Revolution*. New York: David McKay Company, 1976.

Bomberger, C. M. *The Battle of Bushy Run.* Jeanette, Pa.: Jeanette Publishing Company, 1928.

Boucher, John H. "Old and New Westmoreland," *American Historical Society.* New York, 1918.

Bouquet, Henry. *An Historical Account of the Expedition Against the Ohio Indians in the Year MDCCLXIV Under the Command of Henry Bouquet, Esqre.* 1766.

Caven, Brian. *The Punic Wars.* New York: St. Martin's Press, 1980.

Connolly, Peter. *Greece and Rome at War.* Englewood Cliffs, N.J.: Prentice-Hall, 1981.

————. *The Roman Army.* London: MacDonald and Company, 1982.

Coughlan, T. M. "The Battle of the Little Big Horn: A Tactical Study," *Cavalry Journal,* No. 34, Jan–Feb 1934.

Dictionary of American Biography (21 Vols.), Vol. I. New York, 1943

Dupuy, R. E. and Dupuy, T. N. *The Encyclopedia of Military History.* New York: Harper and Row, 1970.

Dupuy, T. N. *Evolution of Weapons and Warfare.* New York: Bobbs-Merrill Company, 1980.

Encyclopaedia Britannica, 1946 edition, Vol. 12 (Ilipa) and Vol. 20 (Scipio Africanus, Publius Cornelius).

Fortescue, Sir John W. *A History of the British Army* (13 Vols.), Vol. III, 1763–1793. London: Macmillan and Company, 1911.

Frost, Lawrence A. *The Custer Album.* Seattle: Superior Publishing Company, 1964.

Fuller, J. F. C. *British Light Infantry in the Eighteenth Century.* London: Hutchinson and Company, 1925.

Godfrey, Edward S. "Custer's Last Battle," *Century Illustrated Monthly Magazine,* Vol. XLIII, No. 3, Jan 1892.

Graham, W. A. *The Custer Myth: A Source Book of Custeriana.* New York: Bonanza Books, 1953.

Grant, Michael. *History of Rome.* New York: Charles Scribner's Sons, 1978.

Grimal, Pierre. *The Civilization of Rome.* New York: Simon & Schuster, 1963.

Hofling, Charles K. *Custer and the Little Big Horn: A Psychobiographical Inquiry.* Detroit: Wayne State University Press, 1981.

Johnston, Harold W. *The Private Life of the Romans.* New York: Scott, Foresman and Company, 1932.

Jones, Douglas C. *The Court-Martial of George Armstrong Custer.* New York: Charles Scribner's Sons, 1976.

Kinsley, D. A. *Favor the Bold, Custer: The Indian Figher.* New York: Holt, Rinehart and Winston, 1968.

Kuhlman, Charles. *Legend Into History: The Custer Mystery.* Harrisburg, Pa.: The Telegraph Press, 1951.

Kurtz, Henry I. "The Relief of Fort Pitt," *History Today,* XIII, Nov 1963.

Lazenby, J. F. *Hannibal's War: A History of the Second Punic War.* Warminster, England: Aris and Phillips, 1978.

Liddell Hart, B. H. *A Greater Than Napoleon: Scipio Africanus.* Boston: Little, Brown and Company, 1927.

Livy (Titus Livius) (transl. Baker, George). *The History of Rome*. Book XXVIII. London: Jones and Company, 1830.

McDonald, A. H. *Republican Rome*. New York: Frederick A. Praeger, 1966.

Marshall, S. L. A. *Crimsoned Prairie*. New York: Charles Scribner's Sons, 1972.

Monaghan, Jay. *Custer: The Life of General George Armstrong Custer*. Boston: Little, Brown and Company, 1959.

Morison, Samuel Eliot (ed.). *The Parkman Reader*. Boston, 1955.

Parker, H. M. D. *The Roman Legions*. New York: Barnes & Noble, 1928.

Parkman, Francis. *The Conspiracy of Pontiac* (2 Vols.). Boston: Little, Brown and Company, 1903.

Peckham, Howard H. *Pontiac and the Indian Uprising*. New York: Russell and Russell, 1947.

Polybius (transl. W. R. Paton). *The Histories*. Books X-XI. Cambridge, Mass.: Harvard University Press, 1960.

Reeve, J. C. "Henry Bouquet and His Indian Campaigns," *Ohio Archeological and Historical Quarterly*, XXVI, 1943.

Scullard, H. H. *Scipio Africanus: Soldier and Politician*. Ithaca, N.Y.: Cornell University Press, 1970.

Sheridan, Philip H. *Record of Engagements with Hostile Indians Within the Military Division of the Missouri, 1868 to 1882*. Washington, D.C.: Government Printing Office, 1882.

Stewart, Edgar I. *Custer's Luck*. Norman, Okla.: University of Oklahoma Press, 1955.

Utley, Robert M. *Custer and the Great Controversy: The Origin and Development of a Legend*. Los Angeles: Westernlore Press, 1962.

Van De Water, Frederic. *Glory-Hunter: A Life of General Custer*. New York: Bobbs-Merrill Company, 1934.

Walkinshaw, Lewis C. *Annals of South Western Pennsylvania*. Chapters XXI-XXII. New York: Lewis Historical Publishing Co., 1939.

Warry, John. *Warfare in the Classical World*. New York: St. Martin's Press, 1980.

Watson, G. R. *The Roman Soldier*. Ithaca, N.Y.: Cornell University Press, 1969.

Windrow, Martin and Embleton, Gerry. *Military Dress of North America 1665–1970*. New York: Charles Scribner's Sons, 1973.

Part Four

ARC: Art and Requirements of Command (4 Vols.). Philadelphia: Franklin Institute Research Laboratories (Prepared for the Office of the Director of Special Studies, Office of the Chief of Staff, Department of the Army), 1967.

Chandler, David G. *The Campaigns of Napoleon*. New York: The Macmillan Company, 1966.

————. *Dictionary of the Napoleonic Wars.* New York: The Macmillan Publishing Company, 1979.

Delderfield, R. F. *Napoleon's Marshals.* Philadelphia and New York: Chilton Books, 1966.

Dunn-Pattison, R. P. *Napoleon's Marshals.* London: Methuen and Co., 1909 (Republished by E. P. Publishing, Ltd., Easy Ardsley, West Yorkshire, 1977).

Esposito, Vincent J. and Elting, John Robert. *A Military History and Atlas of the Napoleonic Wars.* New York: Frederick A. Praeger, 1964.

de Marbot, Marcellin. *The Memoirs of Baron de Marbot: Late Lieutenant-General in the French Army* (transl. Butler, Arthur John). London: Longmans, Green and Company, 1892.

Thomason, John W., Jr. *Adventures of General Marbot.* New York: Charles Scribner's Sons, 1935.

Warner, Richard. *Napoleon's Enemies.* London: Osprey Publishing Co., 1977.

Part Five

Asprey, Robert B. *War in the Shadows: The Guerrilla in History* (2 Vols.). Garden City, N.Y.: Doubleday and Co., 1975.

Chandler, David G. *The Art of Warfare on Land.* London: The Hamlyn Publishing Group, 1974.

Dolbey, Robert V. *Sketches of the East Africa Campaign.* London: John Murray, 1918.

Encyclopaedia Britannica. Edition of 1946. Vol. 7 (East Africa, Operations in).

Gardner, Brian. *German East: The Story of the First World War in East Africa.* London: Cassell and Co., 1963.

Hordern, Charles (compiler). *Military Operations East Africa, Vol. I, August 1914-September 1916.* London: His Majesty's Stationery Office, 1941.

Hoyt, Edwin P. *Guerilla: Colonel von Lettow-Vorbeck and Germany's East African Empire.* New York: Macmillan Publishing Co., 1981.

von Lettow-Vorbeck, Paul Emil. *Heia Safari!: Deutschlands Kampf in Ostafrika.* Leipzig: R. F. Koehler, 1920.

————. *East African Campaigns.* New York: Robert Speller & Sons, Publishers, 1957.

Meinertzhagen, Richard. *Army Diary 1899–1926.* Edinburgh and London: Oliver and Boyd, 1960.

Miller, Charles. *Battle for the Bundu: The First World War in East Africa.* New York: Macmillan Publishing Co., 1974.

Mosley, Leonard. *Duel for Kilimanjaro: An Account of the East African Campaign 1914–1918.* London: Weidenfeld and Nicolson, 1963.

Young, Peter. *A Dictionary of Battles, 1816–1976.* New York: Mayflower Books, 1977.

Epilogue

This selected bibliography is intended for the reader who wishes to: one, gain an appreciation of the scope of military history and the battles considered in seeking examples of leadership—good or bad; two, consider works that reveal vistas looking into broader fields of the art of war.

The sources marked with an asterisk are actually encyclopedic collections of abstracts of battles or leaders. They represent good starting points for appreciating the scope just mentioned. Of particular value in considering world history are the indices in the Dupuy's *Encyclopedia of Military History*.

The anthology *Men at War* heads the list because it contains so many keen insights into the hearts and minds of men in battle. The ten suggested readings are most in keeping with the ideas developed in this book. The reader, however, may take my suggestions as biased samplings—which indeed they are.

*Boatner, Mark Mayo III. *The Civil War Dictionary*. New York: David McKay Company, 1959.

*———. *Encyclopedia of the American Revolution*. New York: David McKay Company, 1976.

*Calvert, Michael with Young, Peter. *A Dictionary of Battles 1715–1815*. New York: Mayflower Books, 1979.

Chandler, David G. *The Art of Warfare on Land*. London: The Hamlyn Publishing Group, 1974.

———. *Atlas of Military Strategy*. New York: Macmillan Publishing Co., 1980.

*Dupuy, R. E. and T. N. *The Encyclopedia of Military History*. New York: Harper & Row, 1970.

Dupuy, Trevor N. *The Evolution of Weapons and Warfare*. New York: The Bobbs-Merrill Co., 1980.

*Eggenberger, David. *A Dictionary of Battles*. New York: Thomas Y. Crowell Co., 1967.

Esposito, V. J. and Elting, J. R. *A Military History and Atlas of the Napoleonic Wars*. New York: Frederick A. Praeger, 1964.

———. *The West Point Atlas of American Wars* (2 Vols.). New York: Frederick A. Praeger, 1959.

Falls, Cyril. *The Art of War: From the Age of Napoleon to the Present Day*. New York: Oxford University Press, 1962.

Freeman, Douglas Southhall. *Lee's Lieutenants* (3 Vols). New York: Charles Scribner's Sons, 1942.

Fuller, J. F. C. *The Conduct of War 1789–1961*. New Brunswick, N.J.: Rutgers University Press, 1961.

———. *Generalship: Its Diseases and Their Cure*. Harrisburg, Pa.: Military Service Publishing Co., 1936.

Goodenough, Simon and Deighton, Len. *Tactical Genius in Battle*. London: Phaidon Press, 1979.

Hemingway, Ernest (ed). *Men at War*. New York: Bramhall House, 1942: SUGGESTED READING:

The Battle of Arsouf, Charles Oman;

The Red Badge of Courage, Stephen Crane;

The Pass of Thermopylae, Charlotte Yonge;

Custer, Frederic van de Water;

Blowing Up a Train, T. E. Lawrence;

Lisette at Eylau, General Marbot;

Gallipoli, J. F. C. Fuller;

The Stars in Their Courses, John W. Thomason, Jr.;

Borodino, Leo Tolstoy;

Oriskany, 1777, Walter D. Edmonds.

*Keegan, John and Wheatcroft, Andrew. *Who's Who in Military History: From 1453 to the Present Day*. New York: William Morrow & Co., 1976.

Liddell Hart, B. H. *The Ghost of Napoleon*. New Haven: Yale University Press, 1934.

———. *Strategy*. New York: Frederick A. Praeger, 1957. (Special Attention is invited to the "Index of Deductions.")

Machiavelli, Nicolo (transl. W. K. Marriott). *The Prince*. Chicago: Encyclopaedia Britannica, Inc., *Great Books of the Western World*, Vol. 23, 1952. Chapters 12–15 and 19.

Marshall, S. L. A. *Men Against Fire*. New York: William Morrow & Co., 1947.

Montgomery, Bernard Law. *A History of Warfare*. New York: The World Publishing Co., 1968. (Special Attention is invited to Chapters 1–2).

Montross, Lynn. *War Through the Ages*. New York: Harper & Brothers, 1946.

Napoleon's Military Maxims (ed. Conrad H. Lanza). *Napoleon and Modern War*. Harrisburgh, Pa.: Military Service Publishing Co., 1949.

Preston, Richard A. and Wise, Sydney F. *Men in Arms: A History of Warfare and Its Interrelationships with Western Society*. New York: Praeger Publishers, 1970.

Sun Tzu. *The Art of War* (transl. Samuel B. Griffith). New York and Oxford: Oxford University Press, 1963.

*Young, Peter. *A Dictionary of Battles 1816–1976*. New York: Mayflower Books, 1977.

Index